Roger Mear (who wrote this book) was born in 1950 and gained a degree in Fine Art at Norwich. He has accomplished a winter ascent of the notorious Eiger North Face and, with two Americans, made the first winter ascent of Mt McKinley's Cassin Ridge in temperatures that fell to 60°C below zero. He has also worked with the British Antarctic Survey in Grahamland. His articles and photographs have appeared in mountaineering journals in Britain and America.

Born in 1956, Robert Swan began to plan the 'In the Footsteps of Scott' Expedition while he was studying Ancient History at Durham University. He met Roger Mear at Rothera Base when he worked there with the British Antarctic Survey in 1980. He has also made a seven-month journey by bicycle from Cape Town to Cairo and circumnavigated the Vatnajökull Ice Cap in Iceland on skis, manhauling supplies.

ROGER MEAR & ROBERT SWAN

In the Footsteps of Scott

With research and additional material
by Lindsay Fulcher

GRAFTON BOOKS

A Division of the Collins Publishing Group

LONDON GLASGOW
TORONTO SYDNEY AUCKLAND

Grafton Books
A Division of the Collins Publishing Group
8 Grafton Street, London W1X 3LA

Published by Grafton Books 1989

First published in Great Britain by
Jonathan Cape Ltd 1987

A CIP catalogue record for this book is available from the British
Library

ISBN 0-586-20688-4

Printed and bound in Great Britain by
Collins, Glasgow

Set in Times

For
JOHN ANDERSON

Contents

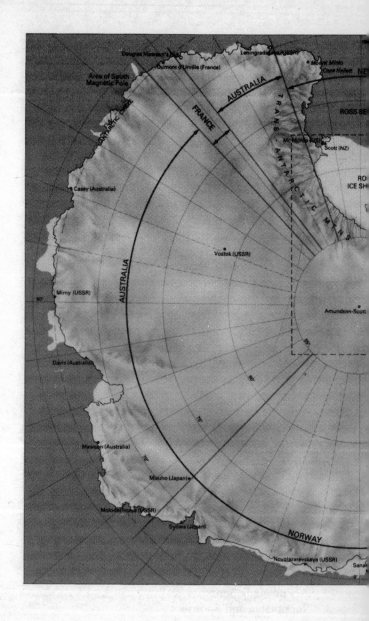

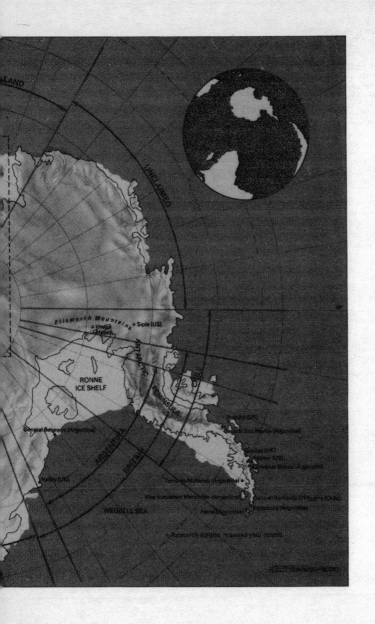

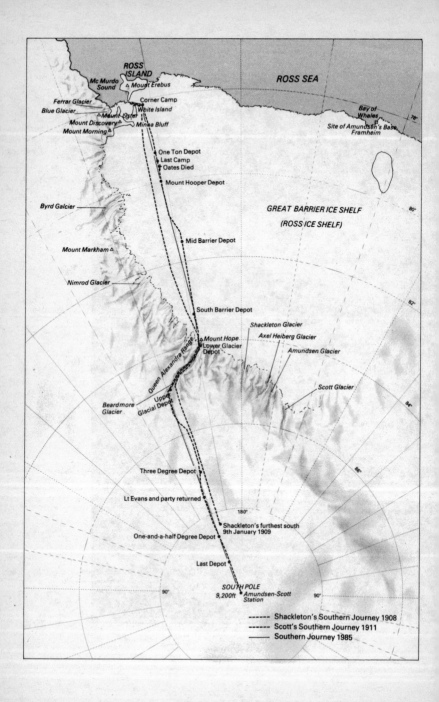

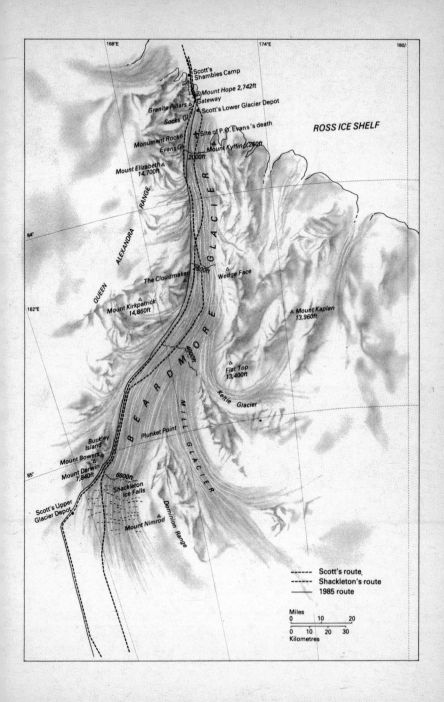

Scott's
Shambles Camp

△ Mount Hope 2,742ft
Gateway

Granite Pillars △
Socks Gl.   ╳ Scott's Lower Glacier Depot

                 + Site of P.O. Evans's death
Monument Rocks △
Evans Gl.   △ Mount Kyffin 750ft
                 2000ft

Mount Elizabeth △
14,700ft

ROSS ICE SHELF

QUEEN   ALEXANDRA   RANGE

84°

2600ft
The Cloudmaker △   △ Wedge Face

Mount Kirkpatrick △
14,860ft

BEARDMORE GLACIER

162°E   △ Mount Kaplan
                                        13,960ft

4800ft

△ Flat Top
   13,400ft

WILL GLACIER

Kettle   Glacier

Buckley
Island
Mount Bowers △
Mount Darwin △
7,840ft   6600ft

Plunket Point

85°

Scott's Upper
Glacier Depot •   Shackleton
                       Ice Falls

Dominion Range

                   △ Mount Nimrod

- - - - - Scott's route
- - - - - Shackleton's route
————— 1985 route

Miles
0   10   20
├───┬───┼───┬───┤
0   10   20   30
Kilometres

168°E   174°E   180°

In the Footsteps of Scott

Introduction
by Robert Swan

We had penetrated to the very edge of the Antarctic continent. My boots crunched on the hard crust of snow as I walked slowly towards the door of Scott's hut, and for one brief, uncanny moment I had the feeling that there were people inside who had heard my approach. It was as if they were holding their breath, hoping against hope that when the door burst open it would be the long overdue Scott and his Polar Party that trooped back in. The hut was deserted of course, I knew that, lined with empty bunks belonging to friends who were no longer there. Yet there was still a feeling of imminent reunion, of excitement tinged with tragedy and awe, a feeling, almost, of coming home.

I had been in Scott's hut many times before in my mind, and in my heart. I knew every detail of its layout, every item on every shelf; I knew every corner so well that I could have re-created it nail by nail. I had known it for almost ten years, in fact; it was as if I belonged there, but still I could not bring myself to walk straight in. I paused on the threshold, wondering if I should knock. I imagined music, soft and sentimental, a record on the gramophone. Then I pictured the faces around Scott's birthday table, their voices rising on the cold Antarctic wind, calling to me from almost seventy-five years ago – Englishmen's voices, from a bygone age: imperative, heroic, defeated.

No human footprints have yet appeared at the south geographic pole . . . but when they do appear, I intend that they shall be British footprints . . .

'How are your feet, Cherry?'
'Very cold, Bill.'

'That's all right; so are mine.'

Great God, this is an awful place . . .

Such were the sounds and the pictures – the imagery of an obsession that had consumed the last decade of my life – that now beckoned me inside the hut. I took a deep breath, and pulled the leather cord. The latch lifted easily.

Mine was a bold dream, conceived in a time when it was fashionable to decry the exploits and achievements of bold men and women. I was going to retrace Scott's footsteps to the South Pole.

Even now, almost ten years later, I can still remember the exact moment in 1977 when that dream was born. I was in my first year at Durham University, having spent two years since leaving school at a variety of jobs: laying a pipeline across the Yorkshire moors, as a labourer on the Heathrow tunnel, as a hospital cleaner, a plasterer, and as a tree surgeon. I had also taken seven months to bicycle from one end of Africa to the other, from Cape Town to Cairo, but it was the tree work that stood me in such good stead, enabling me to pay my way through University by selling logs. I had just been out on one such logging expedition around the streets of Durham, and had gone to the library for some books. By chance, the ancient history shelves were right next to those on Polar exploration, and my eye was caught by the cover of one particular book – *Scott's Men* by David Thomson. I stared for a long time at the picture of four men on the cover, their eyes sunk in their sockets, skin stretched tight over cheekbones; but it was less these physical manifestations of starvation and privation that told me they had suffered than the haunted expression in their eyes, a look that Thomson described as the 'flawless gaze of young men in the South'. What the hell had gone on, I asked aloud, to make that happen? I began to read:

Between the middle of January and the end of March 1912 five men died in the attempt to return from the South Pole to their base on the edge of Antarctica. Their leader, the last to die and the man whose diary described the pitiful difference between vanquished strength and remaining miles, was Robert Falcon Scott. Their journey back began with broken morale in that they had been narrowly beaten to their objective, the Pole, by a band of racing Norwegians, led by Roald Amundsen. The Norwegians were hauled along by dogs, while Scott and his men themselves wore harness and pulled their sledge through ice and snow, across ridges and crevasses.

The bodies of the last three to die were found seven months later and, ever since, Scott's men have been British heroes. It is the legend, as much as their ordeal, that is the subject of this book . . .

It was the legend as much as their achievement that was to take me over completely and to occupy the next ten years of my life. From that moment, I became totally obsessed by the last expedition of Captain Robert Falcon Scott.

I visited the Scott Polar Research Institute in Cambridge and asked if anyone had ever retraced Scott's footsteps. Their answer was to turn my life upside-down. The fact that no one had ever dared to venture upon Scott's journey again began to channel my energy and ambition. Before long the University film society arranged a private viewing for me of the 1948 Ealing Studios epic, *Scott of the Antarctic*. Watching the film was a profoundly moving event in my life. I identified closely with its portrayal of the simple bravery of men against the elements. Scott symbolized qualities of courage, determination and single-mindedness that struck a chord in me.

The film did not seek to analyse Scott's mistakes; it was content to re-enact their tragic outcome. What caught and held my imagination then – and still do – were the haunting aspects of that last expedition which transcend mere history and turn the story into an epic, almost a myth: the terrible idea of Scott and his companions doomed in that remote, howling wilderness of snow and ice, the victims of bad luck and blizzards and lower and lower temperatures as their strength ebbed, only eleven miles from a depot that might have saved their lives; the long silence of more than a year, broken suddenly in February 1913 when the *Terra Nova* at last reached New Zealand with the tragic news.

In a peculiarly British way, Scott's failure far outshone Amundsen's success. Scott's achievement was timeless. He created a legend in the face of overwhelming odds. His expedition also did a great deal of useful scientific work, while Amundsen thought of little else but his meticulous plan to get to the Pole, which he accomplished quickly and comparatively easily by a better route, with skilful use of skis and fifty-two dogs. For him the journey went like clockwork and there is not much more to say about it. Scott's motor sledges (let no one say he was not innovative) broke down, his ponies were a disaster, his dogs too few, and the worst part of the journey had to be done on foot, pulling a sledge with insufficient food. Scholars, I soon discovered, were taking this as their cue to attack Scott's judgment. Certainly he had appalling bad luck, but it did not seem to me that his plan to manhaul was ill-considered, and the words in Scott's last journal still speak to us in our more cynical age, across the intervening years and the experience of two World Wars, of loyalty and courage in terms that remain as poignant today as when first they were written. It was those words which produced in me the first stirrings of a powerful urge to set the record straight on the gallant man's behalf.

So it was that the idea slowly came to me of retracing Captain Scott's footsteps to the South Pole, and the expedition started to take shape in my mind. I wanted so much to bring all the photographs alive. I wanted to defend Scott's judgment and the noble sacrifice of Captain Oates, and in so doing, to uphold the tradition of Polar exploration and draw attention to the pressing need for conservation in the last great wilderness on earth. It was a tall order.

'Scott used to say that the worst part of an expedition was over when the preparation was finished.' With these words, Apsley Cherry-Garrard began his book, *The Worst Journey in the World*, and after many hard years of planning and organizing, I could believe him. In terms of sheer effort, our walk to the Pole was just the tip of an enormous iceberg. It was the culmination of thousands of hours of sweat and slog and sheer heartache that was a credit to the entire team.

Antarctica is a breathtakingly beautiful place, but it is also daunting and very dangerous. No one had seen it until 1820, or wintered there until 1898. It is the coldest, highest, windiest continent on earth. If it was my dream that got us there in

February 1985, there is also no getting away from the fact that, like Scott himself, I was an amateur. I was totally dependent on the friendship and willing dedication of scores of others more expert or experienced than I in many fields in which our very lives were at stake. Not everything went well. We had our share of hardship and adventure and loss. We had our eyes opened to the mischief of political gamesmanship. But we did what we set out to do, and Roger Mear gives his account of it in the pages that follow.

I went back to Scott's hut in the morning of our departure for the Pole. It was early November, towards the peak of midsummer, nine months since we had disembarked from our ship on to this other planet. The sun takes its time to travel down the sky in this season, seems to hang suspended there indefinitely. Time seemed to hang there, too, inside the hut that day. It was November 1985, but for all I knew it could have been November 1912, with Scott about to set out across almost 900 miles of wilderness for the remotest undiscovered, unmarked spot on the globe – the South Pole.

I lay down on Scott's bunk and looked at the ceiling. 'Well, that's what you looked at the morning you set off,' I thought. Then I left the hut with tears streaming down my face. I felt I was saying both greetings and farewell, for I had a sense as I stumbled outside that the spirit of those people would be with me, Scott, Bowers, Wilson and the others, and that we would all be going to the Pole together.

1

Sea of Dreams

The second ice circle enclosed us. It was New Year's Day 1986. In every direction the snow stretched away to come hard against a faultless blue sky. The horizon, flat as the sea, remained always the same distance from us, and though we moved each day it moved with us. So it appeared as if we remained fixed and the world rolled beneath our striding skis. Each day we pulled our sledges for nine long hours. When we stopped, it was at a place indistinguishable from the one we had left that morning or from where we had stopped on all previous evenings since the last snowy peak had slid out of sight, behind us, many days ago. The sun circled as if we were the centre of its orbit. The terms day and night, morning and evening, had long ceased to have any connection with the cold, light-filled world in which we moved. Yet we clung to them and carried them with us as we carried our own time. For they gave us a structure by which to order the endless round of marching, sleep and food. But the food, we knew, was not endless, and that was a fact which was never far from our thoughts. If the food ran out before the journey was completed, then the marching would continue until sleep took its place.

The daily routine enabled us to draw a veil over the infinite scale of the landscape and our pathetic insignificance, a fabric that would occasionally be pierced by the thought of what would happen if some part of this cavalcade, this machine we had created, malfunctioned. Through the rent would rush a vision of an ocean without a shore, of distances measured in single steps that reached over many horizons, out of reach. We were as alone as it is possible to be anywhere on the surface of the earth. There was no way back and no way out other than that which had brought us this far. We had entered a race in which it was no longer possible to step from the track. Behind us lay more than 700 miles of ice. The journey began with sledges heavy with food. Now, when the temperature rose to −20°C, warming the dry snow from the texture of sand, or when descending from the crest of a rolling wave so large as to be imperceptible, we seemed to fly. The pull of the sledge had become so familiar that, like gravity, we did not feel it.

Today, blowing in our faces is another 'searching wind', as Scott called it. There is blood where the cold rims of my glasses have continually burned the skin, and all our lips are split with sharp vertical lines of red. Our faces have become theatrical. Beards hang with ice, and yellow scales flake from a cheek on which, in a moment of inattention, had grown a small white disc of frozen skin. I follow the track made by the thin runners of a sledge, in dry dunes of snow, winding in and out of a silent overfall of frozen waves thrown up by invisible winds. The sastrugi, sculpted waves of snow, curling as if about to break, or swelling up to sharp peaks, are held in a time that is nearer to the wind-eroded change of desert mountains than to the motion of a sea at storm.

Three hundred yards ahead, Gareth stops, and brings his skis together, stands erect, arms wide from his sides, leaning back into his harness as if against a rail. Over the many days I have come to know the message of all such movements. In that momentary pause there is relief and satisfaction, and it tells me without the use of words that this is not a halt to sight the compass, when all attention remains fixed on a distant point, or a hurried stop to adjust a boot. This is the stop in which the last seconds of three hours come to an end and with it comes the promise of food. His pause is as long as two of my strides. After that, as I near, follows a routine of practised actions: pulling back the sleeve of a gauntlet to check the time, removing each hand from the strap on the grip of the ski-sticks which are left standing erect on either side, and with both mitted hands raising his goggles over the peak of his cap before beginning to unfasten the buckles of the harness.

By the time I arrive, Gareth is seated astride his sledge, back into the wind, face into the sun, the food he is allowing himself spread before him and a Thermos of soup in the snow by his booted foot. He is chiselling fragments of butter from a tin with a spoon, and balancing the splintering shavings on one of his three biscuits. He chews the white fat of a leather-hard slice of pepperoni sausage, torn in half with his teeth and soaked in the oily soup. He is engrossed in the struggle to save one of his four squares of chocolate for the moment, tonight, before sleep, when he lies warm in his bag. Soon we are both astride our sledges, lost in the sensations of food. To have a piece of chocolate release its sweetness into your mouth and dissolve without attention, because your mind is elsewhere, is to be robbed.

Robert draws alongside and we are one, two, three in a row peering from the deep recesses of furry hoods, back the way we have come to where our trail meets the white horizon. Nothing is said. There is energy only for what is essential.

'What's the mileage?' Robert asks after a time, and Gareth leans carefully forward, so as not to dislodge any crumbs of biscuit, over the back of his sledge to read the numbers on the wheel.

He answers, '5.36 miles,' without a hint that he can remember when we struggled all day to make that distance on the Barrier.

The cold has crept through our clothing by the time the food is finished and one by one, signalled by the movement of whoever is to lead the next three hours, we get ready to go on. In the short time it takes to step into our skis and strap the harness around chest and hips, we are cold. The fingers of my right hand are stiff and the tips numb. For the first twenty minutes I ski hard, waiting for the flush of heat that the food and exercise will generate. Inside my mitten I have drawn my hand into a fist, which I clench and unclench until the circulation is restored. Then, before sweat begins to mist my dark glasses, I slacken to the pace that I know will carry me through the rest of the day. I am breathing heavily.

Stopping, I turn to look over my shoulder along the trail shining in the sunlight. Fifty yards behind, Gareth has also stopped, at a point where my track bends left. Further behind, the distant figure of Robert, dark in his own shadow, ploughs on, and seeing me look back, raises a ski-stick vertically in the air to signal all is well. Gareth too, raises a stick, but points right with his arm straight and the pole level, indicating a correction to my course. Then an exaggerated shrug of his shoulders tells me he is unsure. Since we entered this area of sastrugi it has become more difficult for the man behind to check our direction. Our track no longer resembles the ruled pencil line on the blank paper that is our map, but weaves through the waves, seeking the easiest path.

Strangely, the red tip of the compass needle points south, for the South Magnetic Pole lies behind us, 1,600 miles to the north. There the needle will stand vertically on end, but here on the Polar Plateau it weakly points our way. Every few days we check its changing variation against the position of the sun at the second of noon and hope that our watches are not slow or fast. I head towards a far white flash of sastrugi, one among many, whose form I have fixed in my mind like a beacon to guide me through the waves. The sledge rumbles along the hard icy crest of a long whale-back, and then I turn over a cornice, with the sledge bucking behind, to descend into the trough. The momentum carries me through a drifting band of dry snow that grabs at the sledge but does not quite halt it, out on to a flat icy ribbon that fills the shallow valley like a stream. I follow its meandering for a time over snow layered in numerous directions, each with an individual colour and patterned with unique textures, like the shoals of firm sand on a beach at low tide. I pull hard up the blue rise of a wave, until ski-tips hang in the air, and then flop over the crest to bridge a deep, wind-eroded channel. The sledge jams beneath an undermined crust of snow, brings me up abruptly, and takes a squandering of power to release it.

For three days we were hindered by this erratic progress, jostled this way and that by sledges tossed by frozen waves. Then, after 56 miles the sastrugi subsided as quickly as they had appeared, with no hint as to why they should suddenly erupt here and not there, a small island of turmoil in a vast, flat plain. Scott had encountered them, 'a sea of fish-hook waves', through which the pulling was 'terribly heavy'. Yet the worst thing about them was the fear they generated – another unavoidable trouble that could appear again without warning and continue, for all we knew, all the way to the Pole. It was a reminder that though there was little more than a hundred miles to go, every delay, every lost yard, ate into the slim reserve we imagined we possessed.

Our bodies are lean, just muscle and bone. A pinch of flesh holds nothing but thin skin between finger and thumb. We have become machines that each day must convert every ounce of food we consume into miles. How good it feels when the sledge glides easily behind and you are able to stretch out, each kick and stride leading into the next in unbroken rhythm. Yet fear is never far beneath the surface, an ever present spur that drives us on.

Shackleton turned back here, 97 nautical miles from the Pole. How close it seemed. The Pole must have taunted him with its closeness. For a few short minutes a large Union Jack stood stiff in a wind that now blew in our faces. Three years later Scott reached and passed this same imaginary point that is distinguished from all other points along the route across the high white desert only by its latitude. 'All ahead is new,' Scott wrote as he climbed on towards an invisible summit that has no physical form and exists only in the abstract notion that through it runs the axis about which the earth turns. For him the attainment was to bring the cruellest disappointment. 'The worst has happened . . . Great God this is an awful place and terrible enough for us to have laboured to it without the reward of priority . . . Now for the run home and a desperate struggle. I wonder if we can do it.'

High above the brown and sluggish waters of the River Wear stand the ancient walls of Durham Castle. It is summer, and the steep slopes of the gorge are shaded under a heavy canopy of sycamore and beech. For seven-and-a-half centuries the yellow stones proclaimed the wealth and power of successive bishops, until that power, eroded like the stones, gave way to a more secular élite.

The students gather now in twos and fours and make their way with difficulty, shod in hard-heeled shoes, up the narrow cobbled streets that converge upon Palace Green. Here, they pause and, in the fading light, watch for a time the close of a ribald game of croquet, before continuing in lax procession under the dipping limes and through the toothed Norman arch of the gatehouse into the Castle bailey. One by one the lights that illuminate this conglomerate of architectural styles come on, and men in dark uniform, with dog at heel, can be seen prowling the ramparts to prevent those without the price of a ticket from gate-crashing the June Ball of University College.

The Great Hall is a press of people, those less active pushed back against the dark oak panelling by the gyrating bodies, sweating in black tie or pearls, whose movements are frozen in a succession of staccato images by a flickering strobe. The walls of the gallery are adorned with Cromwellian armour, racks of pikes, and the frail remnants of regimental flags. Below these stand two banks of speakers that are the source of a prepotent sound that fills the Hall and pervades the farthest rooms of the Castle. Around the entrance to the Great Hall, the milling crowd of undergraduates spills out on to the wide oaken steps of Bishop Cosin's Black Staircase, and they sit on its ascending flights, or lean against the ornate balustrade, talking and drinking.

In 1977, a student at the Castle, Robert Swan, had purposely removed himself from the social whirl and found seclusion in the Senate Room behind the walls of Tunstall's Chapel. There, alone in the darkened room, he viewed a film in serious contemplation. He wore a dinner jacket of a style older than his years, and though he was well enough accustomed to such dress, disliked the constraint it placed upon his body. Above the tight, winged collar of a greyed and suspiciously rumpled linen shirt, sat an incongruously powerful head. His hair was short, shorn as close to the skin as is possible without recourse to the razor. He was hot and his scalp sweated.

Grasping the last inch of a small cigar between massive fingers he watched as the smoke formed a thin blue veil that hung, with sluggish motion, in the beam of light emitted from the movie projector. He heard but did not heed the sound of the madly flailing reel, a signal for attention that few could have disregarded. Outside the ball continued unaware of his absence, and though he knew that his isolation was a self-imposed gesture, he resented the intrusion of frivolity.

The film that Robert Swan watched was made at Ealing Studios in 1948, with John Mills in the title role as 'Scott of the Antarctic'. It was in all probability not his first encounter with the story of Captain Robert Falcon Scott. How could that be possible, educated as he had been at a public school that upheld Scott as the highest expression of its most noble principles? It was the heroic myth embodied in the film that inspired Robert and provided a channel for his energy and ambition. Perhaps it did not happen in exactly the fashion I have related, but there can be no doubt that he left the University not only with a degree but also with a dream.

Even at Durham, Robert Swan was larger than life. His fellow students, observing ice-blue eyes and his heavily muscled figure astride a big Kawasaki motor-cycle, roaring over the cobbles of the Bailey, must have realized he was not destined for a career in accountancy. But how could anyone, when they heard him speak of his ambition to re-enact Scott's epic journey, believe that he would ever fulfil his boast? While studying for his degree, he spent much of his time reading and re-reading the Polar diaries of Scott and Shackleton. He found in those pages stories of endurance, courage and acclaim to which he aspired. The Norwegian explorer Roald Amundsen, Scott's rival in the race for the Pole, recalled his first impulse to lead the life of adventure after he had read of earlier Polar exploits: 'A strange ambition burned within me, to endure the same privations . . . I decided to be an explorer.'

The film does not dwell on the horrors of scurvy and frost-bite or the fatal chain of events that led to the demise of Scott and his party returning from the Pole in 1912, but dramatically portrays the heroic story that symbolized the romantic aspiration of an era, the ability of Englishmen to triumph over adversity and even death. We are a more cynical nation now and our heroes have been toppled from their pedestals. They have been denounced because they have been revealed as men with weaknesses and failings. Scott fell to the biased pen of Roland Huntford in his book *Scott and Amundsen*. Yet the truth lies somewhere between the two extremes. Robert's dream was not simply to walk to the South Pole but to rediscover Scott and bring alive the histories of those men that so inspired him.

A dream, like water, can run through your fingers. Frozen into the solid, cold reality of ice it can be held but, even then, if held too long it will begin to melt away and, as Robert was to discover, so could his dream.

As soon as he had graduated, Robert set about getting to grips with the practicalities of acquiring Polar experience. His Arts degree was hardly the best qualification for work with the British Antarctic Survey: a grounding in the sciences, some mountaineering experience, a basic knowledge of two-stroke engines and the ability to muck-in were what was required. To improve his credentials, he joined an expedition to Mount Kenya, worked part-time in a garage and plagued his family and friends to obtain suitable references. By 1980, he felt ready to apply to BAS and also to the New Zealand Antarctic Division. In June, he appeared unannounced in Christchurch and was given an interview by Bob Thompson, Director of the New Zealand Antarctic Programme, and was gratified to hear that he could join them the following season. Returning to London, he found that the British were also willing to accept his services in Antarctica if he could be ready to leave almost immediately. Impatient as ever, he accepted the BAS invitation and sailed from Southampton on the RRS *John Biscoe* in September 1980.

That year I too had joined the Survey, attracted not by the deeds of Scott but by the mystery of a continent of ice and mountains. I saw Robert for the first time at the annual BAS conference held for new recruits in Cambridge. His formidable stature, close-cropped hair and what appeared to be a police-man's collarless shirt, made me wonder if he had recently been released from prison. He had spotted me, too, it seems. 'You looked a different animal from the rest,' he later told me. We got to know each other during the monotonous fourteen-week voyage south. Our boisterous antics were not always appreci-ated by others on board. I remember a riotous food fight in the mess, watched critically by some of the scientific staff, puffing on their pipes, who asked, 'Are these the right men for the job?' – for we would be responsible for their well-being once we reached the glaciers of the Antarctic. We were seen, I think, as unprofessional, irresponsible, high-spirited adventurers, a charge which would be levelled at us from some quarters throughout our expedition to the South Pole.

Robert told me of his dream of following Scott's route even before the ship had left the Solent. At first, his plan did not interest me greatly. He wanted to re-create Scott's expedition, using men and dogs to haul tons of supplies from the coast to the bottom of the Beardmore Glacier, and from there to manhaul to the Pole, returning through the pre-laid depots. I was not interested, as Robert was, in vindicating Scott and his heroic, or tragic, place in history. But his words sparked an idea, a possibility that excited me: why not dispense with all the clutter and go alone and unsupported, in one push, with a minimum of food – no depots, no air support, no dogs, ponies or mechanized vehicles – just two men, hauling sledges on the longest white walk in history? Of course, it could never be a two-way journey on foot as Scott's had been, for no one could drag the weight of five months' food, but the thought of being out there, in such awesome isolation, with just a pair of skis, a sledge and a tent, made the artificiality of a one-way journey acceptable. To a mountaineer like myself it offered all the mystery and challenge of an unclimbed ridge on Everest or K2 or the perpendicular granite walls of Yosemite. I promised to investigate the practicality of such a plan as soon as we returned home.

Our time with the British Antarctic Survey at Rothera Base passed quickly, Robert shovelling concrete and humping stores with great zeal, while I bumped around the glaciers of the Arrowsmith Peninsula on a skidoo (a kind of motor-scooter with tracks and ski) with the geologist Dan Hamer. A Fid, as those who work on British Antarctic bases are traditionally called, needs to be able to turn his hand to the most unexpected tasks. One of the Twin Otter aircraft, landing heavily, had punched one of its skis through its fuselage and could not be flown out of Antarctica when the season was over. The plane had to be dismantled and its component parts, wings, engines and tail-plane, crated so that it could be loaded on board ship. Robert set to work with his usual energy, hammering and banging a hotchpotch of scavenged timbers and bent nails, until he proudly announced that his piece of the aircraft was successfully boxed. When he came to move his creation, with guttural cries and veins bulging on his forehead, he found that his own unaided efforts were futile. The crate would not move. Four of us gathered, one at each corner, and in unison, one, two, three, hup! we lifted, but to no avail. All four of us, heaving on one corner, managed to raise the box a fraction of an inch, enough to force an iron crowbar under the wood. With this lever the crate grudgingly rose sufficiently to reveal a number of the several hundred nails that Robert had pounded through the planks of his construction right into the wooden floor of the hut.

In March 1981, with the damaged aircraft loaded safely on board the RRS *Bransfield*, we left Antarctica bound for South America. It was during this voyage that we met Dr Michael Stroud, who had been employed at Faraday, another British base, and who was to join us three years later as our expedition doctor. The First Mate on the *Bransfield* was Graham Phippen and he was destined to become the captain of the expedition's ship. Robert and I then disembarked at Punta Arenas to travel up through South America to Rio de Janeiro, where we would rejoin the *Bransfield*. There were just four weeks for a whistle-stop tour and, we hoped, an ascent of Mount Aconcagua, the highest mountain in the southern hemisphere. The latter was a spontaneous and unplanned adventure. There was no time to negotiate the labyrinth of Argentinian bureaucracy for the required permit, and that gave it a clandestine flavour. We were a little unsure of exactly where we should be going, for our road map of South America showed the mountain as no more than a small black triangle. At Puente del Inca we bought potatoes and tins of tuna from a restaurateur who had closed his business for the winter. He was suspicious of Robert in a tee-shirt proclaiming 'The Falkland Islands are British and Beautiful', but pointed us in roughly the right direction. We left the road in the dark and crept past armed sentries at a military base on the sensitive Argentinian border with Chile before picking our way up the arid valley we hoped would lead us to Aconcagua.

In five days we ascended from sea-level to 18,500 feet, and predictably both of us suffered from altitude sickness. It was as if a thin steel band were being tightened irrevocably about my head. Robert, who had been in front, striding ahead for most of the way, became increasingly ill. He felt acute nausea and immediately vomited anything he ate. However upset Robert was at the thought, it was obvious that we had to go down. I suppose we both thought of the climb as a sort of trial, but while I set little store by our inevitable retreat, Robert saw it as his failure. I think he believed that I would now judge him unfit for the Polar walk. In fact, the opposite was true: later, when I became worried that his single-minded obsession to reach the Pole would kill us both, I remembered this incident and reassured myself that he could recognize his limitations and was capable of turning back.

After our return to England we resumed our separate lives, but the seed was sown and from then on everything we did, everyone we met, was viewed with an eye to the Pole. Our preparations took different forms. That winter I went to Alaska on a pre-arranged attempt to climb Mount McKinley, and there I quickly learnt about survival in extreme cold. I returned on crutches, with a knee torn in a crevasse fall, to take up my new job at Plas-y-Brenin, the National Mountaineering Centre in North Wales. Robert joined two Royal Marines officers on a circumnavigation of Iceland's Vatnajökull Ice Cap, manhauling over 150 miles. Slowly we began the process of raising both sponsorship and credibility for what we then called The Scott Antarctic Expedition.

The first decisive step was taken when Robert wrote to the son of Captain Scott, the naturalist Sir Peter Scott, telling him of the expedition and asking if he might visit him at his home in Gloucestershire. Robert recalls: 'I was extremely nervous and it was difficult to gauge whether or not he was sympathetic to my story. We were interrupted by three Everest double-glazing men who had arrived to fix the windows. They looked even more nervous than I felt. How boring, I thought, to be surrounded by people in awe of you. Seeing their diffidence somehow increased my confidence and I asked Sir Peter outright if he would agree to be our Patron. He looked thoughtful, picked up the telephone receiver and spoke to his wife. "Darling," he said, "do come down here for a moment. I'd like you to meet a very interesting young man called Robert Swan. He is going to walk to the Pole in my father's footsteps." His words "in my father's footsteps" rang in my head: at that moment I knew the expedition had become more than a dream, it was happening.'

Afterwards, Sir Peter's secretary told Robert that one of the reasons he had agreed to the meeting was that the swan was his favourite bird. How often, I wonder, does the outcome of a great enterprise hang by such a slender thread of coincidence?

Sir Peter made one request, that we should change the name of our endeavour from The Scott Antarctic Expedition, since he had rightly pointed out that there was no Scott among us. The week before I had attended a lecture by John Beatty, who had recently walked across Greenland. His talk was called 'In the Footsteps of Nansen'. I never did apologize for the blatant plagiarism. We added 'In the Footsteps of' to our literature.

When Sir Peter agreed to become Patron to the expedition, he did more than provide the credibility we so badly needed. Suddenly, the incorporeal figure of an Edwardian hero became a tangible presence. The father at the last had written to his wife Kathleen: 'Make the boy interested in natural history if you can; it is better than games; they encourage it at some schools.' Here was that boy, now a man, dedicating his life to the study and protection of our natural heritage, founder of the Wildfowl Trust, whose intuition is recorded in his mother's diary: 'I woke up having had a bad dream about you (her husband), and then Peter (aged two) came very close to me and said emphatically: "Daddy won't come back . . ."'

2

A Timeless Place

It was in the spring of 1912, after a second winter, eight months after their expected return, that the fate of Scott and his companions was confirmed. Apsley Cherry-Garrard was one of the search-party of eleven which found them:

> That scene can never leave my memory . . . Wright came across to us. 'It is the tent.' I do not know how he knew. Just a waste of snow: to our right the remains of last year's cairns, a mere mound: and then three feet of bamboo sticking quite alone out of the snow: and then another mound of snow, perhaps a trifle more pointed. We walked up to it . . . someone reached up to a projection of snow, and brushed it away. The green flap of the ventilator of the tent appeared, and we knew that the door was below. (*The Worst Journey in the World.*)

Peering inside, it was dark and still, they could see nothing until the snow was dug from around the tent. Then, in a soft green light, three forms dusted with snow crystals became visible. They lay, wrapped in the thick skins of their reindeer sleeping bags, Bowers on the left, Wilson to the right, his head towards the door and his hands folded peacefully across his chest. In the centre was Scott, the flaps of his bag thrown open and his left hand stretched out over Wilson.

Cherry-Garrard's account continues:

> Near Scott was a lamp formed from a tin and some lamp wick off a finnesko. It had been used to burn the little methylated spirit which remained. I think that Scott had used it to help him write up to the end. I feel sure that he had died last – and once I had thought that he would not go as far as some of the others. We never realized how strong that man was, mentally and physically, until now. (Ibid.)

Letters, diaries and scientific notes were recovered, among them a letter addressed to King Haakon of Norway, which

Amundsen had left at the Pole with the request to Scott that it should be delivered. On their sledge, buried under three feet of snow, was found Bowers's meteorological log and 35 lbs of geological specimens, gathered from the moraines of the Beardmore Glacier. Tryggve Gran, the Norwegian member of Scott's expedition, thought that 'they might have saved themselves the weight', and he was not the last to fail to see the enormous significance that the rocks must have assumed for those doomed men. The prize of being the first to the South Pole had been taken from them and therefore, if their labour was to retain any purpose, it would have to be in the knowledge that they won for science. Frank Debenham, the expedition's geologist, regarded the specimens as 'perhaps the most important of all the geological results', and seventy-five years later eminent scientists of the British Antarctic Survey could still write:

The plant fossils collected . . . from the Beardmore Glacier and found with their bodies, were of particular significance. Although the expedition failed to reach the Pole first and ended in tragedy its scientific achievements were more than sufficient to justify it. Amundsen won the race but his efforts provided virtually nothing in terms of scientific information. (Walton and Bonner, *Key Environment: Antarctica*.)

The tent was collapsed over the bodies and a huge cairn of snow, twelve feet high, was built over it. On top was fixed a wooden cross fashioned from a ski. It was a simple and impressive monument, visible from more than 8 miles on the flat white plain. Cherry-Garrard thought that it 'must last for many years. That we can make anything that will be permanent on this Barrier is impossible, but as far as a lasting mark can be made it has been done.'

The cairn was never seen again. Slowly, abraded by the drifting snow and ablated by the sun, it would have sunk beneath the surface. The bodies, preserved from corruption by the frost, are still there, locked in ice which moves interminably towards the sea until, one day, an iceberg will carve from the edge of the Great Ice Barrier and carry them north.

The Antarctic holds 90 per cent of the world's ice. At its deepest, it is 15,669 feet thick. If it were all to melt, the rising sea would flood London and New York. Water would splash the dome of St Paul's and lap around the waist of the Statue of Liberty. The continent is bigger than either Europe or the United States of America and its mean altitude of 7,500 feet is three times that of any other land mass. It holds the record for the lowest temperature ever recorded on the earth's surface, $-89.6°C$, yet during the summer the South Pole receives more solar radiation than the Equator in any equivalent period. It is an incomparably barren land; in its interior only lichens and algae survive. The largest permanent inhabitant is a wingless midge, *Belgica antarctica*, and that is found only in the more temperate areas, and of all the birds that frequent the coasts in summer only the Emperor penguin remains throughout the long dark winter.

The existence of a southern continent had been postulated by the Greeks. Legend has it that in 750 A.D. a Polynesian warrior, Ui-te-Rangiora, in a great canoe named 'Te Ivi-o-Atea', voyaged south until the way was barred by ice and the sky was streaked with serpents, which we now call the Aurora Australis. James Cook circumnavigated the region, crossing the Antarctic circle on 17 January 1773, but saw no land. It remained as Terra Australis Incognita until 28 January 1820, when the Russian, Thaddeus von Bellingshausen, became the first to sight the Antarctic mainland. The men who came after, piece by piece unlocked the secrets of the frozen land.

In January 1841 an expedition sponsored by the British Admiralty and led by Captain James Clark Ross, with two ships, the *Erebus* and *Terror*, penetrated the pack-ice and emerged into an open sea. They sailed south, discovering a land of magnificent snow-covered peaks and what the ship's surgeon, Robert McCormick, described as 'a stupendous volcanic mountain in a high state of activity'. Ross named the peak Mount Erebus, and a slightly lower summit to the east he called Mount Terror. To the most eastern rocky point of Ross Island he gave the name Cape Crozier, honouring his second-in-command, Francis Crozier, captain of the *Terror*. There Ross found the way barred by a wall of ice. He said, 'We might with equal chance of success try to sail through the cliffs of Dover.' It was the edge of the Ross Ice Shelf or what became known as the Great Ice Barrier, an area of ice the size of France. It extended 'as far as the eye could discern to the eastward . . . a perpendicular cliff of ice, between one hundred and fifty feet and two hundred feet above the level of the sea, perfectly flat and level on top, and without any fissures or promontories on its even seaward face'. Though the Barrier was impenetrable to shipping, it was across its surface that the way to the South Pole was to be found. The Norwegian Casten Borchgrevink, who led the first expedition to winter on the continent in 1899, also became, along with William Colbeck and the Australian physicist Louis Bernacchi, the first to walk upon the Barrier. Bernacchi described the ice shelf as 'stretching away for hundreds of miles to the south and west. Unless one has actually seen it, it is impossible to conceive the stupendous extent of this ice-cap, its consistency, utter barrenness, and stillness, which sends an indefinable sense of dread to the heart.'

The early years of the twentieth century heralded the dawn of the Heroic Age of Antarctic exploration. It culminated with the attainment of its greatest prize, the South Geographic Pole, and was brought to a close with Shackleton's attempt to traverse the continent and his epic voyage to South Georgia after his ship *Endurance* was crushed by ice in the Weddell Sea. The stage on which much of the dramatic saga was performed is the Great Barrier Ice Shelf, the great sweep of the Trans-Antarctic Mountains, through which a way had to be found, and the high Polar Plateau, where lies the Pole. The players brought time to a timeless land, named its features and gave it a history.

On Ross Island still stand the winter quarters of the main protagonists, though Amundsen's base, Framheim, at the Bay of Whales, is lost. On the tip of Hut Point Peninsula is the base of Scott's *Discovery* expedition of 1901–4. From there with Dr Edward Wilson, a young Lieutenant Shackleton and nineteen dogs, Scott pushed south until, exhausted, low on food and fuel and with Shackleton suffering from scurvy, they had to retreat. In fifty-nine days they had probed 380 miles across the Barrier towards the Pole, establishing a new Farthest South.

Shackleton returned in 1908 with his own expedition and

built his base at Cape Royds, 21 miles north of Hut Point. The successful ascent of Mount Erebus (12,448 feet) boded well for his attempt on the Pole. The southern journey began on 29 October. It took them only twenty-nine days to pass the point he had reached with Scott: twenty-four days later they had discovered what was then thought to be the greatest glacier in the world, the Beardmore, and climbed it to the Polar Plateau. On 9 January 1909, with their resources stretched to the absolute limit, Shackleton was forced to turn and face defeat. He wrote:

Our last day outwards. We have shot our bolt, and the tale is latitude 88° 23′ South, longitude 162° East.

They were 97 geographical miles short of the Pole. How little that is and how hard it must have been to accept failure when success was so near I only now begin to appreciate. But we can have no real comprehension of how great was the attraction of that prize, with its promise of prestige, fortune and immortality, unless we think of it in terms of the greatest trophy of modern exploration, the moon.

Since the day when the news of Scott's death reached the world, the argument has raged as to why he and his companions died. In his 'Message to the Public', Scott blamed 'misfortune' and the unexpected harshness of the weather they encountered on their return.

The causes of the disaster are not due to faulty organization, but to misfortune in all risks which had to be undertaken . . . our wreck is certainly due to this sudden advent of severe weather, which does not seem to have any satisfactory cause, [and] the storm which has fallen on us within 11 miles of the depot at which we hoped to secure our final supplies.

The pundits added other reasons: the devastating effect on morale that finding themselves forestalled by Amundsen must have had; the mysterious shortage of fuel; starvation, scurvy, dehydration; and the last-minute decision to take five men, not four, on to the Pole. All must have played a part, but for me there is one underlying cause on which all other factors depend, and that is the overwhelming attraction of the Pole. It caused

Scott to stretch behind him a trail of supplies so thin that all reserve was gone and with it the ability to cope with any delay. Scott was not the first to overstep the line of caution, and he will not be the last. It is easy to sit in a comfortable chair and with hindsight judge another's failings, for in the end the final arbiter is success.

In 1958, Sir Vivian Fuchs led the last of the great journeys of discovery, traversing the continent from shore to shore. Since then the needs of science and adventure have moved steadily apart. Technology has usurped the pioneer, satellites have mapped every corner of the land and provide instant communication with the outside world. The mystery has gone. Helicopters whisk geologists to remote rocky nunataks and aircraft drop fresh milk and fruit to the South Pole station, even in the middle of winter. Those who seek adventure can no longer set out under the banner of science and close communion with the great forces of nature is no longer possible from within the restrictive protection of the modern Antarctic base.

So it was that we looked back for our inspiration. Scott had written:

No journey made with dogs can approach the height of that fine conception which is realized when a party of men go forth to meet hardships, dangers and difficulties with their own unaided efforts, and by days and weeks of hard physical labour succeed in solving some problem of the great unknown.

Roland Huntford, in his scholarly but absurdly biased castigation of Scott, focused his condemnation on Scott's choice of manhauling as the primary means of reaching the Pole. His book, *Scott and Amundsen*, contains numerous pronouncements that damn the method and those who would be fool enough to employ it. To the Norwegians, Huntford claims, the man-hauling harness 'was an instrument of torture', and 'Amundsen used the harness to symbolize the penalty of failure.' Yet it was the greatest of all the Norwegian explorers, the mentor of both Amundsen and Scott, Fridtjof Nansen, who first demonstrated the efficiency of manhauling in his crossing of the Greenland Ice Cap in 1888. Huntford uses this remarkable journey, which inspired Amundsen, to begin his reasoned attack on the entrenched attitudes of British Polar exploration and its 'self-perpetuating clique of mediocrities'. He states, quite rightly, that in the technique of Polar travel, 'Nansen broke new ground', that 'Nansen had moreover introduced a startling new concept into Polar exploration', with the launching of the Norwegian school of Polar exploration, 'the school that for an intense, fertile period was to supplant the British and dominate the field'. Yet strangely he neglects to mention the fact that Nansen and his five companions manhauled their sledges every inch of the 323 mile journey.

The relative efficiency of manhauling should not be underestimated. Even with the recent introduction of a new generation of turbo diesel vehicles, manpower compares favourably with the potential range of all forms of land transportation used in the Polar regions. That is, men pulling all their own supplies on sledges could go almost as far as a skidoo pulling its fuel and the provisions of the driver, and further than dogs if they are not fed off the land, as in the Arctic, or used as walking food for both the men and the surviving animals. All this is conjecture, however, for no one has yet dared to prove the superiority of machines by setting out on a Polar journey of any duration without the organized support of aircraft. This fact points to the primary disadvantage of mechanized vehicles, the likelihood of mechanical failure – an affliction to which men and dogs are not prone, and human beings, it seems, have a range equal to, if not greater than, dogs, if the animals are not to be sacrificed.

Of course it is permissible to build a pyramid of supplies, which would extend the range of any form of transport (in this way Everest was first climbed), and neither Scott nor Amundsen intended that all their animals should return. Scott began his journey south with 16 men, 2 motor sledges, 10 ponies and 23 dogs and the previous summer he had laid provisions at One Ton Depot, 140 miles along his route south. Amundsen, 400 miles away at the Bay of Whales, had likewise moved 1.5 tons of fuel and food to within 480 miles of the Pole. Five men and 52 dogs left his base, Framheim, on 20 October 1911. Ten dogs died crossing the Barrier, and when they were no longer needed 24 more were shot. At the Pole a further six were slaughtered to provide food for the remainder to return. Eleven dogs survived.

Modern Polar expeditions – like Fuchs's Trans-Antarctic Expedition, Ranulph Fiennes's Transglobe and Wally Herbert's crossing of the Arctic – have been able to replace the need for pre-laid depots and food on hoof or paw with the enterprising use of aircraft. It was my belief that it would be possible to reach the South Pole independently of such support. Our brochure proudly proclaimed, like the opening lines of an episode of 'Star Trek':

An Expedition whose intention is to retrace Captain Robert Scott's footsteps to the South Pole and to restore the feelings of adventure, isolation and commitment that have been lost through the employment of the paraphernalia of modern times. Without recourse to depots, dogs, air support or outside assistance of any kind, two men alone will manhaul the 883 mile journey to the Pole.

The Times of 12 February 1913, reporting Scott's tragic end, praised him and his expedition and concluded: 'It is a proof that in an age of depressing materialism men can still be found to face known hardship, heavy risk and even death, in pursuit of an idea, and that the unconquerable will can carry them through . . .'

That is what our expedition was all about.

3

A Question of Access

It is one thing to dream of walking the 900 miles of Scott's route from the sea-ice at Cape Evans to the South Pole and quite another to mount an expedition capable of achieving such a goal. Few places on earth are as remote and none more inaccessible.

Antarctica is international territory. Britain, France, Norway, Australia, New Zealand, Argentina and Chile lay claim to segments of the land, measured in radii from the Pole itself, but their sovereignty remains unrecognized. Other nations, including the Soviet Union and the United States, though they do not make territorial claims, reserve the right to do so. In 1958 President Eisenhower, before an international conference convened to discuss the future of the Antarctic, stated, 'We propose that Antarctica shall be open to all nations to conduct scientific or other peaceful activities there.' The Antarctic Treaty which was drawn up as a result in 1959 stipulates that the continent should for ever 'be used exclusively for peaceful purposes' and should never become 'the scene or object of international discord.' It is, however, the Antarctic itself, its harsh climate and its isolation, that has caused a tradition of co-operation to grow between the twelve original signatories to the treaty. (Japan, Belgium and South Africa make up the dozen.) When the treaty was drafted it was assumed that Antarctica did not contain exploitable resources and no provision was made to control such a development. Several nations have since demonstrated their interest in the Antarctic's minerals and technology can no longer be regarded as a limiting factor to their eventual exploitation. It has been estimated that the extraction of oil will become economically viable by the 1990s. Seismic surveys of the Ross and Weddell

Sea areas have already been conducted by the USA, USSR, West Germany, Norway and Japan for purportedly scientific reasons. Traces of gold, silver, lead, manganese, platinum, uranium and other minerals have been located. Despite the growing likelihood of eventual commercial exploitation there still exists no internationally agreed framework by which such work could be prevented or regulated and the Antarctic remains unprotected from the inevitable destructive consequences of uncontrolled drilling and mining.

Since its ratification in 1961 the Antarctic Treaty has only frozen the unresolved questions of sovereignty. The Falklands War of 1982 highlighted the potential for future conflict in the Antarctic. During the war, Argentina occupied Gritviken, the British Antarctic Survey base on South Georgia. The islands are part of an area claimed by Britain that stretches from the Pole to the tip of South America. It includes the Antarctic Peninsula which is also claimed by Argentina and Chile. Norway and Australia claim areas in which the USSR have permanent bases and the New Zealand sector is dominated by American activity. These contentious issues will have to be faced before 1991 when the Treaty is open for review. If at that time disagreement causes the Treaty to become unworkable it will be the nations with the strongest presence who will cut the choicest slices of the cake.

In 1923 the British Government handed the Ross Dependency – the region in which Scott and Shackleton had conducted their explorations – to New Zealand. Thirty years later the president of the New Zealand Antarctic Society, Dr R. A. Falla, in an eight-page memorandum, advised his Prime Minister of the urgent need for some action which would strengthen New Zealand's claim to the territory. He stressed the ease with which other nations, if they were to set up a base in the region, could establish an equally valid claim.

'It is significant that every successful expedition to the South Pole, whether by land or air, has had its base in the Ross Dependency, using either the McMurdo Sound area or the Bay of Whales. These two harbours form the most accessible gateway to the interior of the Continent, and as such they would attract any foreign power seeking a base in the Antarctic.

If a [New Zealand] scientific station is set up, even with token administrative facilities, our sovereignty will be greatly strengthened.'

'Effective occupation' is the strongest basis for any territorial claim and the only one recognized by international law. Scott Base was established by New Zealand in 1957 at Pram Point, following advice from the Americans, who had already established their McMurdo Station in the bay where Scott's *Discovery* hut still stands. The two bases would be only two miles apart, separated by a low pass called by Scott the Gap. It was a proximity that the Americans encouraged because of the interwoven nature of the two operations. This interdependence has developed into a strong dependence by New Zealand upon the support of American aircraft and shipping.

It was also in 1957 that the United States constructed a permanent base at the South Pole. A CIA publication states that America 'stressed its neutrality by placing its Amundsen-Scott Station at the South Pole,' but its strategic position will provide a strong basis for claims of 'effective occupation' standing as it does at the hub of the continent. Few can doubt that the furtherance of science is not the only motivation for the expensive upkeep of Antarctic stations.

Though we did not require permission from any authority to visit Antarctica, the difficulty and expense of reaching its shores independently prompted Robert to seek help from the National Science Foundation in Washington. Our first thought had been for the two of us to fly into McMurdo with our two sledges, food and equipment and to set off immediately for the Pole. Three months later we would fly home again. It was a simple, uncomplicated plan, and we were willing to pay the asking price for transportation.

In 1984 American aircraft operating from McMurdo's Williams Field logged 3,417 hours of flying, airlifted 2,900,000 pounds of cargo and carried 3,833 passengers, and the Hercules LC 130 aircraft which supply the Amundsen-Scott Station regularly returned empty from the Pole. What we were asking seemed very small indeed by comparison.

The Director of the National Science Foundation's Polar Division, Dr Edward Todd, made it clear that it was not

American policy to assist private expeditions, and that signatories to the Antarctic Treaty had agreed not to encourage such ventures. 'If I help one I must help them all,' he explained. Yet his parting words – 'You know, if you get to the South Pole you can expect more than a cup of tea' – led us to think that if we got there under our own steam we would not be unwelcome.

The setback did not deter Robert. With his girlfriend, Rebecca Ward, he set off on a world tour, in search of publicity and support. They had no money and sold family trinkets in America to pay their way. In South Africa they were labelled as vagrants and were threatened with jail, until Theopil Steinmann, their first sponsor, rescued them with a cheque for $5,000. While Robert continued to promote the expedition in New Zealand and Australia, Rebecca supported them by working as a waitress, dressed in short skirt and high heels. Their hopes were raised when Robert found an airfreight company in Melbourne from which, at a cost of a quarter of a million dollars, we could charter a Super Hercules equipped for ski landings. It was a shortlived solution that vanished when the company which owned the aircraft suddenly closed their Australian operation, for it was the only one of its sort available in the southern hemisphere. The dream was beginning to melt away.

While in Sydney, Robert came across an old friend from University who had led the expedition to Mount Kenya in which Robert had taken part. Peter Malcolm has a rather flamboyant taste in shirts and a shock of curly hair which seems to express his energy and unquenchable optimism. His passion is tall-masted sailing ships. His own dream, which had been fired when he sailed on the training ship, *Eye Of The Wind*, in 1981, was for a life before the mast of his own ship. His idea was to sail to the Antarctic following the route of Scott's ship *Terra Nova*. Could anything better fulfil our needs? It was one of the remarkable qualities of the expedition that it became the vehicle by which the dreams of many people could be realized.

Peter at once set about looking for a suitable ship. In Adelaide he found a seventy-foot steel-hulled yacht called *Patanela*, which had been sailed by Bill Tilman to Heard Island in 1964. She would take a crew of twelve and sixteen tons of cargo which at the time he thought would be sufficient. How naïve we were in those days! We ended up with double that number of crew and sixty-four tons of cargo. It was only when Peter came to London and saw what we were planning that he realized his beautiful *Patanela* would be much too small.

It was in the winter of 1983 that both Peter Malcolm and I began to question our involvement with Robert's dream. Because we could not fly to the Antarctic the whole concept of the expedition had to change. In the south, summer arrives in December, but as a rule the Ross Sea only becomes navigable towards the end of January, when the pack-ice begins to break up. By the end of February, the sea is once again starting to freeze. If we were to make it to the Pole the overland journey would have to begin at the end of October or in early November at the latest, just as Scott's and Shackleton's had done. It would be disastrous to set out as the summer drew to a close. There was no alternative to setting up a base in which to spend the winter before beginning our journey the following spring. Not only would the duration of such an expedition be four times as long as the one originally envisaged, it multiplied the logistics out of all proportion. We no longer required a couple of pairs of skis, a tent, two sledges and some food, but what amounted to a mini British Antarctic Survey, a base, a ship, an aircraft to return us from the Pole, more personnel and tons of provisions, fuel and equipment for a year on the ice. I doubted then if it was worth it.

Peter's dream of yards and canvas had to be replaced by the nightmare of noisy throbbing engines and the smell of diesel. Yet the growing scale of the venture only made Robert the more determined, and he pounded on, determined to surmount any obstacle. With such a force in the van, everything was possible. I left my job in Snowdonia and moved to the East End of London, where the expedition had set up its head-quarters in an old dockland warehouse that overlooked the Thames at Wapping's Metropolitan Wharf. It was cheap, unheated and near the City. There William Fenton, another Durham graduate, who had given up his comfortable life in public relations to devote himself to the expedition, presided over the draughty cavern, behind its heavy iron doors, and attempted to keep order at a desk in the middle of the bare concrete floor, a cigar in one hand and a telephone receiver in the other. In one corner of the echoing space were stacked 2,000 cans of Vaux beer, the expedition's first evidence of successful sponsorship. Few cans ever reached the Antarctic. The beer served us well at the end of the many hectic days that were to follow. A trickle of sponsored goods began to arrive, the volume of mail increased and soon the telephone was in constant use.

To find a ship, Peter Malcolm sought the advice of Ken Cameron, who had been the engineer on Ranulph Fiennes's Transglobe Expedition. He suggested that a trawler might suit our purpose. Peter toured the east coast of Britain on a motor-cycle, searching the rusting fleets of a depressed fishing industry for a suitable ship. In the docks of London, Faversham, Lowestoft, Grimsby, Hull, Newcastle and Aberdeen, rows of battered trawlers lay idle and forlorn. It was a buyer's market, but the ships were either too expensive or in such poor condition that even he at his most optimistic thought twice when he considered where we were bound. Then, in the little port of Fraserburgh on the north coast of Scotland, he found a North Sea trawler originally named *Yesso*. Walking around the harbour, he passed her twice before he realized that the ship was not the rusted hulk he had grown to expect. The bright red and white vessel, re-named *Cleanseas I* after a conversion costing half a million pounds two years previously, brought an end to his search. The owners, Salvesen Offshore Services Ltd, wanted £65,000 for the vessel, but Peter was convinced this had to be our ship. He wrote: 'The brass work shone in the engine room, the interior was pristine, there were even cups and plates in the galley and blankets in each berth . . . I imagined her as our expedition ship sitting next to Tower Bridge, then we would have a story to tell . . .'

A ship like this would act as proof that the expedition was more than a crackpot notion. We had already been offered a free berth at Irongate Wharf a few hundred yards from where Scott's first ship, *Discovery*, was moored in St Katharine's Dock. Robert rushed up to Fraserburgh to meet Peter King, Salvesen's managing director, who was so infected by his enthusiasm that he offered to reduce the price to £50,000, and allow us time to pay, providing we put down a deposit, there and then, of £10,000. Peter Malcolm signed a cheque, risking his own money, for as yet we had no means of providing the balance, and *Cleanseas I* became the expedition ship.

After a three-day voyage from Fraserburgh, *Cleanseas I* hit London, quite literally, on 29th March 1984. A reception had been arranged for friends and sponsors in the forecourt of the Tower Hotel at Irongate Wharf. There was a fast flood tide running. The pilot's intention had been to come in square and, when a bow line had been secured ashore, to let the current swing the stern around and bring her gracefully in. There was a piper from Captain Oates's regiment and lots of cheap champagne. Press photographers jostled with the crowd for the best positions as the ship neared. The bow was on them before it was realized anything was amiss. She struck the wharfside hard and a shower of bricks flew into the air along with the champagne corks. Robert stepped ashore, and coolly announced to an amazed audience: 'That, ladies and gentlemen, was a demonstration of our ice-breaking capability.'

The ship would get us to the Antarctic but it could not return us from the Pole. With the Americans refusing any assistance we still needed to find not only an aircraft but a pilot to fly it. There was one man in Britain to approach. Giles Kershaw had been flying in the Antarctic since 1974, when he was a pilot with the British Antarctic Survey. In the northern summer he flew in the Arctic, in the winter in the Antarctic and in between he flew for Britannia Airways. He had acquired a reputation for achieving what others regarded as impossible.

When we met at his house in High Wycombe, Giles carefully outlined the numerous possibilities open to us. Because we were now looking for an aircraft to fly us from the Pole to the Antarctic coast, we had a wider choice. The most attractive was to charter a Tri-turbo DC3, which was booked by various research units and mountaineering groups to be in the Antarctic from October 1984 to February 1986. He had used the Tri-turbo only a few months earlier flying an expedition to the Vinson Massif, when Chris Bonington had climbed the Antarctic's highest mountain (Giles himself climbed it the following year), and it had performed extremely well. It was the ideal aircraft. It would be in the right place, at the right time and, from Giles's estimates, the cost looked reasonable. With this aircraft we could secure our independence from the Americans and have the added bonus of our own search and rescue facilities if we got into trouble.

Giles made it clear, however, that he could not guarantee the plane would still be operational in two years' time when we required it. In the Antarctic, as I had seen myself, aircraft were easily damaged. He also warned that if we were not wanted in the Antarctic pressure could be brought upon the owners to make the plane unavailable for private expeditions, a possibility that I then thought excessively suspicious. But there were other options. Twin Otters could fly from various points around the Antarctic using pre-laid fuel depots. That would certainly avoid placing a reliance on one aircraft. All Giles could give me was his word that if we got to the Pole he would be there to pull us out, and I accepted it. It was time to make another visit to Washington.

In January 1984 Robert and I took our new plans for an expedition that had no need of any American support to Dr Edward Todd. Because we would be based in an area of the Antarctic in which the Americans were operating, and to prevent any misunderstanding, we explained every detail of our operation, except the uncertainty concerning the Tri-turbo. We asked again if he would allow us to fly out from the American station, Amundsen-Scott, at the South Pole on board one of his aircraft. It seemed unnecessary for us to fly our own plane when so many of their enormous Hercules, after unloading their cargo, were returning empty from the Pole. Todd told us bluntly that he thought our plan absurd. There could never be any co-operation between us. Their attitude towards us was no longer neutral. In American eyes expeditions like ours had no place in the Antarctic and were unwelcome. By way of emphasis, Todd even gave us a dramatic account of an occasion when he had stepped from a Hercules at Williams Field into a white-out and found that the ice runway beneath his feet was invisible.

He seems to think this commonplace experience so terrible that it will deter us, I thought. How can we convince this bureaucrat that what we propose is possible, when such a thing is beyond his comprehension?

'What you don't seem to understand,' I said, 'is that we are going to the Antarctic. Without your base at McMurdo we would still go. In fact, its presence detracts from our adventure.'

From now on, we were to become fiercely independent. Upon returning to England we consulted John Heap at the Foreign Office about our plans. He was astute and sympathetic. Though the British government would not directly assist the expedition, he quietly defended its right to go to the Antarctic and, in the spirit of the Treaty, kept the Americans and the New Zealanders informed.

4
Gathering Momentum

The expedition was like a great granite boulder, which for several years Robert had been trying to move. Gradually as more individuals came and added a shoulder to its massive side it began to roll, until it seemed that he had set in motion a thing of such weight it could not be stopped and over which there seemed little control. Recent events had prepared a receptive and fertile ground for the expedition's growth. A spate of television documentaries and historical dramas about the icy continent, which followed the Falklands War, brought public interest in the Antarctic to a peak. Ironically, the critical biography of Scott by Roland Huntford also helped, for many people were rightly indignant at its bias and were looking for a means to redress the balance.

By the spring of 1984 there were gathered a score of people determined and strongly committed to the expedition. Five of us would winter in the Antarctic in a hut we would erect at Cape Evans, a few hundred yards from where Scott's own base still stands. Gareth Wood was a 34-year-old Canadian who had given up a secure city job to live in a log cabin in the wooded mountains of Vancouver Island. I had met him at Plas-y-Brenin in Wales and we had climbed together there and in Scotland. Behind his tall, gracious and polite exterior was hidden a tenacious grit, and he brought a systematic attention to detail that we sorely lacked. He set about the unenviable task of organizing and acquiring everything an Antarctic base would need. Doctor Michael Stroud, whom Robert and I had met on the *Bransfield*, was to look after our health. A lively and at times even ebullient Londoner, he was torn between a desire for adventure and the demands of a medical career.

John Tolson, until recently Mate aboard one of the British

Antarctic Survey ships, was steady as a rock. He would be our calm centre through the winter. Always the last to offer an opinion, his words were ever full of down-to-earth wisdom. Undogmatic and open-minded, he was slow to pass judgment on others. A different side of him, however, was reflected in his nickname, Mad Jack. At first this seemed wildly inappropriate, but when I witnessed his transformation on the dance floor I saw how apt it was. For us he became a one-man film production unit. Despite the desperately hard conditions, he was to shoot more than 26 hours of film, of which only fifty minutes would be seen on television.

When we first sought the approval of the Royal Geographical Society, which had launched Scott's *Discovery* expedition, we were turned down because we were not a scientific expedition. Yet many of its most illustrious members gave us their uttermost support. It was only then that I understood the trust they were placing in us. How could Sir Vivian Fuchs be so sure of us when my own mind was still so full of doubt? By backing us he staked his reputation on our ability to make an unaided journey which even I was not sure was possible. He was not alone. Wally Herbert, the first man to cross the Arctic, mountaineer Chris Bonington and the leader of the first successful Everest expedition, Lord Hunt, all added their names to Sir Peter Scott's in support of the expedition.

No hesitation of any sort ever entered Robert's head. We had survived so far on the impetus of his energy, but we lacked a powerful voice in industry to turn goodwill into material help. Robert decided that Lord Shackleton, son of the Antarctic explorer Ernest Shackleton, was the ally we needed, but he was not so easily won over to our cause. After all, our expedition was named after Captain Scott, and Scott and Shackleton had not always seen eye to eye after the *Discovery* venture. The rift widened when Shackleton in 1907 was forced to break a promise to Scott that he would not make Ross Island the base for his attempt on the Pole. The wound had distanced the two families ever since.

When Robert left after his first brief interview with Lord Shackleton, he took with him nothing but a flat refusal to help or support the expedition in any way. Robert was not to be deterred. He continued to lobby by letter and telephone, enlisting anyone he could think of to help persuade Lord Shackleton to lend his name to the expedition. Lord Shackleton later described Robert as 'the most persistent young man I have ever met.'

'I was against this at the beginning, but, now I have been persuaded, you will find no stronger supporter of your cause. What can I do to help?'

After that the Royal Geographical Society subjected us to the most rigorous scrutiny and finally gave the expedition its blessing. It was the final seal of approval, but much else was still to be done. Robert plunged into the business of fund-raising with a round of lectures, as Scott had done. He talked to his old school, Sedbergh, and to Rotherhithe Primary, and many others up and down the country. He was introduced to gatherings at gentlemen's clubs by Colonel Patrick Cordingley, who today commands the 5th Royal Inniskilling Dragoon Guards. It had been the regiment of Captain Oates, 'the very gallant gentleman' whose memory is still a vital part of its tradition. Patrick Cordingley, who has written a biography of Oates, lent us a squad of men to help load supplies aboard, and dispatched one of his officers, Captain Michael Hough, to represent the regiment on the voyage south from New Zealand to Antarctica.

Wherever he went, Robert's message was a potent one: donations began to arrive, from fivers to cheques for £1,000, hand-knitted sweaters to keep us warm during the Antarctic winter, and paintings from the classroom with which to decorate the ship's mess.

Robert's obsession grew. He would let nothing and no one prevent the fulfilment of his dream. His one idea was to march to the South Pole. It seemed that he had no ambition or thought beyond it. His life appeared to end with its conquest, and I began to wonder whether he was looking for an heroic death. Success was so important that he no longer contemplated failure, while I spent each day trying to imagine every hazard we might encounter walking the 900 miles to the Pole. Out there one mistake, one wrong decision could cost us our lives and I no longer believed that Robert in his fervour would not be driven solely by ambition, the same ambition that had killed Scott. It was then that I asked Gareth Wood, much to his surprise, to join us on the walk. I wanted his caution and practicality to balance Robert who, although shocked, accepted. Only the three of us knew of this change of plan, though later Lord Shackleton told me that he had dreamt that three of us, instead of two, would be walking to the Pole. Was it a premonition or simply his way of suggesting that we needed a greater margin of safety?

The expedition became an ogre consuming our days with an insatiable appetite and still its demands continued to grow. We were later labelled as 'enthusiastic amateurs' and we all agreed that without a touch of professionalism we would never attract the sponsorship we needed. All that changed when Richard Down appeared on the scene. His company, Interaction, had been successful in promoting sporting and adventurous projects. He had raced five times at Le Mans and driven the British bobsleigh team. He had read in *The Times* about two 'madmen' and their plan to walk to the South Pole, and the idea excited him. His approach was businesslike and pragmatic. It was clear that we had found someone with the capability of bringing order to the task of raising money and of capitalizing on the expedition's potential for publicity. After looking through our estimates, he saw at once that we were hopelessly under-budgeted. We had thought that another £170,000 would see us through. Richard came up with a figure closer to £600,000. By the end the cost rose to more than a million! Scott's expedition had cost in the region of £87,000, or in today's terms, close on three million pounds – £170,000 might have got us to the end of West India Docks!

There was no doubt that we had to temper our romantic dream with commercial reality. A glossy brochure was produced that would not be immediately consigned to the wastepaper basket like so many requests for sponsorship. The Press were provided with regular news bulletins and material for feature articles. Television and radio coverage was cultivated, culminating with a unique deal that gained the expedition two years of reportage on Independent Television News. The regular TV newscasts of our preparations brought us to the

attention of millions. The effect was immediate and tangible:
no longer was it necessary to justify the expedition, and
prospective sponsors even began to approach us.

Many of Scott's original supporters, among them Burberry's,
who had supplied wind-proof clothing, Rowntree Mackintosh,
whose tins of Elect Cocoa are still to be found in Scott's hut at
Cape Evans, and Shell, whose fuel powered Scott's tractors,
were approached on the strength of these historical links. We
would need a good deal more than a few drums of tractor fuel
to get our ship to the Antarctic, fly an aircraft and power the
hut's generator through the long southern winter. At Lord
Shackleton's recommendation, Shell was ready to listen to the
expedition's request.

When Robert and Richard were summoned by the chairman,
John Raisman, to Shellmex House, overlooking the Thames,
they knew the viability of the expedition hung in the balance.
Lord Shackleton had arrived early to prepare the way for
Robert to present his case. There was no prevarication. Lord
Shackleton launched straight into what seemed to be an attack
on the venture, saying that when he first heard of it, he thought
it an utterly hare-brained scheme! Then, very skilfully, he
turned his criticism into a vote of complete confidence. The
colour gradually returned to Robert's face as he realized that
in laying out all the possible objections at the outset, Shackleton had acted as the canniest of negotiators. Shell offered to
supply all the fuel and lubricants that the expedition required,
more than 600 tons of diesel.

'We walked into the Strand in a trance,' Robert said afterwards. 'I looked at Richard and he looked at me. Neither of us
spoke a word, but we both knew that without that fuel the
expedition would have ended. I took a taxi back to the
warehouse. We had just negotiated a deal worth £135,000 and
I hadn't the fare in my pocket.'

Hard as it was to believe we could fail now, Richard Down
knew better than most that we were not home and dry. He
returned to the telephone with a renewed vigour. Another
£150,000 was promised a few days later. As he received the
good news he could hear at the other end of the line another
telephone ringing in the background.

'Will you excuse me a moment, that's my private phone,' the caller had said. 'I'll call you back.'

While he waited Richard phoned Robert to tell him that the expedition was almost solvent. Five minutes later the phone rang again.

'Mr Down, I'm afraid that you'll have to forget our previous conversation.'

'I beg your pardon?' said Richard.

'I've just spoken to the chairman, and he considers that he was railroaded by his board last night and he's changed his mind. We will not be supporting your expedition. I'm terribly sorry.'

'But it's too late,' said Richard, thinking quickly. 'I've just phoned Robert with the news and you know what he's like. I'm sure that he will have told a number of very influential people how generous you've been.' The point was well taken by the caller. Subsequently the expedition received a substantial contribution.

Although a robust trawler, *Cleanseas I* was hardly fit for cutting through Antarctic pack-ice, yet the vessel did have qualities which suited our purpose well. When she had been converted for the control of oil spillage in the North Sea, the forward fish-hold had been divided into six watertight tanks. These compartments would be ideal for the stowage of our stores and equipment. Time was short and the ship had to be strengthened to Lloyds' Ice Class III standards, before it could be fully insured for the task ahead. The plan was to begin the 14,000 mile voyage south on 4 August in order that the ship could enter Antarctic waters in the relatively ice-free weeks of January and, after establishing our base, depart before the sea began to freeze again at the end of February.

With seven weeks to go, the ship left her berth beside Tower Bridge and sailed to Newcastle. By the beginning of July she was in dry dock at Readhead's in South Shields, looking very small beside the massive black side of a large container ship. There was much to be done. As well as strengthening the hull, six watertight hatches had to be added to give access to the holds. The fo'c'sle had to be cleared, the funnel, superstructure and hull painted, the fuel and fresh water tanks drained and cleaned and the mess room enlarged and panelled. The crew worked side by side with the men of the shipyard, scraping, cleaning and painting. Peter Malcolm set up a second expedition office and persuaded local companies to sponsor wood, steel and paint. A bakery in the town gave them all the bread and pastries that remained unsold at the end of each day. To escape from the phone for a while, Peter set to with a steam blaster, cleaning the hull of barnacles. He came upon a particularly encrusted outlet pipe into which he thrust the high pressure jet. The effect was not discovered for several hot summer days, for the lavatory was kept locked and out of bounds while the ship was in dry dock. When the door was eventually opened pieces of pink paper and excrement were found clinging to the walls.

A television news team arrived to film Readhead's men as they strengthened the hull and reinforced the rudder. By coincidence, the British Antarctic Survey ship, RRS *Bransfield*, happened to be in a rival dry dock next door. The engineers sneaked in to take a close look at the three steel fins which act as ice-deflectors on either side of the propeller. They then produced a scaled-down copy to suit *Cleanseas I*. The conversion was commissioned before we had the money to pay for it, yet Readhead's went ahead with the work despite the risk. Even the ship was not yet ours. The balance of £40,000 was still to be paid. Eventually, to secure ownership, Peter Malcolm invested a further £10,000, and Robert took out a personal loan of £20,000 backed by Mark Fox-Andrews, who was to become one of the saviours of the expedition. The rest came from the pockets of the crew. On 25 July Robert signed the cheque, and an exuberant Peter leapt about the deck shouting, 'She's ours. She's ours!'

The jubilation was short-lived. Jerry Thompson, the conversion engineer, led Peter down to examine the propeller. There was a fine but unmistakable hair-line crack running round the base of a blade. Another £16,000 would have to be found if Salvesen's had not come to the rescue.

Modifications to the ship were of course included in Richard

Down's revised budget and the publicity had generated promises of sponsorship that would cover the costs, but there was always a gap to be bridged between the time when money had to be paid out, and when it actually came in. Without Don Pratt of Barclays Bank, the expedition would have floundered. He was like a father guiding our passage through the bleakest moments yet trying to ensure that we understood the hard realities of the financial world. It was Don's belief in Robert and in Richard's financial acumen that enabled the venture to survive.

As the work went ahead at Readhead's, it forged the nucleus of a crew. Some had never been to sea before, others were hardened merchant-men. The mixture required the direction of a skipper who could provide much more than strict naval discipline. 'No pay, no prospects' was what W. H. Tilman had offered on his voyages to the Polar seas and this expedition was no exception. Captain Graham Phippen, whom Robert and I had met when we sailed on the *Bransfield* in 1981, took on the unenviable task. Under his guidance those who lacked experience began to acquire the skills of seamanship and the old salts learned to appreciate an energy and enthusiasm that they had never before encountered as members of a paid crew. They lived and worked on board among the grime and disorder of a ship undergoing a major refit. Berths were occupied as fast as Mike Seeney, the ship's carpenter, could build them. The Bo'sun, Tim Fryer, taught the secret art of splicing to Robin Barthorp and Debra Overton, who before she had joined the expedition had designed sets for Yorkshire Television. All worked like slaves and were rewarded only by the knowledge that they were caught up in an organization that was generating its own momentum, and by the adventurous food that Bernard Levy, with his love of chillies, prepared in the galley.

On 25 August, three weeks after she should have sailed for the Antarctic, the ship left South Shields and returned to the Thames. She had been re-named *Southern Quest* by Robert's mother, in memory of *Quest*, the ship on which Shackleton had died. She arrived in London only a few hours before Princess Anne was to visit her. There was a frantic mêlée of last minute tidying. The *Southern Quest* looked fresh and bright in her new paintwork, unlike the crew on whom the month in dry dock had had a less favourable effect. Richard Down, in a smart blue suit, strode on to the bridge.

'Where the hell's Robert? There's only twenty minutes to go.'

'He went to buy a suit,' said a calmly beaming Graham. 'He'll be back.'

'Classic!' Richard fumed. 'Hasn't even got a ruddy suit.'

At that moment Robert was spotted trying to talk his way through the police cordon. He was wearing a crumpled khaki safari suit bought from an Oxfam shop and originally made for someone at least four inches shorter. His hair was greased back hard against his scalp. He waved when he saw the group waiting on the bridge. Graham was smiling. Richard looked exasperated.

Robert escorted the Princess, who was accompanied by Lord Shackleton and Sir Vivian Fuchs, down the line of expedition-ers. It was the first time that everyone had been assembled in one place. Robert could be justly proud of the extraordinary assortment of individuals he had gathered. Lieutenant-Colonel Cordingley represented Oates's regiment and his immaculate uniform contrasted with the tall athletic frame of ship's carpen-ter Mike Seeney, dressed in a tee-shirt, ragged denim shorts and sandals. He in turn towered over the squat, weathered figure of Eddie Davidson, wise old sea dog, master navigator and, at sixty, the oldest member of the crew.

As the Royal party boarded the ship Richard leaned forward to offer the Princess a pair of white gloves. 'Would you like to wear these, ma'am? Everything's a little dirty.'

Princess Anne looked from the gloves to her hands.

'Oh, I think these will be easier to wash than those.'

Below decks Richard was relieved to find that the ship was tidier than he had dared to hope, and the tour proceeded without embarrassment. Then, as the Princess was about to leave, Peter Malcolm asked with an impish smirk, 'Would you like to see what life on board is really like?' as he opened a cabin door to reveal the chaos behind it – a jumble of boxes, unmade bunks spread with dirty washing, books and the pieces of a bicycle strewn across the floor. Richard groaned inwardly, but the Princess was highly enthusiastic about the whole project and stayed longer than her official schedule, obviously enjoying everything.

Southern Quest spent another week beside Tower Bridge before being moved into West India Dock where Blackwall Engineering Ltd were to fit her new propeller and replace the pintelbush on which the rudder turned. The ship was proving to be a greedy consumer of funds, but though money was a major concern, time was now the greater worry. Unless the ship sailed soon she would not reach Antarctica before the sea began to freeze. The worst was yet to come.

The expedition was brought under the public microscope for the first time at a press conference held at Canary Wharf. The polished public image nurtured by Interaction and our new suits donated by Burberry's hid the frantic turmoil of those last few weeks. The Press turnout was formidable and the coverage far exceeded our expectations. Our stores and equipment had long since overflowed the warehouse in Wapping and were now stacked in profusion in a derelict transit shed at West India Dock. The London Dockland Development Corporation had given the expedition the use of shed 34; seventy-four years earlier Scott had assembled the stores of his last expedition in the nearby shed 13. The place was crammed with tons of supplies which had to be sorted into those for the ship and those for the winter base. Everything had to be packed into watertight bags and sealed inside Tri-wall boxes or tea-chests, ready for loading. Items that could not be allowed to freeze had to be marked, as did those that would spoil in the heat of the Equator or precious things that were fragile. The order of loading had to be carefully calculated, for it was no good finding that items vital to a safe landing at Cape Evans were at the bottom of the hold. Gareth Wood and I slept among the crates and boxes. At night, the wind would rattle the steel doors and rats could be heard scurrying on the concrete; during the daytime, all sorts of curious and distinguished visitors came and went. Complete strangers would turn up to help, sewing name-tapes on clothes or vacuum-packing food with a vacuum cleaner. Local characters, such as Keith Stanwyck, spent week-

ends, sometimes weeks, working for the expedition for no
tangible reward, as did the spritely seventy-year-old Stan
Werner. Emma Drake visited us almost daily, bringing bottles of
her home-made elderberry wine or thimbles, woollen socks or
tins of goose-grease that would protect our faces from the cold.
Emma claimed to be psychic and confidently predicted we would
arrive at the Pole at eleven o'clock. When we had begun our
walk, she would report her visions of our progress to the Interaction office, and often they were presciently correct.

With his Merchant Navy background, our cameraman John
Tolson found that he could not avoid becoming involved with
work on the ship. He had been studying its theoretical stability
with various amounts of cargo. His arithmetic unearthed a
snag. He asked the British Ship Research Association to carry
out a computer analysis that took into account a complex of
interrelated factors, the shape of the hull, the weight of ice on
the superstructure and the water that would wash the deck in
heavy seas. At the final hour, just when we were ready to begin
loading, they came up with the shattering news, that, as John
Tolson had feared, there was a dip in the ship's G/Z curve! In
layman's terms, this means that under extreme conditions, if
the ship rolled beyond a certain angle, it might not be able to
right itself again. It was a major setback. The *Southern Quest*'s
stability was below the standard laid down by the Department
of Transport and Industry for commercial vessels. No DTI
approval was necessary so long as the ship was registered as a
'pleasure yacht', but we wanted to fulfil the highest standards
of safety before facing the roughest seas in the world.

The *Southern Quest* was perched high in a floating dry dock
when an emergency meeting was called in the Captain's cabin.
Every alternative was examined and it looked as if we would
have to postpone the entire operation for a year. Richard was
certain that such a move would bankrupt the expedition,
sponsors would pull out and creditors would gather. In the end
we decided to gamble on our luck turning. With an enormous
effort, it might be possible to complete the necessary work in
time to allow a departure from London that would still enable
us to meet the deadline imposed by the ending of the Antarctic

summer. It was imperative that the base be established at Cape Evans before the encroaching ice prevented the ship's escape.

The cost of the work was suddenly a secondary consideration. This was not a time for caution. A staggering £70,000 was added to the expedition's budget. The work had to be done and somehow the money found. After several days of worry the financial pressure was partially relieved by a timely donation from the patriotic benefactor 'Union Jack' Hayward. Blackwall's began at once, their welders working round the clock enclosing the port and starboard alleyways to increase the ship's buoyancy. Our departure date was reset for 3 November.

With some ten days left to go, the ship was re-floated and moored alongside the transit shed. It had been many years since this dock had seen such activity. Along the wharfside grass grew in the rails on which once had run cargo-cranes, and the rows of empty sheds were now beginning to find new life as homes to a few small businesses. Work on the ship continued uninterrupted day and night. There was the smell of acetylene, flashes of bright blue light and sprays of yellow sparks as steel was cut and welded into place. The wharf was crammed with fuel barrels, each with its little yellow Shell sticker, stacked with the prefabricated sections of the hut and littered with dunnage. Lorries driven by bemused drivers delivered the mountain of foodstuffs that Bernie, our cook, had organized almost single-handedly. 'What', I asked him, 'are we going to do with four dozen bottles of anchovy essence?' The weekend before departure saw seventy volunteers, under the direction of John Tolson, operating in chain gangs to move the stores into the six holds and a refrigerated OCL container which had been welded firmly in place on the foredeck.

At last it was finished. The activity stopped while a Lloyds' surveyor inspected the work closely. I think he enjoyed keeping us in suspense until he was finished. Cheers of relief followed, as he gave the go-ahead. At 9 A.M. on a sunny November morning, the crew cast off. A small cluster of friends stood before the open doors of the empty transit shed and waved goodbye. The mooring lines were pulled in and the decks vibrated as the churning propeller pushed the *Southern Quest* gently away from the quayside. Then, as a last wave was exchanged, the engine fell silent, the ship lost way and drifted aimlessly across the dock. It was unbelievable! Fortunately, the trouble was soon rectified and, tended by the Chief Engineer Dave Gillam, the engine ran smoothly for the next 35,000 miles.

The first port of call was Cardiff, where the ship was loaded with sixteen tons of Welsh coal, and the crew were fêted by the Captain Scott Society in the room at the Royal Hotel in which Scott had once addressed the fathers of the city. On 10 November began the long journey south. Peter Malcolm's journal reads:

Just a handful of people and a dog witnessed our departure today from Cardiff. I spoke to one woman whose father, as a Boy Scout, had stood on the deck of *Terra Nova* and sounded his bugle on the day that Scott's expedition had sailed. It marks the end of an incredible struggle. When the seven people sat round a table in January at Metropolitan Wharf I never thought it would take so long or use up so much energy. But, if the venture ended now it would all have been worthwhile because of the people it has brought together.

The *Southern Quest* left behind the five men it was to transport to Cape Evans. We would fly out to join the ship when it reached New Zealand. There was still a great deal to be done.

5
Looking South

Before his trans-Atlantic flight, Charles Lindbergh is reported to have said: 'Safety at the start of my flight means holding down the weight for take-off. Safety during flight requires plenty of emergency equipment. Safety at the end of my flight demands an ample reserve of fuel. It's impossible to increase safety at one point without detracting from it at another.' His words expressed exactly the problem posed by the Polar journey. An aircraft can only fly as far as the fuel it is able to take off with will carry it. The question for us was: how much could a man pull? Scott's party had already covered 400 miles before they began manhauling. At the bottom of the Beardmore Glacier their sledges had weighed 800 lbs, and were each pulled by four men. Shackleton and his companions had pulled 250 lbs per man. Scott took seventy-seven days to reach the Pole at an average speed of 11.5 miles per day. If we were to match his pace I estimated it would mean beginning our journey with sledges that each weighed 300 lbs. If I had known then that they would in fact weigh 353 lbs, I would have considered the journey impossible. Could we maintain Scott's average, pulling such monstrous loads? If not then the journey would take longer and we would need more food. Then the sledges would be heavier, and as a result we would be slower. I could find no comparable precedents. Myrtle Simpson and her two companions, who had attempted to haul a sledge weighing 900 lbs to the North Pole, had given up after fewer than 200 miles. Nansen's journey across Greenland had been less than half the distance we proposed. British expeditions that went in search of Franklin and the Northwest Passage had manhauled over very great distances. In 1853 McClintock's six-man party travelled 1,210 miles in 105 days and the following year Mechamp, with seven men, covered 1,157 miles in 100 days. These journeys, though they were remarkable, gave me no assurance, for they had relied heavily upon depots and the killing of seals for food.

I had expected, as I delved deeper into the problem, gaining knowledge that would improve our diet, and refine and lighten our equipment, that I would become more confident that what we were planning was at least theoretically possible. Yet the more I learnt, the more I understood that no one could answer my questions. Often I was forced to disregard the conflicting advice of experts and go my own way. I spoke to Professor Dilly, of St George's Hospital, who had conducted research in Greenland on the energy expenditure of manhauling. He maintained that the 5,100 calories per day given by the diet I proposed were grossly insufficient, and that 8,000 calories was a more realistic figure. Not only would this add a prohibitive amount to our loads; I doubted that it would be possible to eat so much each day. He also maintained that the quantity of fuel we intended to take would not melt enough snow to provide all the drinking water we would need to stave off dehydration.

In July, Gareth Wood and I went to the Swiss Alps for a week to try out our equipment. We set up camp in Concordia, a few hundred yards from the Jungfrau Joch restaurant at the top of the biggest glacier in Europe. To test our down clothing we climbed the Monch at night, but were in greater danger of heat exhaustion than of feeling cold. The prototype tent sat on the snow, looking much the same as it had when we had erected it in the park in Wapping. It had been under far greater threat of destruction when Arabel, the six-year-old daughter of its designer, Ian Liddle, had bounced upon its top and slid down its walls. We did learn, however, one valuable lesson in manhauling. Harnessed to a sledge weighing 240 lbs, we were unable to travel a hundred yards on the soft summer snow without gasping for breath. The prospect of hauling even this partial load more than 10 miles each day for two-and-a-half months seemed absurd.

Meanwhile the Austrian mountaineer, Bruno Klausbruck-ner, had approached the expedition about the possibility of chartering the *Southern Quest* when she made her second voyage to the Ross Sea in 1986. When we met in London to discuss his plan for an Austrian Antarctic expedition, he told us of three South-Tyrolean alpinists who had recently man-hauled across the north of Greenland. Their route was more than twice the length of Nansen's, who had crossed the ice-cap in the south, and furthermore they had been without support, pulling all their own food, just as we intended.

To learn more, Gareth and I flew to Innsbruck where we were met by Klausbruckner and driven to Bozen, the small Dolomite town where the leader of the Tyrolean expedition lived. There we spent the day talking with Dr Robert Peroni about his experience, questioning him in detail, seeking his advice and approval. His tall, lean figure, gentle manner and the tasteful aestheticism of his home set him apart. I felt like a student sitting with his mentor or an initiate at the feet of the mahatma. On the wall was a beautiful, polished, ivory tusk of a narwhal.

The journey, he said, had changed him, for he had glimpsed a truth. He had felt 'like a bird that rises from the lake and shakes off the droplets of water'. Now, though he found it difficult, he had to try to live with this knowledge in everyday life. His companions did not seem to have shared his mystical experience. Wolfgang Thomaseth had joined the expedition to discover his physical limit. He found it in the first few days; after that there was only pain and torment. Fear never left him. Three times during their march he sat down in the snow to wait for death, and was only made to continue by force. Each day they were faced with the same white landscape, no sound, no living creature, only an endless plain with a flat horizon that never came closer. After four weeks, Peroni was the first to begin hallucinating. He was convinced they were being fol-lowed. 'Don't you hear,' he whispered, putting his finger to his lips, 'the Porsche comes.'

After eighty-eight days they reached the Eskimo settlement of Nuussuaq. They had come through after 838 miles with only a single day's food remaining. It had been no ill-conceived adven-ture; Peroni had examined every aspect with mathematical precision and taken every possible precaution. There had been no room for error. The three men had had their appendixes removed, and they had made a pact that if any one of them became ill or injured, so he could not continue, he would be left. They took with them only those things which they regarded as absolutely essential – not even a rope. If one of them had fallen into a crevasse there would have been no means of rescuing him. Peroni said, 'even a spare button is too much.' Every extra ounce had been pared away. At the beginning of their journey each of their three sledges weighed 321 lbs, but they had been too heavy to move, and 24 lbs of food had been thrown away.

The visit to Peroni confirmed many of the things we planned. With his advice we made improvements to our equipment, but there were also disparities which my own experience would not allow me to accept. Peroni sensed that these differences worried me, for I regarded him as the master, and as we left he said, 'Be confident. There is always more than one way to the same goal.' Through Peroni I had a glimpse of what we were to face. The knowledge that they had survived was a reassurance. Yet we would be going farther and for weeks we would be at greater altitudes. They had spent only a few days at their highest point and in temperatures not as low as those which we expected to encounter. Once again the question of whether it was possible to walk to the South Pole without assistance remained unanswered. We seemed balanced on a knife-edge between success and failure, and the answer would not be found until we were finally committed to the walk.

As *Southern Quest* crossed the Equator, the temperature in the engine-room rose to an unbearable 53°C. There developed a rivalry, traditional in the Merchant Navy, between those below in the noise and heat and those on the bridge who stand (or so it seems to the sweating engineers) in their cool shirts idly watching the rolling ocean. A grease-covered William Fenton took to ambushing unsuspecting crew who passed the engine-room hatch on their way to the bridge, laden with slices of melon and ice-cold lemonade. Almost everyone slept on deck in sheets sticky with salt, while flying fish skipped across an oily sea. In Cape Town the frenzied activity of the last days in London were repeated. South African Seaton Bailey and Scottish ornithologist Steve Broni joined the crew and in seven days the ship was serviced and reprovisioned. Left behind was 'Albert', the old clinkered rowing boat that Peter Malcolm had bought in Fraserburgh, which found a last, dry home in a children's playground.

From Cape Town the *Southern Quest* followed a great circle route which took it across the Antarctic convergence into the cold waters of the Southern ocean. She arrived in Lyttleton, New Zealand, on 15 January. The tiny port has a long and proud association with the Antarctic. The ships of Scott's first expedition, *Discovery* and *Morning*, Shackleton's *Nimrod* and Scott's *Terra Nova* had all made final preparations there. Scott's Cape Evans hut had been given a trial erection on the town's recreation ground, and both of these latter expeditions had set their Manchurian ponies to graze on Quail Island before embarkation. Among the small crowd gathered on the wooden quay to greet *Southern Quest* was a man who remembered these events. Bill Burton had been a stoker on *Terra Nova* and, at ninety-six years of age, he is the last surviving member of Scott's expedition. His mind was sharp with the memories of his youth, and his massive hands gestured powerfully as he recalled how Taff Evans, after a night of drinking with the locals, fell into the harbour in his rush to board the ship on the morning of her departure for the Antarctic.

Lyttleton nestles under a ridge of grassy hills that rise dramatically from the sea and divide it from the nearby city of Christchurch. Driving down the winding road that descends from Evans Pass to the town, Ken Marshall and his family were intrigued by the unusual sight of the red North Sea trawler entering the harbour. 'That will be the ship of the English expedition with those silly beggars who are going to walk to the Pole,' he said, little thinking that in a few days' time he would be joining the *Southern Quest* as First Mate for the voyage to the ice.

Antarctica also figures prominently in the daily life of Christchurch. Scarcely a day passes without local press and radio carrying some mention of the southern continent. From the city's airport the enormous American Hercules and the Starlifter jet transporters of Operation Deep Freeze fly the 2,400 miles to the McMurdo Station. A proud statue of Captain Scott modelled by his wife Kathleen stands on the willow-hung banks of the river Avon, which winds on through the city past the offices of the Polar Division of the Department of Scientific and Industrial Research. Bob Thompson, its director, who had offered Robert a job in 1981, had called our venture 'bloody stupid', and was reported in the *Daily Telegraph* as saying, 'In this day and age, for anybody to suggest walking to the Pole is idiotic because there is nothing to it.' Scott, too, had faced similar criticism: *Vanity Fair* said, '. . . there is no need to associate it (Scott's expedition) with rubbish about human progress and the advance of civilization.'

When the five Antarctic winterers flew in to join *Southern Quest* before she sailed, Gareth and I went to see Thompson in the hope of a reconciliation. We had no idea why the enmity had developed. Was it all a misunderstanding inflamed by the press? Thompson was polite but made it immediately clear that we could provide no justification for our expedition that he could understand. Science is the cloak under which the political and commercial motivations of government-sponsored Antarctic programmes hide; without its sanction we were condemned as irresponsible. That anyone would wish to expose themselves to the rigours of the Antarctic with no purpose other than to experience its primeval forces was beyond his comprehension.

Not everyone who worked for DSIR in the Antarctic shared Thompson's opinion of the expedition, but such was the fear of disciplinary action that expressions of support were made only surreptitiously. Once we got to the Antarctic, we were privately assured we could regard our New Zealand neighbours at Scott Base as friends. One man who worked on a freelance basis with the New Zealand programme offered to join the *Southern Quest* as Mate. He possessed an invaluable local knowledge of the waters around Cape Evans. Unfortunately, a few days before our departure he was forced to withdraw when he was reminded how 'uncomfortable' life might be upon his return if future employment with DSIR was not forthcoming.

The sour taste of relationships with Antarctic authorities did not tarnish the welcome we received from the community. Like Scott, we could say that the expedition found in New Zealand a 'second home and those who would think of them in their absence, and welcome them on their return.'

The apparent disorder that prevailed on the morning we were due to sail made me doubt that the ship would be ready in time. Well-wishers had already begun to arrive and there were still many jobs to complete. I had reckoned without the change that the long voyage from England had wrought in the crew. While the skipper joined a group of Morris men dancing on the quay, the deck cargo of fuel drums and timber was quickly secured and soon the gangway was brought aboard and stowed with an expertise that spoke of practised efficiency. At 2 o'clock on that sunny afternoon when the mooring lines were cast off, handshakes and kisses were exchanged with a colourful crowd over the slowly increasing gap between ship and wharf. The Skellerup brass band played the 'Monty Python March' as the vessel gained way. The old steam tug *Lyttleton*, which had similarly escorted *Terra Nova*, led the way with a billow of smoke to a cacophony of hoots from cargo ships, tankers and Russian trawlers that all dwarfed the *Southern Quest*, as she departed for Scott's last port of call.

Port Chalmers received the expedition with a warmth that belied the size of the community. There were many people who recalled *Terra Nova* or whose parents could and one 83-year-old man, who used to cycle past Scott's Devonport home on his way to school, brought us jars of marmalade and home-made prunes. The *Terra Nova* Scout Group loaned the ship an ensign sewn with a piece of the flag of the ship from which they took their name, and the mayor, Sir John Thorn, brought us much more than civic dignity when on the morning of 30 January his voice led the crowd singing 'Now is the Hour'. The sun was beginning to break through the cloud as we slid across the mirror waters of the channel that reflected trees and green hills along its margins, and out into an even rolling swell before turning south.

From the day we left New Zealand the ship had its flock of attendants. Initially Pintado petrels and Bullen albatross were our companions, but slowly as our latitude grew the species changed. Great-winged petrels, Antarctic petrels and heavily mascaraed Black-browed albatross soon predominated. There were also visits from Royal, Wandering and Sooty albatross, which flew, in motionless form, wheeling above the waves, skimming the peaks, until they seemed to be flying the flowing border of air and sea, and then turning on a wing tip into the wind and soaring to turn again, level with the windows of the bridge, long wings stiff with air.

In the galley a great squawking could be heard as Bernard Levy mimicked the sound of gannets to the many hungry hands thrust through the hatch from the mess. Appetites had returned after two days of gales in which the rearing decks were awash. 'I find it impossible to get through eight hours sleep without something to eat,' Gareth said.

The first skua was sighted at 53° South as we entered an area of fogs that marked the meeting of warm northern waters and cold southern seas. It became colder. On the fifth day we crossed the Antarctic convergence and the temperature of the green-grey waters plunged to 2°C. It began snowing. I wrote: 'Mike Stroud gets the magnum for sighting the first iceberg, but he'll have to get his own ice!' Through the gloom, we could make out its tall band of blue cliffs, with rough waves breaking against the windward side. More and more icebergs appeared, flat-topped islands of ice several miles long. There were fantastically shaped fragments, no bigger than a house, and water-washed growlers, sea-tumbled boulders of green ice that remain unseen until the ship is almost on them. Then, two days later, we were through the chain of bergs that garland the edge of the Ross Sea and there were no more to be seen. The albatross too had gone. Instead Adélie penguins kept pace with the ship, porpoising in and out of the water at tremendous speed and darting under the bows. A Snow petrel appeared, the pure white herald of the Antarctic, fluttering above a ship's rail that was hung with long icicles. The decks, mast and fo'c'sle were encased in a frozen crust of spray, that shone in the bright sunlight of endless day.

A little before midnight on 7 February, we sighted Mount Erebus against a soft rose sky, fine on the port bow. Though still 125 miles away the translucent grey mass towered above the horizon, its summit wrapped in cloud. It was the light refracting in the cold air that caused a mountain of 12,448 feet to appear as if it were higher than Everest.

We were approaching Ross Island, and while it is usual to find, at this time of year, the Ross Sea clear of pack-ice, McMurdo Sound, formed between the island and the mountains of the Scott Coast, is less predictable. Our last information, now more than eight days old, reported fast-ice around Cape Evans and five-tenths pack in the Sound. Even if the ship could penetrate the pack, it could mean hauling tons of cargo over miles of fast-ice to the beach. If the sea-ice had broken out, would the water between ship and shore be blocked with brash-ice, which is impossible to walk across and impenetrable to small craft? Or would the bay be clear, with a convenient ice-edge, a few yards from land, against which we could unload?

At 4 A.M. *Southern Quest* passed under the pall of cloud that hung over the island. Behind us the sun shone. Penguins and seals plopped and lumbered into the water off ice floes nudged by the bows. We slid past Beaufort Island, its grim dark rocks hung with glaciers. People began to gather, clambering to high points on the ship, Robert and Peter in the barrel at the mast head, others on the roof of the bridge or entwined in the railings of the fo'c'sle. All eyes were turned towards the desolate land that was nearing. The ship glided into North Bay with a far-reaching swell from the bows the only disturbance on the water.

It was as if the ceiling of cloud had risen to reveal a scene that was lost in time. A barren, black land of windswept cinder lay beneath the giant cone of Mount Erebus, and at one end of the dark beach was Scott's hut, bone grey and silent. It seemed a chill, dismal place, arid and devoid of any snow that would have softened its desolation. Everyone who went ashore that day, while the 400-yard ice ropes were pulled out and moorings prepared, was left with deep impressions. There was not a footprint on the beach, only the hollow trails of Weddell seals that had dragged their heavy bodies through the pea-like scoria, and the only sound the occasional angry cry of skuas. Scott's hut stands a few yards from the water's edge, for tides in the Sound are very small. It is a large hut, bigger than I expected.

The grain of its timbers was weathered proud. A lead-coated nail protects a small disc of green canvas under its big flat head. The stables on the seaward side are filled to within a foot of the roof with ice, and stacked against their northern corner is fodder for the ponies, bales of hay rounded by the wind. The debris of an expedition is scattered about, discarded fragments which time has transformed into historical relics. I peered through the only window in the long east wall, into a russet shaded world of another age that was to open itself to us over the coming year.

6

On the Black Beach

'Pontoon's on its way,' said carpenter Mike Seeney, glancing through the open flap of the Bokz tent that had first seen use in the Western Cwm of Everest. The frame for years since had been used as a greenhouse before being erected on the beach at Cape Evans. Mike himself had built the oil drum raft which could be seen setting out from the ship, moored some 300 yards offshore. He had named this eccentric craft *Spirit of Incompetence*, and now its deck was awash under the weight of its cargo. Spray from the great wave thrown up by its square bow was driven by the wind into the faces of the two men perched stiffly upright at the stern. They were both encased in ice. Engineer Andy Ashbridge at the tiller, a frosty beard protruding from beneath his yellow sou'wester, peered over a heap of boxes, bags of coal and fuel drums. Wild-bird man Steve Broni stood coiling ropes, seemingly bemused by the harsh conditions in which they worked.

We gulped our tea and one by one stepped out into the snow that streamed down the beach and out across the dark grey sea. That morning the wind blew 30 knots off the shore, and at times the ship became obscured in the blizzard.

Work kept us warm. By the end of the first day we were all exhausted. First Mate Ken Marshall, who organized the discharge of cargo, discovered towards the end of the afternoon that, once the stores were ashore,

everything had to be carried up the sloping beach and laid out in numbered lines among the beds of lava where the wind will keep the boxes clear of snow . . . I stepped ashore to lend a hand, and it was bloody hard work. I must be getting old because I couldn't keep that up all day. An hour was enough for me.

Work on board was equally gruelling. The failure of the windlass meant that muscle was the only power available to move the sixty-four tons of cargo out of the holds. Robert revelled in lifting 600 sacks of coal above his head to the first link in the chain of hands that conveyed them over the side to the waiting pontoon. Coal dust was everywhere, and at the end of the day he emerged looking like a white-eyed Othello at his most manic.

In the evening, before dinner, we would gather in the mess for hot whisky or mulled wine and cinnamon and sink into a haze of pleasant tiredness. The smell of damp wool, and voices embroidering the day's events over the deep throbbing sound of the ship's generators, added a sense of comfort. Then came the bedlam of the meal, a squash of elbows round the table, plates piled high with food, people calling out for second helpings in a confusion of plates misdirected, puddings eaten before the main course. 'I haven't got a fork.' 'Is there any tea?' 'This custard tastes of fish.'

The first of the prefabricated hut sections came ashore after three days and erection began. A level site had been selected at the northern end of the beach, some 200 yards from Scott's hut. All sixteen tons of coal, enough to keep us warm for two years, all the food and most of the equipment now stood in their appropriate ranks, but the labour was beginning to take its toll. Once dinner was over the ship fell unusually quiet. Next morning people began to drift in for breakfast later than usual, or not at all. The twenty-four hours of daylight had disrupted the sleep of many. There were rumblings of discontent.

'Why is it so necessary to keep up this frenzied pace?' someone asked Captain Graham Phippen. 'Does it matter if the unloading takes a day or two longer?'

Graham pointed to the two heavy iron anchors buried in the black sand before Scott's hut, witness to the unpredictable nature of the Antarctic, which was at the heart of his concern.

In May 1915 four men occupied Scott's hut at Cape Evans and six more camped 17 miles away at Hut Point. They were members of the Ross Sea Party whose task it was to lay depots for the last stage of Shackleton's Trans-Antarctic expedition across the continent. Three hundred yards offshore, in much the same position as *Southern Quest* now occupied, their ship *Aurora* had been moored with seven steel hawsers from stern to shore, and the bows made fast to the two anchors buried in the beach. She had been allowed to ice-in and was considered safe for the winter. On 6 May a violent storm tore the *Aurora* from her moorings and, still trapped in the ice, she was carried, helpless, out to sea. The ship drifted for 1,100 miles, and it was ten months before the pack-ice released her. The account is one of the forgotten stories of Antarctic exploration. They were the last to spend a winter at Cape Evans. Only six survived.

Inevitably it was the weather that dictated the rate at which the unloading could continue. On the morning of 13 February word went round the ship that the boats could not be launched. Winds of Force 9 and a temperature of −11°C provided an excuse for a leisurely start to the day. Sea-smoke evaporating from the warmer water and condensing in the cold air raced across the bay. The black lavas of the Cape had been stripped of what little snow there was. The ship, broadside to the wind, was pushed taut against the lines at bow and stern, and the large bosses of ice which had formed around the ropes where they entered the water were lifted high into the air. Out in the Sound, a little more than 2 miles away, a stream of pack-ice hurried past the western tip of Inaccessible Island.

In contrast, the following day was calm and the sun warm, despite an air temperature of −10°C. By late afternoon the last of the seventy-four drums of generator fuel was rolled off the pontoon and up the beach. Apart from one or two boxes that Gareth was hunting for in various corners of the ship, the unloading was complete. It had been a remarkable five days. All nineteen of the ship's crew had laboured like demons to get the expedition safely ashore and could feel justifiably proud.

During the first day's reconnaissance of the Cape, when it was decided where we would build our home, we became aware of a difficulty that we had not anticipated. There was no convenient source of fresh water. None of us had expected that there would be any shortage of snow in the Antarctic. That evening, just before dinner, a dull roar from the direction of the 300-foot-high ice cliffs of the Barne Glacier drew our attention to a temporary solution.

With boatman Robin Barthorp at the helm of the inflatable rubber Gemini, I set out across the bay towards a section of the towering cliffs that had collapsed. Vehicle-size blocks of ice bobbed in the water. An ice-piton driven into the side of one small berg provided an anchor to which we attached a line, and with the Gemini under full power, slewing from side to side, we towed the reluctant lump of ice to the beach. It was to provide our only source of fresh water until 1 March, when the debris from another fall of ice was blown on to the beach by a northerly wind. After that, as winter approached, a snowdrift which formed around the hut supplied our needs.

The ship remained in North Bay for another four days while the hut was completed. The weather had grown noticeably colder since our arrival. When the air was still, a thin film of ice formed on the surface of the sea, like a shining slick of oil. Shadows grew longer, and though it was still light throughout the day, the sun had begun to drop beneath the southern horizon. In the evening the ice cliffs of the Barne Glacier reflected the soft light, changing from bronze to gold, lavender and rose, and when the sun slid behind Mount Discovery, way to the south, the colours suddenly vanished, leaving a mile-long wall of shadowless white, cold and terribly austere. The summer was drawing to an end. The last of the ships that supply the American base at McMurdo had sailed north several days ago, and the mood aboard *Southern Quest* was for leaving the Sound before the sea began to freeze.

On 19 February *Southern Quest* began to pick up its anchor. With the windlass broken, this was a long and arduous task. All hands were gathered on the foredeck and for five exhausting hours we took turn and turn about, winding in the 500 feet of chain. At five P.M. we were underway, heading south for as far as it is possible for a ship to go, towards Hut Point, the site of Scott's *Discovery* hut, to visit our neighbours at the New Zealand and United States bases. Gareth Wood and Mike Stroud remained at Cape Evans and began the process of turning the hut's empty shell into the home we would call Jack Hayward Base, after the man who had rescued us in London.

It was only now, as we steamed out of North Bay, that the magnitude of the land began to be apparent. The hut quickly disappeared against the dark background of volcanic moraines that demarcate the Cape from the Barne Glacier. Soon the Cape itself shrank to insignificance beneath the great spread of ice that flows outwards over every contour, from the rearing slopes of Mount Erebus to the coast. The ship passed among the Dellbridge Islands, where Edward Atkinson, the surgeon on the *Terra Nova* expedition, had become lost in a blizzard. He had set out to read the thermometers that were but a few hundred yards from the beach in North Bay. For six hours he stumbled across the sea-ice in the winter darkness, 'the snow a raging blanket around him'. It was easy to imagine the rocky cliffs of Inaccessible Island looming up before him, or was it Tent Island or Razorback? He had no way of knowing, until the moon broke through the storm and he saw a flare of tow soaked in petrol that had been lit on the hill behind Scott's hut.

We cruised slowly past the islands, through patches of newly formed ice that rippled like viscous liquid as the bow wave travelled across the water. Where the surface had not yet frozen, sea-smoke hung like the mist on a pond. It was −17°C. As the ship slid between Razorback and Tent, I climbed the icicle-encrusted steps to the bridge. Ken Marshall was at the helm and Graham Phippen was striding from port to starboard and back again, peering intently at the way ahead, checking the echo sounder and the chart in quick succession. These are poorly charted waters, which always demand attention, but Graham's silent preoccupation hinted that something was amiss. Across our path stretched a wall of blue-green ice, taller than the mast and honeycombed with half-submerged caves. Graham rang 'full astern' and then 'stop engines' on the semaphore, and we drifted into a small cove of ice. The chart showed only open water.

The Erebus Glacier Tongue points its thin finger into the Sound from the northern corner of Erebus Bay, less than a mile wide, partly grounded on the sea bed, partly floating. On modern charts it is shown to be little more than six miles long; in 1901 it was nearly nine miles in length and remained so until 29 February 1911 when, to Scott's astonishment, several miles of the ice tongue broke away and carried north. In seventy-four years it had regrown to its former stature, for it was the tongue, Graham soon realized, now two miles longer than the chart indicated, that obstructed our way.

The ship turned west, squeezing between the ice cliffs and Tent Island. On the snout of the floating glacier the Americans had placed a notice that warned: 'DANGER CREVASSES'. As we sailed out into the centre of McMurdo Sound, the long arm of Hut Point Peninsula came into view, and soon we were approaching the amorphous slopes of Arrival Heights.

Fast-ice, less than a foot thick, covered the whole of Winter Quarters Bay except for a narrow channel of open water running alongside the wharf. Despite regular attempts to speak to McMurdo Station since our arrival at Cape Evans, radio calls from the ship had remained unanswered. We were not at all sure that the expedition would be well received at the American base. Rather than attempt to use their empty mooring, Graham steamed straight into the ice, ploughing on until the ship was safely lodged.

Our fears were unfounded, for two days earlier the last of the NSF officials had departed by Hercules for New Zealand, and hospitality prevailed. Within minutes of what must have seemed a rather eccentric entrance into the bay, the distinctive southern drawl of Lt-Commander Roger Orndorff of the fighting Sea Bees, who was to command McMurdo through the coming winter, hailed us on the radio:

Southern Quest, Southern Quest, this is McMurdo. When you have finished playing in the ice, perhaps you'd like to come alongside. You're all most welcome in Mactown. We were fearing that you'd be leaving without paying us a visit.

McMurdo Station is far removed from the rustic simplicity of the traditional Antarctic base, having the unlovely appearance of a mining town. Orange painted four-wheel-drive pick-ups, tracked vehicles and giant bulldozers rumble down the dusty streets, which are edged with rows of rough pine poles draped with heavy cables and telephone lines. A sprawl of prefabricated buildings, chalets, Nissen huts and wooden sheds house workshops, laboratories, accommodation for military and civilian personnel, a fire station and a hospital. There is a chapel, a television station, a barber's shop, three bars and a liquor store, and all the services required by a population which swells to more than 1,200 people in the height of summer. It is by far the largest of all Antarctic bases, and nestles in the shelter of black volcanic hills between Hut Point, where Scott's *Discovery* hut now sits among pipelines and fuel storage tanks, and the steep rise of Observation Hill, on top of which stands the cross of jarrah wood, erected by the men of Scott's last expedition in memory of the Polar party. The surrounding landscape is heavily scarred, the surface having been scraped down to the permafrost to provide hardcore for buildings and roads. Ground surrounding the nuclear power station (closed in 1972), which had been contaminated by radioactivity, had been removed. It is impossible to disregard the ugliness of the town, which is a discredit to the sensibility of the men and women stationed there. As the slums of a city reflect the concern a nation shows for its people, so does McMurdo proclaim how little regard those responsible for its establishment have for the fragile beauty of Antarctica.

That evening while the Captain, Robert and the crew were entertained with Budweiser and coffee in Mactown, I gladly accepted the invitation of Leo Slattery, the jovial postman in charge of the New Zealand station, to look around Scott Base and meet the ten Kiwis who were to keep it running over the coming winter. We chatted as we drove up the graded road out of McMurdo, Leo pointing out the smouldering dump where refuse is first burnt and then bulldozed into the ground, and the silver tanks that house six million gallons of fuel. As we crossed the Gap to the southern side of the peninsula, we fell silent. I think he sensed I knew what was waiting round the bend in the rising road. To our right the rocky ground dropped steeply down to the frozen sea, into which reached the stubby promontory of Pram Point, where the sap-green buildings of Scott Base were neatly arranged. Beyond that was the view that had haunted me since Robert had first suggested walking to the Pole: the Great Barrier Ice Shelf.

I had tried to imagine the scale of the thing, exaggerating

beyond belief its enormity, so that when this moment came the reality would seem less daunting. I knew that this flat feature-less plain was the size of France, that it had taken Scott forty days to cover the 400 miles to the Beardmore Glacier. I had seen photographs and satellite images. Yet, those images were as nothing before the sight of that infinite horizon, soft blue beneath the red sky of midnight. In nine months' time we would set out to measure that incomprehensible distance step by step.

After a last sweep of the bay *Southern Quest* made her departure, silhouetted against the backdrop of glaciers and bright mountains across the Sound. All five of us stood at the water's edge watching the ship grow small, and then one by one we walked back up the beach to our hut, leaving Robert alone with his thoughts, gazing after the ship until it disap-peared over the northern horizon. Yet we were glad to see it go, for we were anxious to begin our life in the Antarctic. With the ship gone we were suddenly isolated from the cares of the world, cut off from our own time, and thrown closer to that when *Terra Nova* had sailed from Cape Evans. At the far end of the beach Scott's hut stood lonely and forlorn in the evening light. It was easy to imagine the activity that had once sur-rounded it: men clambering up Wind Vane Hill to the meteor-ological instruments, walking the ponies or struggling with heavy boxes from the lines of stores set among the weathered rocks, and the dogs whining with excitement, leaping and straining at their chains whenever a figure approached.

Cape Evans is an insignificant, wind-swept triangle of black lava, bounded on two sides by sea and on the third by a high embankment of moraine pushed up by the flank of the Barne Glacier and called by Scott the Ramp. Often, during the ensuing months, after periods when blizzards confined us to the hut, or when the effect of the three large meals we ate each day began to become too apparent, Robert and Mike and some-times John, but never Gareth, and I, in my sloth, only once, would run around the Cape's three-mile perimeter.

From the hut their circuit took them over low mounds of lava set in flat gravel-beds to the foot of the Ramp. The reward for the lung-tearing climb up ice and rubble was a level jog along the crest of the embankment with fine views across the miles of glacier that cream in gentle undulations from the sudden dramatic upthrust of Mount Erebus. This narrow belt of boulders, high above the Cape, bleeds in even gradation into bare glacial ice, like the transition from sand to sea on a gently shelving beach. Scattered about are concave cones of ice and sharp grit, symmetrical and twice the height of a man. Strange blocks of Kenyite lava stand like a surreal menagerie of topiary animals or a collection of Henry Moore's heavy, black bronzes. After 400 yards the ground begins to descend toward the southern coast. To the right is the head of a tiny glacier, over which you could throw a snowball, if it were possible to make such a thing with the dry crusty powder from the drifts. It slides back under the Ramp to peter out on the edge of a broad alluvial plain. From here it is still possible to see the grey ice of Skua Lake, and beyond it the partially obscured roof of Hayward Base. To the left the rocks of the Cape stretch east, above perpendicular cliffs, until they are overwhelmed by ice at Land's End. From there the coast is formed by nameless glaciers that meet the sea in sheer blue walls and shallow coves, until rock appears again at the great bastion of Turk's Head. Turning west, a short and steep descent leads into the gully which Scott used to gain access to the sea-ice that invariably remained in South Bay when the ice in North Bay had blown out. It was here, or perhaps a little farther on among the broken crags and shelves of ice forming the southern shore, that Mike, trotting round the Cape in the dim twilight of a winter noon, ran into and tumbled over a solitary Emperor penguin. It let out a blood-curdling shriek, which scared them both, and they fled in opposite directions.

The run continues up hill and down dale, over loose ash and sheets of scalloped ice with pockmarked boulders, past the Whale Cairn, to the rocky tip of the Cape. Then there comes a gruelling 100 yards of deep coarse sand across the secluded West Beach. Adélie penguins gather here in summer, and there are fragile skeletons of tiny starfish scattered among the black sand. A narrow path, between cantilevered plates of sea-ice rafted on the shore and the icy spur that descends from Wind

Vane Hill, leads out on to Home Beach. Scott's hut appears, the gable-end mirroring the shape of the distant smoking cone of Mount Erebus that rises above the roof. Now there is a choice: a steep climb to the cross on Wind Vane Hill and a swift descent to Skua Lake, or, if enough exercise has been taken for one day, a final sprint of 200 yards, through the gap between Scott's hut and the rickety latrine, and then up the beach, past a slumbering Weddell seal lying in its own filth, to finish with the hurdle of a double row of fuel drums outside the door. It took thirty minutes to circle the Cape if you ran up all the hills, and the cold air left you coughing.

The days raced by, filled with the work of turning our hut into a home. Slowly, the empty 16-by-24-foot shell was transformed in a frenzy of sawing and hammering. The bare walls disappeared behind shelves loaded with stocks of food, equipment and tools. To erect the chimney, John and Gareth worked on the roof in a 25-knot wind and temperatures of −20°C. Robert sealed draughty gaps around the walls through which the wind blew little piles of spindrift. The Esse stove was lighted ceremoniously four days after the departure of the ship and we ate a first meal cooked on its cast-iron hob – steak and kidney pie, dehydrated mashed potatoes, tinned carrots and onion sauce, with baked apple and syrup to follow. Left-overs were consigned to a large pot which each day provided lunch, a thick soup the flavour of which seemed to change little, as the remains of Mike's Boeuf bourguignonne, a stew made by a cook tiddly on the pretext of cooking with wine, was added to yesterday's fish pie.

We began baking bread, with unpredictable results. When gales blew strongly from the south the stove would roar out of control, incinerating anything in the oven in a matter of minutes. I remembered that Gareth's first attempt was 'helped' by Robert's unsolicited advice. 'I was taught to bake bread by the man who has baked more bread in the Antarctic than anyone else – Big Mac McMannus.' Gareth's bread was light, soft and crusty. At lunch Robert, sitting in his place at the table, was quiet.

Our world shrank to the confines of the hut and its immediate vicinity. More than a month went by with none of us venturing farther than the few yards to the meteorological screen or with the slopping bucket from beneath the sink down to the steadily growing shelf of ice that had formed at the water's edge. Each day slid unnoticed into the next. John Tolson's diary records one among many:

As a result of a very late night, I didn't get up until 10 o'clock. It was blowing hard again and the cloud level was indeterminable. It was a day of odds and ends. Roger hung the dark room door, while Gareth continued his never-ending battle to erect the radio masts that the winds, which blow incessantly over the Cape, regularly destroyed. As the more essential jobs have been completed, we can begin work on our tiny sleeping places in the roof space. Rob spends much of his time pottering about his den. It's more of a lair, for to gain entry he has to crawl on all fours beneath the plywood desk he has built, and the chair which sits in the passage-way and all but blocks the entrance to Mike's home opposite. Our cubby-holes are now complete, barring some refinement, with shelves and reminders of home. This afternoon I began to furnish my room, laying out the ridiculously luxurious sheepskin on the floor and setting out the Mary Quant bed linen. We live in a comfort far from the traditional image of an Antarctic base. The temperature in the hut has risen to 28°, and it is amusing to think of the people back home who imagine we are suffering the harsh extremes of Antarctica.

The lighting of the oil lamp earlier each evening marked the approach of winter, as did the departure of the skuas, and the blood-red northern skies in which floated black mirages of the Western Mountains far beyond the horizon. I was restless and eager to travel the island before the encroaching darkness prohibited such explorations. Only Mike seemed to share my thirst. Gareth's priorities still centred on his work around the hut, and John and Robert were spellbound by the history of Cape Evans, and for the moment felt no need to venture farther afield.

'Don't you realize where we are?' Robert asked me one evening. 'Isn't it enough to be here on the edge of the Antarctic? And look' – he pointed out of the window – 'that is Scott's hut.'

'That's just the point,' I said. 'Out there beyond the hut is all Antarctica, and we sit here in our cosy little home protected from the very world we came here to experience.'

On 18 March Mike, Gareth and I set out with heavy sacks and Nordic skis to traverse the summits to Cape Crozier at the far end of Ross Island. Two days after our departure John wrote in his diary:

The weather is good for the walkers. They must have made the descent from Erebus by now and be on their way to Terra Nova. I really don't envy them at all. Rob too is glad to be here and not tramping about. His philosophy is that the Polar journey is essential for his credibility and future, but no other travelling is vital, apart from some training. Neither of us derives any satisfaction from humping rucksacks up mountains.

Having eaten a rather large lunch neither of us wanted any supper barring a plate of delicious ice cream. It's most pleasant having only the two of us in the hut, and interesting being alone with Rob, for he says a great deal more than he would otherwise, and I begin to understand his motives, problems and anxieties.

With their chairs drawn up beside the iron stove, whose open door revealed the deep red heart of the burning coal, Robert ruminated on the reasons that had brought him to Cape Evans.

'This Erebus lark is a bore, the history of this place is reason enough for being here. I often feel alone in my obsession for its history. What is the real story of Scott? I have a feeling that we may find it out there on the journey. The Pole will be a great experience, but already I can't wait to be back in the real world. There one can follow the line of least resistance, but here I will have to become a different person. Restraint does not come easily to me, but I suppose that is a cross I must bear, and for the first time in my life not even I can talk my way out.

'At home, during all the work to get here I felt like a boxer on the ropes, staggering from the punches, somehow standing up, drunk in a dream with a slight smile on my face, knowing that whatever I did it mattered not. It was just a game. But walking to the Pole is frighteningly simple, and without radios there is no way out. It is an opportunity for truth.

'The Pole will unshackle me from the awful fear of failure and the burden of having to win at all costs. I have to feel that life is worthwhile. If or when we pull this off, I will have done something extraordinary which will give me the opportunity I long for.'

Mike, Gareth and I returned to crowd the hut after eleven days of travelling the island for 130 miles in the low sun of late summer. For Robert and John there was some regret that the interlude of uncongested domesticity should end so quickly. John wrote: 'Robert and I are like a couple of schoolboys on their last day of holidays. The others return tomorrow so it will be back to routine, normality and no doubt within a couple of days' time Roger's moodiness.'

7

Winter Darkness

My first impression on entering Scott's hut was that we were intruding into the home of someone whose absence was only temporary. There is a strange lack of dust. Often it was colder inside than out, yet the hut felt strong and secure, as though at any moment the door would burst open and with a stamping of heavy boots upon the wooden floor the occupants would return. It was impossible to feel at ease in the shadowy hall, and though the atmosphere was not malevolent, the feeling of reproach never left me while I pried into its dark corners. None of us, during the eleven months at Cape Evans, ever mustered enough courage to sleep a night there.

The hut is filled with possessions. These were not the sanitized objects found in a museum. Like favourite shoes which take on the shape of the feet that wear them, every item was pregnant with ownership. Even the monkey's fist which finished the rope that lifted the wooden latch on the door was a reminder that the men who had lived here were part of a naval expedition.

In Scott's day the hut was partitioned into ward room and mess deck, but much of this wall of boxes was removed by the Ross Sea Party. Today there is an unobstructed view the length of the room, which is dominated by a long oak table. Shafts of light from two small windows on the western wall break the darkness, but they are too high to give any reminder of the cold world outside. From the door one's attention is drawn immediately to the galley. Behind the iron range shelves groan with tins of food and bottled preserves, and colourful labels proclaim many familiar names – Lyle's Golden Syrup, Colman's Mustard, Heinz Tomato Ketchup, Bird's Baking Powder, and Huntley and Palmer's Biscuits. Opposite, where the bed of

Petty Officer Evans once stood, is a sledge with deeply scoured runners and a green canvas tent that had been used in 1915 on the crossing of the Ross Ice Shelf.

Mid-way down the room are two areas of bunks. On the right are the berths of the Norwegian, Tryggve Gran, and the geologists, Frank Debenham and Griffith Taylor. Across the table are the 'Tenements' where the 'scallywags' lived, Cherry-Garrard's bunk on the lower left, with a heavy reindeer sleeping bag rolled out upon it. Beside it is a chair on which Bowers used to stand, using his bunk above as a desk, as he planned and calculated the weights of stores for the Southern Journey. A plank nailed diagonally across the narrow aisle supports Titus Oates's bunk, which is built on wobbly stilts. It was all still as it had been when Herbert Ponting captured the scene in a photograph – Cecil Meares relaxing with his pipe and Surgeon Edward Atkinson on the lower bunk with a large spoon suspended on a string, looking as if it protruded from his ear.

The dark-room in which Ponting worked and slept dominates the northern end of the hut. Inside, hidden among the debris of broken glass plates, developing trays and water clocks, is a tiny cardboard altar and a rosary belonging to the Reverend Spencer-Smith, who died on the Barrier in March 1916.

Each area of the hut holds its secrets. There are rough clothes made from sail cloth by the marooned Ross Sea Party, black with soot from the seal blubber they were forced to burn for light and heat. A collarless linen shirt with thin blue stripes bears the name of Lieutenant Edward Evans, after whom this Cape was named. There are ragged copies of *Illustrated London News*, *Tit-bits* and the autobiography of Babbacombe Lee, 'the man they could not hang', and a stuffed Emperor penguin. Only Scott's enclosed 'den' is a disappointment. It is bare and empty. The rusting wire bed is stripped and sagging. The books have gone and the framed pictures of his wife and son have been removed. The few things that remain are not Scott's. It is as though he wished to remain an enigma. There is only a pipe-rack made from lamp-wick and a small, curling sepia photograph, spiked on a nail driven into a beam beside the bed, of a young and smiling Kathleen, his wife.

* * *

Mornings in our own hut began with the sound of Gareth, who was invariably the first to rise, raking the ash from the stove and stoking it with coal. Then, while he waited for the kettle to boil, he would begin to brush his teeth vigorously. Robert was usually the next to stir. He would pound past, crouching under the low roof, down the narrow alley from his den to the trap-door and then descend the creaking ladder to the room below. A third of the hut was partitioned into four small cubicles – a boot-room where outdoor clothes were hung; a lavatory, its walls hung with tools and skis; a pantry with deep shelves loaded with tins of peas, corned beef and peaches in heavy syrup, and a dark-room. The area that remained measured sixteen feet square, and in this cramped space the five of us lived and worked. John had made a table by rounding the corners of a sheet of marine plywood, and this filled the centre of the room. Shelves lined the walls from ceiling to floor. Between them were crammed work-tops and the two large fuel drums in which we melted snow. Two windows overlooked the beach, and while washing dishes it was possible to watch the ever-changing colours of the Barne ice cliffs, or the sun setting behind the mountains across the Sound. Mount Erebus was visible from the window at the northern end of the hut, where Gareth had set up his radio corner, and the single window in the eastern wall overlooked the lunar landscape of the windswept Cape.

Twice a month we were woken by Mike, who had been known as Dr Shroud when he worked in Dubai. He would greet us with a breakfast of two pints of lukewarm Complan. It was lumpy and flavoured with chocolate. When we had forced down the sickly goo, he had us wired up to a cardiograph and breathing into a mask. Then he made us lie for two hours, without moving, listening to threats that if we fell asleep we would be fed more Complan. It was Robert's privilege to inflict this same study of 'metabolic adaptation to cold' upon Mike, who began to refer to him as Doctor Heavy Hands.

Our evenings were spent quietly, writing diaries. John logged his day's film and cleaned his cameras. Gareth took care of the Base and was always busy with the generator or the radio. We listened to the World Service or to voices from Japan and Greenland while we waited for the wind to destroy his latest aerial. Sometimes, when we had opened a bottle of Scotch, we talked late into the night, about anything that came to mind, from Indian railways and the Swinging Sixties to the demise of the Health Service and God.

Our diaries record the passing season and the difficulties of living in each other's pockets.

'Today', I wrote on 5 April, 'has been one of the most beautiful we have had at Cape Evans. Bright clear skies and the weightless sun drifting across the northern horizon. Ice daisies garland the mosaic of cracks in the thickening sea-ice, which has lost its translucent quality under a sprinkling of snow. The clear water at Cape Barne is visible as mirage, and there are mirages across the bay towards Granite Harbour. Mountains beyond the horizon appear as islands floating in shimmering air. I rode the Mountain Bike out across the sea-ice to where the ship had stood, feeling as guilty as if I'd walked through a field of buttercups at the snaking trail I left behind me.'

8 April: 'The wind began at five o'clock and the sea-ice on which we had played left the bay in minutes. We have been given a warning. Any journey that puts us more than an hour from shore is potentially very dangerous.'

The walk to the Pole was never far from my thoughts. It hung over most things we did, and the constant reminders of the dangers of the Antarctic were sobering when we thought how alone the three of us would be. Yet I felt now more than ever that I wanted to make the journey without radios, for with them we could never come close to the commitment Scott had found.

9 April: 'I am in a sombre mood, quiet and sullen. For a time, following our return from Cape Crozier, I felt fulfilled and content, but Cape Evans is a frigid place, and the wind does not encourage us to leave the hut. Robert, Mike and John appear considerably more stable emotionally than I. Gareth has a fragile cheerfulness about him that I find disturbing. He is vulnerable and edgy. Perhaps it is the talk of not taking radios to the Pole.' For without radios it is a different game.

Robert had rescued a skua with frozen feet that remained at the Cape when all the other birds had long departed. 'He shows such tenderness to the skua that, it seems, is with us for the winter. Its time of sanctuary will be but a brief postponement of its inevitable death at the hands of a continent that will tolerate no misfortune.'

Gareth's diary, 9 April: 'I find it difficult living in the hut at times. It feels like I'm the only one with any cleanliness or organization. The clean tea-towel is used as an all-purpose rag, then screwed up in a ball and deposited on the shelf. Am I the only one who uses the towel rail?' Three days later he added, 'What is wrong with these guys? I cleaned up again this morning and received several sarcastic comments. The tea-towel is screwed up in a ball again.'

My own diary of the 9th continues: 'I am closest by a large degree to Mike; he is the only one with whom I share any interest that is not centred on the expedition. Gareth with his conscientiousness I find the most irritating, more so even than Robert, whose relationship with me is one of mutual tolerance fostered by the inevitability of our involvement with each other in the journey to come.'

Robert's diary, 10 April: 'I am in a furious temper with Roger, his moods poison the atmosphere. I will write to him tonight. Serious stuff, but I do not really care about the consequences because this time I know I am right.'

My own diary describes the scene that evening: 'Once again we were all in bed before ten. When I climbed the stair Robert was standing by his candle-lit desk. There was no signal of communication and he rather quickly entered his room. I found beside my bed the product of Robert's pensiveness and remoteness over the last two days – a manilla envelope bearing signs that it had been handled by a force that could never be contained by the task of sealing envelopes.

'The letter I think was sincere. I hope that is the case. I have spent a long morning listening to the grievances of all. It all boils down to the fact that my ephemeral moods are impossible to fathom. We are so much affected by others' deeds and thoughts. The hut vibrates to the movements of each of us. I must learn to control my emotions, which I seem to have in an intensity not shared by the others, and learn to be as they are, more guarded in expression and yet more generous.'

Mike remembers that we 'launched into the discussion with some trepidation, but the upshot was that Robert and Roger talked honestly together . . . At about midnight, after Gareth and John had gone to bed, Robert decided that we must have a celebratory drink and the three of us sat down and demolished a bottle of Scotch.'

My diary, 21 April: 'Robert took the skua from the hut and put an end to its misery. Every day he has tended the animal. He splinted its legs to prevent further damage to its lifeless limbs and fed it, from a tin, a concoction of our leavings mixed with snow and butter. He would take it outside and hold it aloft so that it might flap its wings and he would leave the kerosene heater on all night, much to Gareth's annoyance because of the fire risk. The bird, which was the only living thing on the Cape besides ourselves and the occasional visiting seal, was called F. E. Smith, after the first Earl of Birkenhead. Robert later ran out his emotion with two circuits of the Cape.'

Theoretically 23 April was the last day of the sun at Cape Evans. At noon its altitude would have been about half a degree. There was only twilight. The sky reddened at sunrise and slowly, imperceptibly turned to sunset without the sun's disc ever becoming visible. The darkness was almost complete; soon there would be only a faint reminder of the sun's existence on the northern horizon, a band of red-grey sky so unremark-able that it did not even provide an incentive to gaze out of the ice-framed windows of the hut. We would not see it again for four months.

On 8 May John and Mike skied to Razorback Island. While he was away it occurred to Mike that conditions might be right now for a cycle ride, and so two days later the two of us set out to bike the 17 miles over the sea-ice to Scott Base. Although not a common method of transportation in the Antarctic, the expedition's two bicycles were not the first to be used at Cape Evans. The rusted remains of the bicycle which belonged to the Australian geologist Griffith Taylor still hangs in the annexe of Scott's hut.

The quarter moon had not risen from behind Mount Erebus when we pedalled away from the shore at a little after 10 A.M., and the stars were hidden by cloud. A strong wind at our backs helped us on our way as we pounded along in the lowest of gears. We were heavily laden, for as well as carrying emergency equipment, we took with us a gallon can of Austrian schnapps which we thought the Kiwis might enjoy. Though the temperature was −25°C we soon became warm, and frost formed thickly around the balaclavas that masked our faces.

Pedalling was harder than we had anticipated. The smooth ice that Mike had previously encountered was now covered by a deep crust of snow crystals, through which the broad tyres of the Mountain Bikes crunched a wobbling trail. The speed of our progress was dictated by the changing surface. At times, sastrugi and furrows of rime forced us to walk. We sped across areas of smooth hard snow with the pedals twirling. Occasionally, pushed by the wind, we coasted, bumping over cracks where the rise and fall of the tide had split the ice. The novelty of riding upon the frozen sea amused us enormously.

It took us eighty minutes to cover the 5 miles to the Erebus Glacier Tongue, and there the moon slid out from behind the mountain and turned the ice to silver. It was a struggle pushing the bikes up the steep snow bank, which had formed against the low ice cliffs, and on to the tongue, but once up we were able to pedal over the glacier. Rear wheels spun on the smooth ice as we climbed to the top of the whale-back. We considered roping up, but the crevasses seemed well-bridged and we reasoned that if the front wheel did break through, we would be thrown over the handle-bars to safety. We free-wheeled easily down the other side into a bay where the glacier merged with the sea-ice.

From there on we were forced to walk more than ride, much to our disgust, for the sea-ice was covered in a deep crust of snow that had collected in the lee of Hut Point Peninsula. The thought of pushing the bicycles for the remaining 10 miles to Hut Point persuaded us to cut directly across Erebus Bay towards Castle Rock and try our luck along the coast. We reached the shore at a place called Knob Point at 2.30 P.M., feeling that perhaps the disadvantages of Antarctic cycling outweighed the advantages. Rather than continue our laborious progress on the sea-ice, we decided to climb to the top of the peninsula, but we had neglected to wear crampons and the ascent was none too easy, holding handle-bars rather than ice-axes. About half-way up the climb, in a moment of impulsive rashness, it seemed to me that rather than continue upwards to the ridge, it might be possible to ride the bicycles across the slope, traversing the ice to Hut Point. Mike foolishly agreed. For about three-quarters of a mile our progress was swift and the rocks of Arrival Heights drew steadily nearer, only once or twice did our front wheels slide out from under us. The slope became steeper and the patches of snow, between which we timorously pedalled, less frequent, until discretion caused us to halt. Below us now the slope ended abruptly in cliffs whose height we could not see but which we fancied were not low. We discovered later that we were in the middle of Danger Slopes. The wooden cross at Hut Point commemorates the loss of seaman Vince who, on 11 March 1902, slipped hereabouts and plunged over the cliffs to his death. We retraced our steps and climbed to the top of the peninsula.

Once there, we were rewarded with a wild downhill ride, bumping and crashing over waves of sastrugi in the half-light, until we reached the hair-pin road that winds from the top of Arrival Heights down into the orange lights of McMurdo. We entered the town at great speed, whooping with the exhilaration of the descent. Encrusted with ice, and with Mike's scarf trailing from his neck, we swept past a snow-cat trundling slowly up the street and saw the occupants wide-eyed with disbelief. An hour later we climbed to the Gap and sped down the road to Scott Base where snow was swirling about the buildings.

We met no one as we tip-toed down the clinically clean and brightly lit corridors in our stockinged feet. The Post Office and radio-room were deserted. It was only when we reached the galley that we found any of the eleven New Zealanders who were stationed at the base for the winter. The diminutive Metman (almost everyone answered to a nickname), grinning impishly, was offering a bowl of seaweed up to tall blond Potek.

'Go on, eat some. It'll do you good. It's full of iron.'

Potek, looking suspicious but willing to try anything once, took some of the dark-green mess with a large spoon. 'Hmmm,' he said after consideration, 'tastes just like – ' and paused while he searched for a suitable comparison, 'like seaweed,' and he washed it down with a glass of ethanol and tonic water.

We passed unnoticed into the bar. 'Well poke me stupid, it's Richard and John!' gargled the Ten-gin-ear as we entered, and he tossed us each a can of Stein lager before we could cross the floor. Both cans exploded as we opened them, spraying Leo Slattery's frizzing mane with beer. The Base commander's hair and beard had grown to become one indivisible mass. We joined Pedro, the weatherbeaten Antarctic veteran, on the high stools round the bar. 'Hallo,' he said quietly as though he had expected us. It was hot inside the base. The cook, Big George, was dressed in running shorts and tee-shirt, and Killer was naked beneath a military flying suit that was unzipped from ankle to thigh and from neck to navel. They were taking turns at throwing darts at each other's bare feet. When I next turned round they were wrestling on the floor. No one paid them any attention. Tussock, the electrician, was playing pool with Brian and in a corner Jock, the carpenter, played his squeeze-box, rocking back in a chair with his feet on a table.

I placed the gallon can of schnapps on the bar. It was labelled, 'Thinners. Highly Inflammable.' Doggo, having returned from a visit to the huskies, entered carrying one of Footrot's six pups. The small bundle of fur scampered across the carpet and leapt on the wrestlers. It was Friday night at Scott Base, and once work was over there was little else to do but get drunk. No one here was allowed the freedom to travel that we enjoyed. The cold, starlit world that lay beyond the confines of the base had ceased to exist. I stood and gazed out of the polished windows and saw only my own reflection.

8

Erebus, Daughter of Night

It was 5 June and the hut had been covered by darkness for nearly a month. Mike cooked a fine breakfast for the two of us, using my imminent departure for Mount Erebus as an excuse for indulging ourselves. Gammon steaks, tinned tomatoes, thick slices of wholemeal bread, toasted with fork and fire, spread thick with a now normal but disproportionately large amount of butter, and eggs, fried eggs. It was almost four months since they were laid, and we took the precaution of immersing them in water before cracking the shells. Those that floated were generally found to be bad. Our original stock of several hundred had slowly dwindled. Few remained, their scarcity raising them to the status of a special treat. Though we were sure that Robert, John and Gareth would be indulging themselves at Scott Base, we ate the eggs with a pang of guilt, which added a little to their enjoyment.

Procrastination delayed my departure. I found it hard to leave the warmth and security of the hut, and waited for the feeling that said it was right to go, until there was no more reason for hesitation. By the standards of modern mountaineering, the ascent of Erebus was little more than a walk, but it was a walk into an alien world where the only warmth would be that of my own body and the only movement the wind and the slow rotation of the stars and moon. The temperature that morning had been −30°C. The summit of Mount Erebus, 12,448 feet above us, would be as much as 30° colder.

The previous day I had packed only those things I thought most essential into a lightweight rucksack: a double sleeping bag (it would be the first time I had used it in earnest for, to save weight, I took no tent), ice-axe and crampons, food for six days, four pints of fuel (enough for at least eight days) and the prototype MSR stove, which weighed less than 1 lb. I left the rope behind, for there would be no one to tie up with, and also my skis. This last was a difficult choice, for without skis I would be significantly slower on the glacier, on the way up as well as down. More important was the increased possibility of a crevasse fall. Breaking through a snow bridge, alone and unroped, was an event that in the circumstances could have only one outcome. Against this had to be weighed the risks of skiing in darkness, upon a glacier of iron-hard ice, and through crevassed terrain. I decided to walk.

We discussed for a time what Mike should do if after four or five days I did not return. If the weather remained fair, I should be back; if it turned foul, then I would be delayed, holed up in whatever shelter I could find, or perhaps safe and secure in the abandoned American hut just below the summit crater. Whatever the circumstances, it was agreed that nothing should be done until the others returned from their visit to McMurdo. Mike would not tell them of my departure before then, for the radio link with Scott Base was a very public affair and I preferred not to involve others in this private adventure. But he insisted that I should take a distress flare. It seemed a futile gesture to me. If only he knew of my climb, was he to spend the days gazing fixedly at the mountain? In winter the streets of McMurdo, 20 miles from the summit of Erebus, are those of a ghost town, a no man's land where Antarctica and America meet. Few venture out except for the briefest dash between buildings, and even then it is in a cocoon of glaring yellow lights that illuminate the deserted streets. No one there would see a flare's red stars fall.

As a compromise we arranged that twice a day, at 9 o'clock, when Mike would be at the Stephenson screen recording temperature and wind speed, I would shine a light towards Cape Evans, and so, perhaps, give an indication of my progress.

We left the hut together at 4.30 P.M., Mike, in a gesture of concern, accompanying me as far as the glacier. He was disappointed at not being a part of this adventure. We could see little as we emerged from the shell of light that surrounded the hut. Then, as our eyes became accustomed to the darkness, the Cape revealed itself, enchanted in the light of the full

moon. It was −25°C, warmer than it had been that morning.
The wind had got up a little and was blowing 15 knots from the
north, but there was virtually no drift. We left the beach and
made our way over and around the humps and bumps behind
the hut, in and out of the contorted rocks, our boots crunching
on the pea-like ash, or squeaking as the rubber made its imprint
on the matt white but faintly luminous drifts that hid in
every lee.

We descended slightly to the flat, alluvial bed of Skua Lake.
In February, when we had first arrived at Cape Evans, the
shallow, stagnant water had been covered in a sheet of ice.
Now the lake was a solid transparent lens, no more than fifty
yards across, shrunken by ablation from the edges of its hollow.
To follow this route in summer meant running the gauntlet of
angry skuas, a bedlam of screeches, gaping beaks and aerial
attacks. Now there was only silence.

Before us, some 400 yards from the hut, rose the steep
embankment of moraine that divides Cape Evans from the
Barne Glacier. Mike scurried on ahead as we began to climb
the slope of loose rock and gravel. I felt unfit and clumsy after
weeks of inactivity, and would soon have become much too
warm if I had attempted to keep up the pace Mike was setting.
He was waiting for me on the level ground beyond the rise,
where the last of the boulders gave way to ice. It was as if he
stood on the shore's edge, unable to go any farther because he
did not wish to trespass on my private adventure. He wished
me well, for which I was grateful, and returned to the hut.

I began to walk, in awe of the wondrous moon-lit landscape
and the uniqueness of the experience that lay before me. No
one had ever climbed an Antarctic mountain in the dark of
winter. From the rocks of Cape Evans, the glacier rose gently
into a shallow re-entrant at the head of which stood Williams
Cliff. For several hours I made my way towards this shadowed
crag, surveying the ground ahead with manic intensity, left and
right, perceiving in the half-light all sorts of phantom signs that
said 'Crevasse!' I knew my anxiety was disproportionate to the
risk. We had all of us walked or skied this route on more than
one occasion, and always unroped. Yet now, despite what
reason said, my fears loomed large.

I arrived at the northern end of Williams Cliff feeling very tired. At 11.30 P.M. I settled for the only spot where the ice abutting the rocks would not cause me to toboggan in my sleeping bag back down the slope to the crevasse on the glacier.

Spread out below was a luminous achromatic world, bleached of colour and lacking the harsh contrast of dazzling snows and ink-black shadows that the sun would bring. The silver half-light made the air as substantial as the mountains. The ghostly summits of the Royal Society Range were visible across the frozen waters of McMurdo Sound. The Dellbridge Islands appeared as dark forms set in a white ground, each with its own particular character – Inaccessible Island, sharp and majestic; the large and ponderous Tent Island; the intriguing stone blade of Razorback Island, which always looked suspiciously man-made, like the sea-wall of a Cornish harbour, terminated in a great rock bastion; and the minuscule, but elegant pyramid of Little Razorback. Beyond these, the eight-mile Erebus Glacier Tongue was visible only by the bright band of the cliffs that weave in florid waves along its length. In each bay, the ice cliffs shrink in height to insignificance, punctuating the line into silver hyphens. Hut Point Peninsula, limiting my southern horizon, shone like bone in the light of the full moon that now circled high in the north as I pulled the drawcord of the sleeping bag as tight as it would go.

I slept, warm and comfortable, without interruption until just before 8 A.M. The only token of a new day was the moon's changed position, now a little lower in the sky and south of Mount Discovery. After a breakfast of hot chocolate, Alpen and soup, prepared and eaten with little more than a hand escaping from the sleeping bag, I dressed still inside the bag and then grudgingly left its warmth to pack. It was −32°C. With the cold no small incentive to get moving, and teetering on crampon points, I crossed to the base of an icy ramp and began to climb. Emerging through broken rocks near the top, I found myself on a level summit scattered with isolated tors. From here, the glacier forms a broad saddle, descending slightly to a point mid-way between Williams Cliff and the sudden steep rise at Erebus. It was 12.30 P.M. by the time I had trudged the 3 miles to the base of the mountain. There, level with the

mysterious Three Sisters Cones, the site of the camp on our
first attempt on Erebus, I sat for a while on a convenient wave
of sastrugi and brewed a Cup o' Soup, tomato flavour, I recall.
While waiting for the snow to melt and then the water to boil,
I rolled a cigarette, and had to remove my gloves for this most
delicate operation, and then, before I could light it, rewarm my
numbed fingers. The temperature was −39°C, with a light wind
blowing from the south.

It was easier to relax now that I had gained the snowfields of
Mount Erebus, with the glacier and the constant worry of
hidden crevasses behind me. I continued climbing until 5.30 in
the evening, when I reached the rocky niche which we had
been so grateful to find in March. As the moon slid behind the
mountain, I unrolled the sleeping bag on the shelf we had
previously levelled for the tent, and, contentedly, began pre-
paring for another comfortable night.

My complacency soon evaporated as I was sharply reminded
of the true vulnerability of my position. The mattress was
punctured. I considered curtailing the ascent. Examination
revealed a small angular tear, perhaps caused by a crampon
point. I attempted to repair it with a patch I carried, but in the
cold the glue would not stick. I tried to restore the necessary
insulation by spreading my rucksack, cagoule and down salo-
pette under the deflated mat, but it was not enough to keep out
the incipient cold. I curled, shivering, into the foetal position.
It was not the prospect of a few nights' discomfort that alarmed
me, but the knowledge that should the wind become too severe,
I might not survive an enforced lay-up lasting several days.

The second warning was the sudden poor performance of the
stove. After taking considerably longer than usual to melt ice,
it finally began to splutter and die. How foolish I had been to
think of testing this prototype in such hazardous circumstances.
Without a functioning stove, I would have no alternative but to
retreat. Fortunately, it proved a simple matter to strip and
clean the stove with the aid of a Swiss Army knife, and its
efficiency was soon restored.

After a cup of hot chocolate the world seemed less threatening. I lay on my back gazing up at the 5,000 feet of Mount
Erebus which eclipsed the moon. Was it coincidence that the

moon's disappearance had brought so many doubts? It seemed unbelievably cold, much colder than the −39°C displayed on the thermometer, and the higher I climbed the colder it would become. I wavered, undecided – up or down? I could not face the prospect of returning so soon over the glacier with its waiting crevasses. The weather was as fine as could be wished, not a trace of cloud in any direction. Mount Discovery was visible and all the mountains of the Scott Coast, seemingly incorporeal. To the south, the Great Ice Barrier, a plain of unimaginable size, stretched in interminable flatness, unbroken and devoid of any feature that could give sense to the scale of its barrenness. To the north the sea was frozen beyond the horizon, for 200 miles, and this more than anything expressed the utter isolation of the land. Deprived of sleep, I watched the moon's glow progress from south to north behind the dark silhouette of the volcano and reasoned that, by midnight, it would begin again to cast its light upon the face. What point was there, I thought, in staying here until convention said that it was morning? I pondered whether I had rested my grossly unfit body enough. At midnight I began again to drink and eat, before packing and making ready to go.

I took a line up snowfields left of a rib of volcanic lava, side-stepping upwards in a succession of tacks, first left, then right, then left again. For 5,000 feet I climbed, avoiding where possible outcrops of rock and bare ice and keeping to the chalk-hard snows that predominated. In places, great plaques of snow, a remnant of a newer, softer layer that had been eroded by the wind, stood proud of the underlying surface. These had to be negotiated with care. Often they would fracture under-foot, and lumps of this slab would slide down the slope into the gloom.

Soon I reached the final steepening rise below the rim of the old crater. Here, at the line between moonshine and moonsha-dow, I had a square of chocolate and a rest. In the darkness the slope which we had climbed before under a bright sun seemed interminable. The ice was marble hard and the points of my crampons skittered ineffectually on its surface. After so many months living at sea level my breathing at this altitude was heavy and laboured, and despite the cold I was soon sweating, unable to stop with such precarious footing. At last the slope relented and I emerged from the shadow on to the great flat expanse inside the ring of the old crater. The ground was littered with large felspar crystals and blocks of pumice into which the points of the crampons sank. The pointed summit cone was still a mile distant, and between me and it loomed several ghostly towers, scattered indiscriminately across the plateau. These polymorphous growths, some of which were twenty feet in height, were the ice-encrusted vents of fumaroles, and clouds of vapour billowed from their tops like organic chimneys.

It took another hour to reach the summit, and I did not stay there long. Though there was only the slightest breeze my hands quickly began to freeze. I stood on the lip of the crater and gazed down into its black depths. Foetid, sulphurous fumes grabbed the breath. Enormous silvery boils of cloud filled the chasm and drifted in majestically slow rises out above my head. Thinner tares of yellow-tainted vapour were pulled by swift currents up the vertical inner walls and over the rim. Nine hundred feet below in that mist-obscured cauldron glowed an iron red heart, and when for a moment the air cleared, I saw rents of soft orange heat. Strangely, the temperature at the summit was only −39°C.

I raced back along the narrow ridge that divides the active and dormant craters of the summit cone and with plunging steps leapt down loose scree into the breach in its northern face and out of the wind. Directly below me was the wooden cabin once used by parties from McMurdo as a base for studies of the crater, but now abandoned due to increased volcanic activity. It was with relief that I realized the vague shadowy block towards which I walked was indeed the hut. I had never been confident of finding it in the dark. As I dug my way into the drift I uncovered a notice on the door which said, 'This is definitely a hard hat area.' I pondered what I would do if Mount Erebus erupted now.

The temperature inside the hut was also −39°C. (Later I discovered that mercury freezes at this temperature.) I lit a candle and soon had the stove purring, and after about an hour the temperature rose to −28°C. Water vapour rising from the pot of melting ice froze before it reached the ceiling, falling as minute particles that covered every surface in the room, as if dusted with sugar. On a shelf in one corner was a bottle of Glenlivet buttressed by its own little snow drifts. Imprisoned behind the green glass was a frozen block of Scotch that rattled but would not pour. I was affected by the altitude to a far greater extent than I had expected. The simple task of unlacing a boot left me breathless. I had no desire to eat and watched the noodles I had cooked freeze in the pan. I forced myself to drink, feeling weak and queasy. It is well known that the relatively low air pressure near to the Poles markedly increases the effect of altitude. Though I was no more than 12,000 feet above the sea, it felt as if I had rushed to a far greater height. Would the 350-mile journey across the Polar Plateau, which rises to over 10,000 feet, be equally debilitating?

I decided to descend without delay. In all probability my recovery would be swift as I lost height, and I knew that the period of calm in which I had snatched the ascent would not last. The 13 miles of polished ice and broken rocks stripped bare of snow that lay between the summit of Erebus and our hut at Cape Evans offered no possibility of shelter. As I strode out across the mile of gentle slope towards the rim of the old crater, the moon cast before me a deep shadow of my rucksack-laden form. The air was absolutely still. It was as if the cold had frozen time. Nothing moved, nothing changed, nothing lived. I felt like a phantom, my passage as insubstantial as my shadow, viewing the world like a dream.

I reached the rim and plunged into the shadow of the mountain. The ground fell away, to slide out of the shade, 8,000 feet below, as a moonlit glacier. Zig-zag, zig-zag, down, down, down, over ribs of rock and sheets of ice, seeking out the soft layer of snow I had avoided on the ascent, because it cushioned my plunging steps. I kept pace with fractured slabs that my heels dislodged. Down, past the pulpit, where twenty-four hours before I had bivouacked. Down the last steep slope of snow, the Three Sisters coming up to meet me, and then I was below the tops of their pointed cones and walking out across the level ice into the moonlight, with the dark face of Erebus behind.

Five hours after leaving the hut I reached the top of Williams Cliff and traversed around its northern side. On the crest the scalloped ice was scattered with fist-size rocks blasted from the crag by the wind. What was it like here when the tranquillity was shattered by a roaring stream of air in which a man could not hope to keep his feet? An icy whale-back laced with chalky ribbons of snow-capped crevasses led steeply down to the Barne Glacier. Stretched out below me were the 6 miles I hated most, the spread of ice cut by crevasses that had to be crossed. I knew that no matter how carefully I probed each crevasse bridge the step from ice to hollow lid always filled me with fear. In the millisecond when the first footfall found only empty air you would know and, faster than the body could react, you would be gone. There were perhaps a hundred crevasses between here and Cape Evans, some only a foot or two in width, others fifteen feet across. Sometimes, where the ice was bare of snow, they were as proud as scars on suntanned skin, but in the gentle hollows of the glacier, where a sastrugied crust of snow had formed, they were hidden.

I was tired now. Cape Evans was close, and though it was a rule I did not like to break, I pushed on into fatigue. Often in the mountains you see an alpinist returning to the valley exhausted, weaving a slow path between thronging tourists. Running on empty is a game I have often played, but not here, where inactivity quickly brings the threat of frostbite and exhaustion hypothermia.

My path was farther to the north than on the outward journey and I managed to avoid the areas of snow-covered glacier that had so concerned me then. Instead I found myself for a time among a series of sickle-shaped crevasses that ran across my path and curved towards Cape Barne. Sometimes it was possible to traverse the upper edge until their converging sides petered out, but often there was no choice but to test the crusted bridge and cross.

Ahead the summit of Inaccessible Island rose and fell beyond my horizon as I walked the rolling undulations of the glacier. During those last hours I saw in the silver light some vivid illusions. Perhaps it was the fatigue, or, more probably, the eye's need to make sense out of its deprivation. I saw, even though I knew it could not be, a scattering of black rocks on the bare ice, and then as I gazed more intently, they rose and flew, turning this way and that, like a flock of autumn starlings or a swarm of dark bees. Twice I saw, in the separated red and green of a 3-D movie, people at a distance of 400 yards. Two figures suddenly multiplied into a group of fifteen or more, shuffling in line and each carrying a pike or an avalanche probe, or a placard which made them reminiscent of delegates at an American political convention. Once I came upon something so beautiful I had to stop, and sank to the snow to watch it play. From the shadow, beneath the cornice of a low sastrugi, emanated a small mandala of pointillist light, viridian and orange. It hovered like a timid pet, and even when I broke the concentration and looked away it reappeared.

In the last painful mile of jarring ice the black moraines of Cape Evans came into view. I tried not to want their arrival too much and make the last moments interminable. Then, crossing the last crevasse, reaching the first rocks and knowing the journey was safely done, I was flooded with the friendliness of the Cape. It was a piece of barren ground claimed by men, it was known, it had a history and its parts were named: The Debris Cones (which flanked the glacier), the Ramp and Wind Vane Hill. Relieved of care, my energy fled and the pain of feet flayed by 13 miles and 12,000 feet of cramponed descent surged forth. I stumbled through the rocks and crusted snow to the flat gravel bed of Skua Lake. The hut did not appear until I rounded the last hillock above the beach. A warm yellow light fell from the windows. I dropped my sack in the pitch-black porch and, still wearing crampons, stepped into our warm and pleasantly grubby home. Mike had risen especially and made tea. I sat down as I was, stripping off icy layers as I became warm. A little over eight hours ago I had been on the top of Mount Erebus, in another eight hours, when I woke from sleep, the experience would be a memory. Robert, Gareth and John were still at McMurdo. If Mike had been with them and not at Cape Evans, no one would have known that my climb was not a dream, least of all me. Other people assure us, as we assure them, that because the experiences we share are not contradictory they are real. On Erebus how could I tell?

9

The Winter Journey

'If you march your Winter Journeys you will have your reward, so long as all you want is a penguin's egg.'
Apsley Cherry-Garrard, *The Worst Journey in the World*

Cape Crozier is the most eastern extremity of Ross Island. It was discovered by Scott's first expedition in 1903 to be the site of what was then the only known rookery of Emperor penguins. Dr Edward Wilson, Chief of Scientific Staff on Scott's second expedition, was determined to obtain freshly incubated specimens of the Emperor's eggs. He believed that a study of the embryo of this primitive bird might help to answer a number of intriguing evolutionary questions, such as whether feathers evolved from reptilian scales. During the *Discovery* visits, it had been deduced from the size of the chicks that these extraordinary birds must lay and incubate their eggs, inconveniently, in the midst of the Antarctic winter.

So on 27 June 1911, Wilson embarked upon what was perhaps the most hazardous of all bird nesting adventures. He wrote that he was allowed 'the pick of the whole party, Birdie Bowers and Cherry-Garrard as my companions whom I had chosen and who were allowed to come by the Owner on condition I brought them back undamaged.'

The three men set off from Cape Evans, to begin what was one of the most fearsome epics of Polar travel ever performed. Hauling more than 750 lbs on two sledges, they soon discovered the serious difficulties of travel in such extreme cold – fingers blistered by frostbite, sweat turned to ice, making their clothes like armour, and snow so dry that it felt as if they were dragging their sledges over sand. For much of the journey they were forced to relay their sledges, pulling one and going back for another, often advancing only 3 miles in a day of exhausting labour. They had several lucky escapes from crevasses, which were impossible to see in the candlelit darkness. Then, when they finally reached Cape Crozier they were caught in a terrifying storm, in which a dark and cold death seemed inevitable. Cherry-Garrard admits he had given up hope, but they survived, and returned to Cape Evans in possession of the eggs which had so nearly cost them their lives.

Many years later Cherry-Garrard described those thirty-six days in his book, *The Worst Journey in the World*. It is a vivid account told with great tenderness and respect for his companions, against a background of a beautiful but savagely cold, sunless world to which men do not belong.

From the moment our first tentative plans for the expedition changed to include a winter at Cape Evans, the idea of repeating this 'Worst Journey in the World' became an intriguing possibility. Indeed, the prospect was as attractive in my mind as the Polar walk itself, for it became apparent that no one had visited Cape Crozier in the depth of winter since Wilson, Bowers and Cherry-Garrard. As well as providing another opportunity to follow 'In the Footsteps of Scott', it would be the perfect opportunity to test our Polar clothing, equipment and diet in the most demanding conditions imaginable.

Originally, all five of us were to embark upon this venture, but as the time approached, concern about the wisdom of making the journey at all grew. Despite the great improvements in Polar equipment since Scott's day, there could be no doubt that we would be exposing ourselves to extremes of climate so harsh that, even discounting blunders or errors of judgment, frostbite would become a distinct possibility and survival questionable. It was an undertaking of such seriousness that each of us had to make up his own mind.

Robert spent many anguished moments battling with his fears, and a letter from the explorer Wally Herbert, urging us not to make the journey, reinforced his decision not to go. He felt he could not afford to jeopardize his fitness for the Pole. John did not relish the idea of manhauling even in the most agreeable weather, and as filming the journey would be all but impossible, he too eventually withdrew. That Gareth, Mike and I should go was perhaps fitting, as three had gone before.

Of course we all had misgivings – for Cherry-Garrard's vivid account of the journey saw to that. We had only to venture outside briefly to realize that he was not given to hyperbole when he wrote:

The horror of the nineteen days it took us to travel from Cape Evans to Cape Crozier would have to be re-experienced to be appreciated; and any one would be a fool who went again: it is not possible to describe it. The weeks which followed them were comparative bliss, not because later our conditions were better – they were far worse – but because we were callous. I for one came to that point of suffering at which I did not really care if only I could die without much pain. They talk of the heroism of dying – they little know – it would be easy to die, a dose of morphine, a friendly crevasse, and blissful sleep. The trouble is to go on.

Despite our fears, preparations for leaving were begun and the days up to mid-winter were spent making numerous adjustments to clothing and equipment, weighing food and poring over charts.

The plan was to leave on the same day as Wilson, partly for historical reasons, but also because, as luck would have it, a waxing moon would light our way, becoming full as we crossed potentially crevassed areas later in the trip. We hoped we could exceed the pace of the original trio, and even thought we might accomplish as many as 10 miles a day, pulling our 200-lb sledges over the flat ice-shelf. In this we were to be proved sorely mistaken.

After the mid-winter festivities, preparations were stepped up. We would take three different sledges: one of the twin-hulled Gaybos we intended to use on the Polar journey, and two flat-bottomed pulks, a six-foot-long Mountain Smith, and a smaller one of the type used by the Royal Marines in Norway. This last we intended to sacrifice on the rocks of Cape Crozier. Each had to be packed with enough food, fuel and equipment not only to see us through the three weeks that we anticipated being away, but to cover us for a month or more if necessary. All this took time, and tension mounted as Mike pushed to get away while the moon was most favourable. He was upset that I did not share his sense of urgency.

By 27 June everything was ready. Outside a shrieking gale rocked the hut and inside we could do nothing but wait anxiously for it to end. We were concerned lest the newly formed sea-ice between Cape Evans and the Islands was carried out to sea by the storm, making it difficult or even impossible to start the journey at all.

In the afternoon the winds diminished, and Mike and Gareth went out to assess the situation. The roar of the storm had been replaced with an eerie quietness, and the moon in its first quarter was surrounded by a circle of iridescence. The ice before the hut in North Bay had blown out, leaving only the blackness of open water. They climbed pessimistically to the top of Wind Vane Hill, to reconnoitre the south route toward the Glacier Tongue. The faint gleam of moonlight on the frozen water confirmed that, there, the ice stayed fast, but they could see the sickle-shaped sweep of the ice-edge stretching out between the end of the Cape and Inaccessible Island; and north of that was open sea. Though we would have to carry our sledges from the hut over the rocks and gravel blown clear of snow, we could depart.

Friday, 28 June   minus 22°C

At 5 P.M., after a last big meal, the three of us set off from the ravine on the south side of Cape Evans, which Scott had sometimes used to gain access to the sea-ice for his ponies. We soon fell into the slow rhythm of manhauling. The sea-ice was a patchwork of large triangular plates set in newer grey ice. To begin with there was only a light covering of snow and we moved easily towards the cliffs of a stranded iceberg. There the surface changed to a deep mat of crystal snow, and the heavy pulling began.

As our eyes became accustomed to the darkness, the magnificence of a heaven full of stars was revealed. The Southern Cross poised high above, the Milky Way an almost solid ribbon of light, and the aurora. For a few moments, soft green trails of luminescence wavered serpent-like across the sky: a billowing curtain, flickering, brightening, fading. This was the Antarctic night.

The dark silhouettes of the islands drifted past, as they had for Wilson, Bowers and Cherry-Garrard. We were, as they must have been, excited by the prospect of adventure in a nocturnal world of surreal beauty but, unlike them, we were not as happy and united as we might have been, for mixed in with the elation and inevitable fears were deeper tensions, conflicts and ambitions.

Mike wrote:

At first sight Roger appeared to pose the worst problem. He was difficult to get along with in the field and both Gareth and I had found him so on our first journey. Confident in his own judgment, he had little time for other people's ideas and failed to recognize that despite his vastly greater experience, our ideas should at least be considered.

This potential difficulty was, paradoxically, exacerbated by his general unassertive nature. He had not imposed himself as 'the leader' and so there was a lot more room for dissent between three strong wills, dissent which under the coming trial was to be inevitable.

He also felt that within limits of safety it was every man for himself. This didn't apply to obvious teamwork such as erecting the tent or cooking, but it did apply to packing up or getting things sorted out in the tent, where he would always grasp opportunities to do his tasks as soon as they arose. In many ways, this is a fair system, but with Gareth and me operating by politer rules, he left himself open to criticisms of selfishness. It was a very irritating trait in the confines of a tent.

Gareth could be irritating. He was meticulous in the extreme. It was a trait that had already annoyed Roger, who, querulous as ever, had made no efforts to conceal the fact. Consequently, a rift had grown between these two old friends that deeply hurt them both. For Gareth, it was a pain that he strove desperately to hide, and he always tried to avoid confrontation by ignoring Roger's digs and criticisms and carrying on in silence. Of course this only served further to exasperate Roger, who believed that such grievances should be aired. By the time the journey began they were dangerously close to confrontation.

But what of myself who had already done much to mediate and avert confrontations at the Base? Was I going to be able to help now to prevent difficulties arising as the pressures exerted by the journey increased? Unfortunately, my own position was not as even as might have been hoped. Unable to go to the Pole, the Winter Journey had taken on a great importance to me as the physical challenge of my year. It had become not only a test of will and strength but also my only proving ground. With considerably less experience than Gareth and far less than Roger, I had felt like a student with two teachers when the three of us made the Ross Island Traverse: but now, with more confidence, I was determined not to find myself in the same position again. I would show them that not only was I strong enough to get to the Pole should the chance arise, but that I could actively and intelligently participate in decision making.

My assertiveness, though largely sub-conscious, had already antagonized both Gareth and Roger when I had pushed hard to get away soon after mid-winter and now upon the journey itself, it inevitably clashed with Roger's self opinionation.

At about 8 P.M. we reached the crest of the Glacier Tongue. To the south-west, towards the tip of Hut Point Peninsula, the lights of McMurdo lent a dull, alien, orange cast to the clouds. We had elected to deviate from the original route by crossing the peninsula, close to where it joined the flank of Mount Erebus, directly on to the Barrier, instead of heading on round the end of Cape Armitage. It shortened the distance to Cape Crozier by nearly 10 miles and made the journey more interesting. More important, it avoided the necessity of passing close to the American and New Zealand bases. If we were spotted, the purpose of our journey would be immediately obvious and only by keeping our intentions secret could we prevent the people there feeling any responsibility for our safety if difficulties arose.

Up on the glacier tongue, the temperature was −22°C and a bitterly penetrating headwind rose to Force 8, persuading us to stop. It was not until the following afternoon, when the moon once more lit our way, that we descended back to the sea-ice and resumed our journey.

Saturday, 29 June   minus 28°C

The weather was dull and overcast and a thin ground fog made visibility, already poor in the darkness, worse still. Taking our direction from the compass, we plodded slowly forward, with the pulling much harder than on the day before. Occasionally, whoever was leading would turn to flash his headlamp into the gloom, and then the others would return the signal to confirm their position and well-being. This system of signalling was used throughout the journey. For the most part, we walked in total darkness or by what light the moon provided.

It was all we could do to maintain a speed of 1 mile an hour. Later the fog thinned, and ahead we discerned a dim darkness on the horizon. So close did it appear that at first we thought it must be a small uncharted island piercing the sea-ice, but we were deceived. It was several hours before we came near the foot of what turned out to be the huge mass of Hutton Cliff.

Here, during the summer, an American field unit studies the population of the Weddell seals which stay close to the big tide-crack to be found at the base of the outcrop. Now, in mid-winter, we were surprised to discover, slumbering in the darkness, thirty seals littered like huge black slugs on the ice. Surprised too were the seals, for the bright light of our head-torches heralded the first winter visit they had ever received. Safety regulations at McMurdo, only 10 miles away, prevent the study of this important colony for over half of the year. We stood and watched the seals, noticing that their breathing had become markedly pronounced, deep and regular. A head popped up through one of the holes in the ice kept open by the seals and reflective eyes surveyed us with mistrust.

We camped beyond the cliffs, beside a band of rafted sea-ice, at the foot of a steep snow slope up which we hoped to climb on to the peninsula.

Sunday, 30 June   minus 27°C

Along the foot of the snow slope, there ran a low ice cliff, hidden by the accumulation of snow drifted against it. Although the snow was soft, it presented no great barrier, but where it abutted against the slope, the sea-ice rising and falling with the tide had maintained a large crack, rather like a crevasse or bergschrund. We skirted the rift, tentatively probing points at which it might be bridged. Eventually we found a place and with an effort heaved sledges up and over on to the slope beyond. Then, with two pulling and one pushing, much slip-sliding, panting and grunting, we moved each sledge one at a time up the steeply convex hill, until the gradient ceased.

Harnessed once more to our own sledges, we began the hard,

two-mile pull to the top of the ridge, almost 800 feet above the sea. The surface was blue ice, necessitating crampons, but it proved good for the sledges. Even so, at times I was leaning almost horizontal in the traces, mitted hands pawing the ground, like an anorexic Geoff Capes pulling a London bus.

In places, crevasses many hundreds of yards in length ran across our path. One at least was more than twenty yards across but, bridged by multi-year accumulations of snow, they presented little danger.

A cold down-draught spilled over from the ice-shelf and where it met the relatively warm coastal air, formed a bank of cloud which ran along the backbone of the peninsula. To our right, the outcrops of Castle Rock and Crater Hill were visible against the warm glow of light from McMurdo, and between them, Danger Slopes, across which Mike and I had tried to ride our Mountain Bikes. To our left Mount Erebus and a distant Mount Terror shone in the moonlight, their southern slopes flowing down to the huge bay of the Windless Bight. Ahead, the great Ross Ice Shelf stretched away, dimly white, enigmatic and cold.

As we gained the crest, the ground levelled out and soon the sledges began to push, not pull. When the lights of Scott Base appeared, we knew we were on the downward slope. We were heading due east when Mike began to urge a more southerly course. He was worried that I would lead us over a band of high ice cliffs that run along the northern end of the Peninsula and demarcate glacier from shelf-ice. I was not aware at the time that Mike had been hurt by my neglect of his opinions and was on the look-out for opportunities to knock me from my smug little perch. In situations such as these, decisions have to be made on something more than correct evaluation of known facts. Which is the safest route? Is the risk inherent in this decision worth the saving of time and energy? Is this the moment to act or wait, continue or retreat? Much is conjecture. Antarctic maps are accurate only in the broadest terms, and in darkness and extreme cold, it is easy to make mistakes. The sparsity of information raises assumptions to the level of truths and when judgment is coloured by the ulterior needs of ego, who knows where the correct choice lies?

After two hours of descent, the terrain began to flatten out into a series of small snow-filled bowls. The moon had slid behind Mount Erebus and in poor light we entered an area of rolling waves that marked the indistinct transition from hillside to Barrier. We stopped to camp, suspicious of the presence of crevasses, and sure enough while we were stomping about, erecting the tent and unloading sledges, our boots found the edges of a number of concealed holes.

Monday, 1 July   minus 45°C 5.2 miles

The moonlight was very bright and it enabled us to see many of the features that border Windless Bight. The Aurora Glacier, descending from the col between Erebus and Terra Nova, Fog Bay and Cape MacKay, the tip of the southern spur of Mount Terror, around which we would pass to reach Cape Crozier. It was a kind and splendid day, with only the lightest of airs from the south-east. Mount Erebus was clear, but attended by two long and slender clouds, attached like silver Remora fish. The orange lights of Scott Base came and went, intermittently obscured by a mist which hung over the sea-ice, between the snow of the Barrier and the white mountains beyond.

We descended the last vestige of a slope on to the unequivocal flatness of the Barrier. It seemed that we were entering a basin of coldness that had been the theatre for the epic adventure about which we had all read. We were moving at a snail's pace. The snow surface was like firm, dry, chalk, which squeaked at every footfall, and the sledges ground badly. The colder it became the more resistant was the snow, until it could be said that the sledges were not sliding at all. I began to wonder if we would not have been better off with wheels.

After four hours of extremely hard pulling, we had covered only 3 miles and Gareth was struggling and began to fall behind. We had anticipated that the flat-bottomed pulks that he and Mike hauled would not perform well on these dry surfaces, and so had tried to load them accordingly. Mike, with the sledge we thought the worst, pulled 178 lbs, but Gareth had only a few pounds less than the 235 lbs in my Polar sledge.

Ahead, less than a mile away, we knew that a line of flags

must cross our path, marking the route from Scott Base to a small hut in the middle of the Bight. It housed a seismographic station which relays data collected from automatic instruments scattered strategically about Ross Island.

In such intense cold, it is not possible simply to wait until those behind catch up. Only by continual movement is frostbite kept at bay, despite the warmest double boots and layers of socks, and hands in bulky mittens and gloves which make even holding a ski-stick difficult. In the darkness, Mike and I discussed the situation before Mike went back to assist Gareth, while I went on ahead to look for the flag line.

About an hour later I found the flags, and leaving my sledge I returned to assist Gareth. I met Mike, coming slowly in my tracks, and informed him that the markers were just ahead. His movements were sluggish and his voice subdued. Now it was his turn to find himself exhausted, and Gareth and I, pulling together rapidly – if such an energetic term can be used to describe our laborious struggle – overhauled and passed him. Mike recalled: 'I was moving frighteningly slowly, reduced to about thirty yards at a time before my thigh muscles went into spasm. At this speed, with all the stops, one gets very chilled and my hands began to get nipped on the fingertips while my feet were going numb. I began to get concerned.'

About midnight, after I had gone back to help Mike, all three of us were together again. We were all very cold and the feeling had gone from my left heel. It is of paramount importance to look after oneself in this environment, for on one's own well-being depends the safety of all. No one else can judge when the limit of control is reached until it is dangerously late. Suddenly we were caught in a race to pitch the tent and explode the stove into life before we suffered real damage.

Each day, breaking and pitching camp were the two periods when we were most exposed to injury, and I cannot overstate the frantic urgency with which we set about the task. Inside the bare shell of the tent, with frost glinting on the walls and the air smoky with our breath, all attention was focused upon the lighting of the stove. Pull it from its bag, the nylon stiff and hard, flood it with petrol, careless of spillage or economy, and then with fingers becoming wooden, quickly remove a mitt and with gloved hand rip the lighter, hanging on its string around the neck, from its warm place next to the skin. Lighting the petrol always provided proof that we were living in a world where normal rules did not apply. No spark would ignite it with a whooph! A flame held against a pool of liquid for several seconds would cause it to flicker slowly into life, like brandy burning on a Christmas pudding. Then the yellow flames would rise, and I would plunge stiff fingers, still inside the glove, into their midst to halt the creeping cold. Eventually the stove would splutter and belch and settle to its comforting roar, and the air would lose its metallic feel. With relief, we could relax. 'We all sat feebly over it,' Mike remembers, 'trying to get ourselves back into action and soon enough managed to get the lamp going as well and then . . . warmth. Feet were uncovered to find socks frozen together, but with care they were nursed back to life and we all avoided damage. Roger popped outside the tent and threw in all our belongings. Chaos ensued as we tried to sort things out, brush snow off, place our sleeping mats. With all three of us in together and a hot lamp hanging in the middle, this was no easy task.'

Tuesday, 2 July   minus 43.5°C   1.3 miles

The moon – high, bright and nearly full – revealed the hut almost immediately we set off, and we reached it at 10.15 P.M. after a little more than an hour's skiing. There we decided to stop, rid our clothes of ice and, having eaten, put in another few miles in the early hours of the morning. That would have left us only a couple of days short of the far side of the Windless Bight. Once around Cape MacKay we hoped to find some easier, wind-blown ice surfaces.

Plans changed a few hours later when, emerging from the hut, we met a deterioration in the weather. The temperature had risen to −24.5°C, it had begun to snow lightly and the radio aerials hummed ominously in a freshening north-easterly wind. It was very difficult to forgo the security of the hut and we were easily persuaded. Looking for adventure we may have been, but none of us was of sufficient character or perversity to want this to become a real 'Worst Journey in the World'.

Six hours later, with conditions decidedly worse, it was clear that we must wait for an improvement. This gave Gareth an opportunity to keep a radio schedule with Cape Evans where John was busy sticking stamps to 10,000 philatelic covers and Robert continued his mammoth task of typing with one finger letters to our sponsors. Although communications were poor he managed to convey our position and that all was well. In return he heard that outside the Windless Bight a major storm was raging, with all the signs of continuing unstable weather.

This news was disturbing, for we had begun with twenty-one days' supply of food and one month's fuel, and now after six days we were only half-way across the Bight. At our present pace, Cape Crozier was still six days away and unless the return journey could be accomplished considerably faster, we would have to extend dangerously our food. Still, we could see how things went in the next few days. We certainly had no wish to give up.

Another twenty-four hours passed and we were still shut up in the hut, eating little and remaining in our sleeping bags, with the hut in darkness to conserve our fuel. Repeated radio contact with base had informed us that the barometer was still falling and hurricane-force winds of over 60 knots had damaged some of the radio masts. Robert wrote in the met-log 'STORM FORCE HELL'. At McMurdo, a Condition One alert confined everyone to the buildings. For us there were intermittent periods of complete calm, punctuated by dramatically sudden bursts of wind from unpredictable directions. Sheltered by the mass of Ross Island, the Windless Bight truly lived up to its name. Even without the hut, the gale was no threat so long as we remained within the confines of the Bight, but once we rounded Cape MacKay we would be as vulnerable as the original trio, who were hit by such a storm at Cape Crozier.

On 5 July, our third day in the hut, our patience was nearly exhausted. Mike, with so much at stake in the journey, became the most restless:

My impatience begins to take control of me as we continue to fester in this place. Conditions have neither improved nor deteriorated, but we have 'hard' information from McMurdo that the storm should disperse within a day or so. Considering that it will take us at least three days to clear the shelter of the Windless Bight I can now see little reason not to go on even if in poor visibility it will be miserable.

Of course I accept that the improvement may not come and if we had gone on after twenty-four hours, as I had wished to do, we should no doubt have been caught by ferocious storms at Cape MacKay and would probably have had to retreat. Still, it seems as if only perfect weather will convince my companions to go on.

Gareth also felt impatient, but he hid all his frustrations rather than further antagonize me, for I refused to budge, regardless of expert pronouncements of imminent improvements in the weather. Anyway, I was reading, with a torch inside my sleeping bag. I was immersed in the tragic unrequited love of *Anna of the Five Towns*. Mike, fidgeting, succeeded in emptying a basin of snow into Gareth's sleeping bag. During the ensuing commotion he added rolled oats to the mess from the packet in his hand and finally cast a pan of uncooked porridge from the stove to the four corners of the hut. Well out of harm's way, I giggled and read the label on the large space-age cylinder beside which I slept:

Radioactive Material, special form
Strontium (Sr 90), 81,500 curies

It was the nuclear battery which powered the instruments in the hut. We talked of close encounters with death, and Mike told us how the silver cigarette case which his grandfather kept in his tunic pocket was hit by a bullet during the battle of the Somme. 'Don't tell me,' I said, 'he was shot in the back.'

Saturday, 6 July   minus 36°C   8.13 miles

The break in the weather eventually came and we set out with a light breeze at our backs. Cloud, hovering over the Barrier to the south, obscured the moon as we walked on, only visible to each other as shadows in a blackness broken occasionally by the yellow flash of a head-torch, lighted to check a compass. Precise sounds punctuated the darkness – the rustle of clothing, the slow click-clack of skis and the creaking of sledges as they slid and bumped over small waves of sastrugi. Sometimes, our passage would cause large areas of snow to settle with a deep, muffled roar which reverberated away in all directions. The slabs would sink abruptly and without warning under our skis, tearing us from our thoughts and leaving us with loudly beating hearts.

After his difficulties on the previous days, Gareth had exchanged sledges with me; now it was my turn to fall behind. Mike, pulling the military pulk, was also finding it difficult. If the journey did nothing else, it confirmed that the sledge we had designed specifically for the Pole, with its slippery Fluon runners, was infinitely superior.

We marched for seven hours, halting for two short breaks at which we drew abreast of each other. Still harnessed and without removing our skis, we stood and passed a Thermos of hot soup along the line, ate lumps of leather-hard pepperoni, and tried not to break our teeth on iron squares of chocolate. The cold deterred inaction. Though these stops were welcome, it was only minutes before the numbness creeping into fingers and toes urged us on. Around us, the only tangible things were the steel-cold air and the silent wind, which sought without respite to steal the precious warmth of our bodies and dissipate it into the belly of the night. We were incongruous, aberrations of life in an entropic world.

Ross Island, its volcanic summits towering 12,000 feet above, was visible as a black area of sky devoid of stars. Slowly, step by step, under the rearing shadow of the island, we moved across the bay towards the dark arm of Cape MacKay, skirting the shore of the plain of illimitable flatness.

We rounded the Cape the next evening, climbing three great ridges of ice the existence of which was betrayed only by the sudden heaviness of the sledge. The snow cover began to decrease and dramatic waves of sastrugi indicated that we were entering an area of high winds. Deep in the heart of the continent cold air sinks heavily over the high Polar Plateau and finds its way through the Trans-Antarctic Mountains, down huge glaciers on to the Barrier. Then, for several hundreds of miles, it flows uninterrupted over the bare ice-shelf towards the coast. Ross Island is the only obstacle in its path. Here the air-stream is deflected around the Windless Bight, pouring out into

McMurdo Sound and blasting over Cape Crozier. From this point on, we could expect no shelter. The consequences would be severe if we were unlucky enough to be caught.

Tuesday, 9 July   minus 41°C   12.8 miles

We reached Cape Crozier at 6.15 A.M. and halted beside a shallow rib of shattered rocks a few hundred feet above the Barrier. Igloo Spur is of no special significance except that it was the site chosen by Edward Wilson on which to build his stone shelter in 1911. It is a barren inhospitable pile of stones, and the hillside of ice on which it lies bears no trace of snow, evidence enough that the area is raked by gales. Of this Wilson was aware, but he nevertheless 'decided to build as close as we could to our work with the Emperor penguins, and take the chance of doing so in the blizzard area.'

Leaving our sledges, we wandered down the stony backbone of the spur to the lonely remains of the igloo that had been the scene of so much drama many years before. We were the first to visit Cape Crozier in winter since that epic ordeal, and it was easy to believe that what they endured had not been exaggerated. Indeed Wilson's diary is remarkable for its detached understatement:

Sunday 23 July. Sixth Sunday after Trinity and quite the funniest birthday I have ever spent. The wind was terrific. It blew almost continuously with storm force – there were slight lulls occasionally followed by squalls of very great violence, and at about noon the canvas roof of the hut was carried away and we were left lying exposed in our sleeping bags.

Cherry-Garrard's account is more vivid:

Gradually the situation got more desperate . . . There was more snow coming through the walls, though all our loose mitts, socks and smaller clothing were stuffed into the worst places: our pyjama jackets were stuffed between the roof and the rocks over the door. The rocks were lifting and shaking here till we thought they would fall.

We talked by shouting . . . And then it went . . . The uproar of it all was indescribable. Even above the savage thunder of that great wind on the mountain came the lash of the canvas as it was whipped to little tiny strips. The highest rocks which we had built into our walls fell upon us, and a sheet of drift came in . . . A few ribbons of canvas still remained in the wall over our heads, and these produced volleys of cracks like pistol shots hour after hour. The canvas never drew out from the walls, not an inch.

Fragments of the green Willesden canvas are still there, weighed under rocks placed around the remains of the rough walls of the igloo. Within its cramped confines, other historic debris abounds: the thick feathered pelt of an Emperor penguin, killed in all probability to provide fuel for the blubber stove; the battered and rusted shell of a small lantern; a woollen sock, perhaps one of those used to stop a draught in the leaking walls; and a sledging box, its thin wood bleached to the colour of bone, blocked full of blue ice in which were set rusting tins of food.

Though there were many similarities between our excursion and the original winter journey – the weights we pulled, the terrain we crossed, the darkness and the cold – it was the disparities that highlighted the fortitude of Wilson, Bowers and Cherry-Garrard. In the relative comfort provided by improved equipment, we could marvel at what they had endured. Even so, we were soon made vividly aware that poor judgment and carelessness could be punished severely.

We returned to the sledges and erected the tent so that we could eat in comfort and warm the ciné camera. I wanted to record our visit to the igloo, though with only the light of a simple kerosene lantern it seemed a forlorn hope. With the camera stuffed inside my jacket we made our way back down the spur. It seemed to take a long time to reach the igloo. Gradually we began to suspect that we had strayed from the crest of the spur. Perhaps we had come too far? We turned and began to retrace our steps towards the dim silhouette of a rounded mound which we presumed was our target. After some minutes the dark form appeared no nearer and we realized that our nearby mound was in fact a distant mountain. We found ourselves wandering over unfamiliar ground.

It had been so easy: in a few moments of foolish inattention we had precipitated ourselves into a situation of acute danger, from which escape would be more a matter of luck than judgment. We had lost not only the igloo but also the sledges and the tent. I was as afraid at that moment as at any other on the expedition. Though we could not be more than a few hundred yards from the safety of our equipment, we knew that if we did not find it we could not survive. We began to circle, hoping that by chance we would come upon a feature that we recognized. Eventually the outline of the spur loomed up before us, but it appeared from an unexpected direction. The five-minute walk to the igloo had taken more than an hour. It was a salutary lesson.

10
Cape Crozier

We had no intention of camping on that exposed and desolate spur, for a few miles away, above the northern tip of Cape Crozier, there now stood a little-used hut which served as a base for visitors to the Adélie penguin rookeries. We had discovered it on our earlier traverse of Ross Island, and those responsible for this and other refuges in the New Zealand Dependency had agreed that we could make use of them, as one would any mountain shelter.

The seven-mile walk to the hut took us across broad plains of stones and valleys and rolling hills covered with scree and boulders. Clearly, sledges are not designed for dragging over rocks, but we had brought the rugged military pulk for this purpose and had to accept that it would be ruined. We loaded it with rations sufficient for one week, four one-gallon tins of fuel, the Hughes radio, a shovel, the lamp and the stove. Our spare clothing, sleeping bags and cameras we carried on our backs. The tent, our skis and the equipment and provisions for our homeward journey were loaded into the other sledges, which we up-turned and secured to the ice with ice screws. We had no wish to lose anything to the wind in our absence.

The promise of the hut invited us to accept a degree of risk similar to that to which we had inadvertently exposed ourselves. We now knew only too well the consequences of separating ourselves from the equipment. Without it we could not return from Cape Crozier. We set out from Igloo Spur intent on crossing an area renowned for storms, trudging in darkness through a complex of hills and valleys with no adequate map, to a tiny hut on a black hillside that we had only visited once in daylight. It was not just the outward journey that posed the threat. The return, when we would be without food and searching for the sledges tethered to an indistinct rib of stones, had an equal potential for disaster. Accidents never just happen; they are constructed from a chain of circumstances, action and decision.

It was a relief not to have the continual gnawing worry of crevasses on our minds. I think we regarded the few miles before us as relatively straightforward. We headed north, all three of us pulling the one sledge, jostling and stumbling into each other as it scraped over rocks instead of snow, and was frequently overturned.

After three hours of halting progress, snowflakes were whirling in the beams of our torches and the wind was rising rapidly. We were unsure of the location of the hut. We were unsure of how far we had come, and we argued as to which way we should go. The terrain was unfamiliar and becoming steadily more difficult – short, steep, boulder-strewn ridges and polished ice slopes sliding off into the darkness. It seemed that there were only two things about which we could agree: that the prospect of surviving a blizzard without shelter was extremely daunting and that in all likelihood we would soon be doing just that. Indecision caused us to continue blindly on in what had become a howling gale. The situation was resolved not by controlled or positive action but by Gareth recognizing that we had stumbled upon the edge of the rocky cwm that held the hut. We had in fact navigated ourselves to the shelter by the most exact and direct route, despite the doubt bred by complacency and disharmony.

The tension eased as we arrived at the hut, but it did not entirely disappear. Behind the laughing and smiling some deep sores were smarting. Privately Gareth had pledged himself 'to get back to Cape Evans without uttering a harsh word'. He hoped that by holding his tongue and avoiding confrontation he could maintain a charade of peace. Gareth seemed the least irritable, but inside he was seething.

Mike was also angry with me, for once again he felt that his ideas had been treated with contempt. He had suggested, when the uncertainty of our position began to be felt, that we were heading in the wrong direction and that it might be safer to turn east and descend to the coast.

'You seem to have no understanding whatsoever,' I had said condescendingly, when Mike muttered that the hut lay way off to our right.

I felt isolated, snubbed by Gareth and threatened by Mike, in whom I sensed a rising hostility. It seemed to me that he had begun to contradict every decision I made, and it caused me to lose contact with the intuition on which I depended. That evening, with a gale rattling the hut we had been so fortunate to find, I wrote in my diary: 'The real difficulty is that staying alive in this environment is an art. There are no hard and fast rules. It is impossible to be guided by reason in all one's decisions, and yet, because I lost faith in Mike's judgment and with little expectation that Gareth will take any line but that of compromise, I am forced to treat all my decisions as infallible.'

We spent a week at the Cape Crozier hut, making tentative sorties over the sea-ice in search of penguins. We had been operating on a nocturnal rota since leaving Cape Evans, but now, with the moon well into its last quarter, we made use of the red noon glow in the northern sky that had begun to provide a few hours of faint twilight.

Cape Crozier is a strange, enchanted place. Its topography is of an intimate, human scale, distinct from the callous vastness of the Barrier and the rarefied grandeur of Mount Terror, under which it nestles. On the northern coast, among the soft contours of rounded hills, are three black cwms. In each, the little Adélie penguins have founded ancient rookeries to which, in the bright light of spring, they return in their thousands to nest. Then the air would scream with their squabbling, and reek enough to make one gag; but now the cwms stood silent, like deserted battlefields. Guano, the colour of warm ochre, painted every rock and stone. Unseen at first, the mummified bodies of chicks protrude, beak and wing, rib and eye, from this excreted earth. Here countless generations of parents have stood and incubated eggs in shallow scoops, their feet treading, unheeded, the pale, ochre-coloured corpses.

On one side of the central cwm, projecting into the sea, is a small basalt promontory, and at its tip, among cantilevered plates of rafted sea-ice, the isolated Williamson Rock. It was on the summit of the promontory in 1903 that *Discovery* left a record of her movements tied to a post, to inform the relief ship *Morning* of their intention to winter in McMurdo Sound. Later that year, a vain attempt to reach the post with further information, by way of the Barrier, concluded with the death of seaman Vince.

The post is a forlorn and pathetic marker, a hurriedly erected joist, leaning from the vertical in a cairn of boulders, its grain blasted into high relief by countless storms. Though it has endured, it has a quality of impermanence that points to the insignificance of man's deeds. The timber has the same colour as the guanoed ground on which it stands. At its base lie the remains of generations of penguins, and the eighty years that have elapsed since the post with its message was erected seemed as inconsequential as the death of the birds that each year add to the ochre fields.

Our first attempt to find the Emperor penguins was soon aborted. There was a light breeze blowing and the temperature of −26°C seemed warm. We descended a thousand feet from the hut at the head of the cwm to the *Discovery* post. As we approached the promontory, Mike remarked that he could hear a noise, like the sound of a distant waterfall. Squalls of drift worried the coast, and the visibility changed continually from miles to yards. Across the sea-ice, running out a mile from the Cape where we stood, we could see the low, vertical cliffs that mark the edge of the Great Ice Barrier. Somewhere under their scant protection we hoped to find the nesting birds. The soft roar we could hear was caused by the wind blasting over the ice-shelf and projecting a great grey plume of snow out to sea. We plodded back up to the hut, over-dressed and sweating, occasionally losing sight of each other in the drift.

The following day was Friday the 13th, perhaps an inauspicious day on which to continue the hunt. Whether or not we had misgivings, the undiminished blizzard deterred any further search. The 14 July found us crunching across the sea-ice, on a breathless day under a sky of sharp stars. It was intensely cold.

From Ross Island the Barrier edge runs east for 400 miles to the Bay of Whales. In Wilson's day the ice-edge began only a little beyond Igloo Spur, 2 miles south of Cape Crozier itself.

Since then it has advanced 3 miles, sliding past the basalt cliffs under which the whaler, launched from *Terra Nova*, had bobbed, looking for a landing. Now the ice-shelf reaches out past the Cape, stretching white fingers like the erectile crest of a cockatoo into the sea. Low ice-walled canyons intrude between each finger and taper to a close in a mile or two. In these canyons, on the frozen surface of the sea, we expected to find the Emperors.

In the dim half-light of noon we entered the first inlet, and before we had gone but a few hundred yards were brought to a halt by an eerie *kaurk*! It was a piercing, primeval noise that cut the silence. We turned and made towards it and there, in the dark shadow, under the ice cliff, a black, amorphous shape seemed to be flowing over the frosted ground. We followed its weaving course, excited, and quickening our pace until our lamps reached out into the darkness and divided the form into individual parts. Here were the Emperor penguins, lords of the night, in their silent brittle corridors of ice, frightened and bewildered by these aliens with their lamps.

There were forty birds in the group, huddled against the ice cliff. If we came too close, they waddled off, shoulder to shoulder, or flopped on their bellies and scooted away, their indignant cries answered by other far off calls. We gazed at them with awe, feeling privileged to witness these strange, majestic, comically pompous birds which had found an uncontended niche on a deserted continent in which to breed.

It was apparent that none of the group was sitting on eggs, nor were there any chicks among them, and indeed the group were all immatures and probably too young to breed. We searched deeper into the inlet but found no other birds, only tracks in the salty crust and specks of blood and green bile around a tide-crack. Wilson had expected a rookery of 2,000 birds but was disappointed to find only a hundred, of which, he estimated, no more than a quarter were incubating eggs. The questions he asked then still seemed pertinent. Were these birds early arrivals? Had a previous rookery been blown out to sea, and was this the beginning of a second attempt? Had the Crozier rookery dwindled because changes in the coastline made the bays unsafe, or was it that during this winter unbroken sea-ice extended too far north?

We crossed to the second inlet, which proved deeper than the first, and a mile's walking brought no sound, sign or sight of any penguins. I felt that it was pointless to continue, but Mike and Gareth were still keen and insisted that we should check to the very end of the narrowing gorge. I found myself plodding behind them for another hour of fruitless search. To the north, a solitary lens-shaped cloud burned the brightest orange in a vermilion sky, like a substitute sun. Eventually the fading light convinced them that we should return.

Disappointed, we slogged back up to the hut. Often on this journey, we beheld sights by which, under more amiable conditions, we would have been transfixed in wondrous contemplation. The cold discouraged inactivity, not merely with discomfort, but with the ever-present threat of injury. As we climbed, we turned and gazed back down the dark cwm and out across the sea-ice to the ragged headland of ice cliffs, wondering which dark corner hid the Emperors. Cape Crozier appeared more mysterious than ever. An arc of light rose slowly over it, gaining brilliance, flowing like the folds of a heavy velvet curtain in transparent shades of red, green and pearl. Then the arc broke, and the writhing fragments began turning back on themselves in whirls and spirals, like paper curling as it burns. My feet were growing cold. I turned my back on the spectacle and headed for the hut.

The question of whether to persist in our search arose. I was convinced that it was a waste of time and wanted to return to our sledges while the weather was good. Mike was altogether against giving up. Though finding the Emperors held slightly less significance for Gareth, he also felt that a termination was premature. To Mike's annoyance I pointed out the dangers of these excursions, wandering miles from a shelter that was difficult to find, even in reasonable conditions, with only a sleeping bag and a pocketful of food to sustain us. He saw this, quite rightly, as a rather feeble rhetoric designed to sway the argument.

'If you think it's too dangerous, then don't come,' Mike

countered, impatient at my obduracy. This only reinforced my mounting feeling of exclusion.

'That's just what you'd both prefer,' I said with indignation.

'Please don't think that, I'd be only too glad if you came with us. Your reactions are almost paranoid, it's really your own insecurity that's the problem.'

'That's your interpretation,' I said, plunging into a silence from which I refused to surface. The last thing I wanted was to listen to Mike wearing his doctor's hat of clinical psychologist.

Gareth recalled that he 'washed dishes and cooked a meal while all this was going on and said nothing. I was feeling very hostile. It requires all my strength not to belt the man. What am I going to do on the Polar trip?'

'So what have I done?' wrote Mike in his diary. 'Apparently I have deeply offended someone I like by telling him a truth about a disagreeable element in his character. I have tossed and turned all night with it and maybe found that some of it is my own fault. Certainly I have been surprisingly aggressive and antagonistic towards Roger. Perhaps part of it is my insecurity rather than his, and in particular my need to show myself as competent, to prove to myself, Roger and Gareth that I could do the Polar trip if I had the chance. The more I think about this, the more truth I see in it. I have been almost as awkward as Roger himself.'

In the morning things remained very strained. No apologies were forthcoming from any of us. I announced by deed rather than word that I would be joining them on our third trip along the coast and we set off ambivalently together.

Down by the *Discovery* post the tenuous peace collapsed. This time it was over Mike's suggestion that we should walk straight out across the sea-ice, to the cliff beyond the second inlet we had reached yesterday, there to resume our search from where we left off. Still convinced that the effort would be pointless, I resumed the theme of unjustifiable risk.

'I'm definitely not going out there,' I declared, sensitive to any hint of conspiracy.

Mike remembered that 'Gareth stepped in with a real brick, not understanding that Roger didn't mean what he said to be taken literally.'

'It's simple,' he said. 'Go back to the hut and Mike and I'll carry on.'

I swore at him in a rage, and sped off across the ice I had just declared I would not cross.

Mike caught up with me after about half an hour and attempted a reconciliation. He explained the misunderstanding and his own analysis of the situation. He referred again to my dark mood. He was genuinely concerned, but I wanted nothing, least of all a rationalization of events that I knew reflected clearly the lost respect of the man whose support I needed for the march to the Pole. I needed space. It is ironic that, in a land of unbroken distances, solitude is so hard to find. For the rest of the day we did not speak as we searched the Barrier edge, finding more small troupes of penguins but no nesting colony.

Disappointed once again, we returned to the hut one by one, Gareth first and then Mike. I followed, last. Slowly communication was re-established. Exercise had taken the edge off my emotion. We were all very worried about the prospect of the Polar journey. Mike ruminated: 'I blame myself, in part, for precipitating these difficulties. Roger is churlish and highly temperamental and needs to be handled delicately. I must forget my own problems of insecurity and assertiveness and just try to keep him calm. God help the Polar Party. He, Rob and Gareth will be an unmitigated disaster.'

The weather next day confined us to the hut, reading by candlelight dog-eared paperbacks found on a shelf over the shuttered window. I got through *The Making of a Psychiatrist* and *The Space Egg*, Mike tackled *An Introduction to Jung's Psychology* and Gareth read Taylor Caldwell's *Dear and Glorious Physician*, the romantic biography of St Luke.

The weather at 6.30 A.M. on the 17th was again uninviting. By 10 A.M. conditions looked better, but it was already too late for us to be able to guarantee that we would reach Igloo Spur before the light faded. None of us wished to risk the possibility of failing to find the sledges. We decided to wait. Mike used the opportunity to look one last time for the penguins. Neither Gareth nor I shared his need, so he went alone. Unless he reached the very end of the inlet, Mike said, he would always live in doubt. Although he returned unrewarded, he was pleased he had done all he could to find them.

Friday, 19 July   minus 51°C

It was a fine day but intensely cold when eventually, in better spirits, we left the hut and without incident reached Igloo Spur in only two-and-a-half hours. The two sledges were recovered and we set off homeward in the early afternoon, optimistic about reaching Scott Base in five days. Surely, we thought, with our much lightened loads we could manage the elusive 10 miles a day? We camped after only 5.03 miles. The pulling had been extremely hard, and that night in the tent ice particles floated in the air and fell as dust on our sleeping bags, even while the lamp burned.

The next day the temperature reached −54°C and the dry, squeaking snow made the hauling worse than ever. Only 5.4 miles were covered that day, and 5.8 the next. Mike's 'unbreakable' plastic mug shattered into pieces when he inadvertently trod on it, and butter, stabbed with a knife, snapped and splintered like brittle toffee. It took four hours to get away each morning and five hours to deal with everything in the evening. With eight hours of pulling, we were left with only seven hours in which to grab a chill, interrupted sleep. For the first four hours we would be warm, but gradually during the night the cold would creep into our bodies and in the final hour we would lie shivering and rub arms and thighs inside our enormous double sleeping bags.

We eventually rounded Cape MacKay into the Windless Bight on 22 July. By a freak of navigation we came upon our outward tracks. It remained very cold. I have heard it claimed that it is difficult to distinguish changes in temperature below a certain level, but it seemed to us that each degree below −50°C became progressively more distinct. People will say with amusement, 'Oh, we had minus forties while skiing in the Rockies', or 'it was almost as cold as that in the Alps last winter', and then you find they were skiing powder in March sunshine, or wedling between drinks of brandy and gluwein on the sunny slopes of Verbier. For us there was no respite and no sun to warm the face, and the only comfort was that Wilson, Bowers and Cherry-Garrard, sleeping in ice-encrusted reindeer bags, experienced a temperature of −61°C. Even the Royal Marines, when training in Arctic warfare in northern Norway, are supposed to stop and erect canvas when temperatures drop to −30°C.

While unloading his sledge that evening, Mike kicked over the lamp in the darkness. No one spoke; each of us stood and looked at the broken glass and saw five days of cold darkness ahead and a real 'Worst Journey in the World' beginning. After replacing the mantle, we got the lamp to work again, but without the glass the mantle was unprotected, and we were acutely aware that there remained only two spares.

Tuesday, 23 July   minus 50.3°C

While Mike cooked breakfast, I was writing in my diary. I asked Gareth why he was avoiding me. Why did he always pull up alongside Mike at the stops and why did it seem that he never directed any of his remarks to me? He disputed that this was the case. He said he had been struggling to remain civil, wanted to remain neutral, so as to avoid provoking me, and that I was over-sensitive. He said the sound of my voice brought him feelings of contempt and my emotional moods he found impossible to follow or accept. I asked him why he bottled everything up until it burst. With a trembling voice he replied: 'What is there to be gained from arguing all the time? To me this voicing of feelings seals a finish to the problem.' In his diary he wrote: 'Was it Roosevelt who said, "walk softly and carry a big stick"?' Even so I saw our heated talk as a way to a new beginning.

The yellow lights of Scott Base miraged on the horizon. 'You've got it in the neck, stick it, you've got it in the neck.' Cherry-Garrard's inane mantra, which he had repeated to himself throughout his journey, ran through my head too. We had it a good deal easier, met little of the hardship they had encountered, yet we came out of it anxious and hurt. None of us could write as Cherry-Garrard did of his companions, 'They were gold, pure, shining, unalloyed. Words cannot express how good their companionship was. Through all these days, and those which were to follow, the worst I suppose in their dark severity that men have ever come through alive, no single hasty or angry word passed their lips . . . We did not forget please and thank you, which means much in such circumstances, and all the little links with decent civilization which we could still keep going. I'll swear there was still a grace about us when we staggered in. And, we kept our tempers – even with God.'

On the 25 July we walked into the light, noise and heat of Scott Base and received a warm welcome from the New Zealanders. A hurriedly erected screen was pulled over the antagonisms between us. It was part of the rules that a pretence of cohesion be maintained. Similar concealed undercurrents could be felt between the Kiwis. The darkness of the winter had crept into both our communities.

'How long has it taken you boys to ski over?' asked Leo Slattery, the Officer in Charge, thinking that we had just popped over from Cape Evans.

'Oh, about a month,' I replied, matter-of-factly.

He looked confused.

'We came by way of Cape Crozier,' I said, trying not to sound too proud.

'Well you'd better come and have a little something to warm you up,' he said. 'I always thought you guys were mad.' And we followed him to the bar.

We enjoyed comfort and hospitality for four days at Scott Base and took the opportunity to telex Richard Down in London. Then it was out and around Cape Armitage and home across the sea-ice, travelling into a bright orange northern sky. The sun was returning. Winter was almost over and spring was on the way. There was much to resolve in the few months that remained before the big walk south.

11
The Return of the Sun

'My decision has been made,' began Robert. 'I don't blame
Gareth for holding on to the hope of going to the Pole, but I
think that it's insane for the three of us to go, knowing the way
we are, and I don't think that is going to change. In my opinion,
we should seriously consider Michael as the third man in place
of Gareth.'

This was the first time the subject had been discussed openly,
yet Robert's pronouncement came as no surprise to anyone.
He had made his feelings clear to John while the rest of us were
at Cape Crozier. Robert had written: 'I will push for a No to
GW, but if I get Yes from RM I will accept it, but I will *push*.'
Indeed, after several celebratory drinks on the night of our
return, he had pointedly remarked to Mike and me as he
climbed the ladder to bed, 'It's about time we stopped messing
about and got this act together. The three of us.' Later, Mike
and John confided that they shared Robert's opinion. I felt
isolated. Everyone seemed so sure that I was making a big
mistake in my preference for Gareth as the third man. Even he
offered me no support, and kept professing to be quite willing
to make way for Mike. For me, there had never been any
doubt. Despite the periods of antagonism between us I was
sure that Gareth, with his great determination, solid reliability
and painstaking attention to detail, was the man I needed for
the Polar journey. Even more important, he was scrupulously
honest. He would remain his own man, as I had found to my
own cost in London, when I had tried to enlist his allegiance in
some private grievance against Robert. I wanted his neutrality
at the third corner of the triangle. It was precisely this remoteness that had made Robert decide against him. Robert wanted
a companion with whom he could share his hopes and fears.

Mike would be more fun to have with us, but he was also a threat to my control. I was looking not for congeniality but for an utterly dependable part to fit the machine we had to become if we were to convert food into miles day after day after day.

I prevaricated, not wanting the decision to be made while everyone was against Gareth. 'It's difficult to weigh up who the third man should be. You can argue it rationally either way. Whether we get to the Pole or not, we are never going to know if we made the right choice, because the other combination will remain untried.'

'Maybe you can't judge,' observed Mike, 'but you have to choose.'

'Well, I still feel that Gareth is the right choice,' I persisted, 'but we have to be convinced. It's no good leaving here with doubts. We must be sure that the situation is as good as we can make it and not leave anything to chance.'

I began to argue my case step by step. 'That Mike is a doctor is a plus, but in practice his medical skills will not be as much use out there as they would be here in the hut or in a city hospital. What he can do will be limited by the facilities he has to work with, and that will be nothing. Right?'

I was looking for his agreement before moving on to the next point.

'Yes, absolutely,' said Mike.

'Then there's the fact that I get on with Mike, Robert gets on with him, everyone thinks that Mike is a great guy. We have things in common. If we get stuck in a blizzard for four weeks we will have something to talk about as we starve. I never expected that this journey would be a pleasure, so having a good time is low on my list of priorities. My gut reaction is still for Gareth. He has the most experience.'

'You were once going alone with Robert,' Mike recalled.

'I doubt if it's possible for two to pull the extra weight,' I said, ducking the real reason for my wanting a team of three.

'You said you didn't want to go with me alone because you didn't like something in my personality,' Robert reminded me.

'Well, I didn't think I could handle it. I didn't feel safe. A lot of things have changed with you since then. At that time your ambition ended with the Pole. I found that very worrying. Your whole being was directed to one point and there was nothing after it. Everything weighed on getting to the Pole, nothing was more important. I was the first to feel relief when suddenly you had ambitions beyond it, for that meant you also wanted to come back. That was a big change.'

'There is a side of me,' Robert admitted softly, 'that wouldn't mind dying out there. In fact I would quite like it in a way.'

We sat in silence for a moment, avoiding each other's gaze, and then I went on as if Robert had not spoken.

'If four people were to go,' I said, knowing that a party of three was the only number we would consider, 'you have the advantage that if there were to be big personality problems it would be easier to remain a little more isolated from the person you have the conflict with. The team could even split, if it came to the point where two people wanted to stick their necks out and go on and the others wanted to turn back. Or you could operate as two independent teams walking side by side 200 yards apart, disregarding each other. You could even race neck and neck to the Pole. Those options will remain open until the last moment. Five of us will leave here and go together the first 50 miles past White Island, or wherever it is that the filming ends. Then the decision will be made. Whatever we decide now, even if we all agree, the final decision will be made out there. If there are conflicts, then they will have their effect. That's the way it is.'

'That would be a terrible beginning to the journey,' Mike said.

'Yes, it would be,' I agreed.

'I never thought it would come to this,' Gareth said. 'You mean that even if we decide round this table that I am going to the Pole, there will be a lingering doubt right up to the last moment?'

'What Roger says is true,' Mike put in. 'It does look as though that is going to be the situation. But I'm sure it's good to talk about it. It's a shame we've left it so late.'

'There have been a lot of things on this expedition that have been left until the last minute, and we've made it this far,' I said.

Gareth sighed. 'I feel worse about it now than I have ever

felt. It's all very well for me to say that if I don't go you would be in big trouble because Mike doesn't have the experience. Is that an honest impression, from my heart, or is it me trying to defend my position? I feel very confused about the situation.'

'What exactly do you feel?' I asked him. 'We all know that you have a position to defend, and we can take that into account, but if you say nothing then we have nothing to assess. I need to know how much you want to go to the Pole.'

Gareth, still unable to accept that it was him I wanted, could only answer my question obliquely. Staring at his boots, he said:

'I thought it was going to be really simple. I thought it would just be a question of swallowing my pride and sulking for a few days and then living with it. I thought that if I called Roger the worst bastard in the world to his face, then the decision would be made. I would have hated it, but at least it would have been settled – but because I think there is still a slight chance, I don't want to tell you now that I don't want to go. It would be a major event in my life.'

'It's not a slight chance,' Mike corrected him. 'Roger reckons that with you it can work.'

'Until a decision is made you are in the same position,' Gareth said to Mike, who also would not acknowledge, even to himself, how much he wanted to go.

For some while the two of them debated the technical problems of the Polar journey and their relative abilities to handle them.

'I think I'll go and get frostbite,' Mike said flippantly, to break an awkward silence.

Gareth continued to take the matter seriously. 'That wouldn't help. Roger entertains you because you are a better mediator than I am. I guess it's your doctor's bedside manner.'

'It's more than that. I think I see both sides. At least, I hope I do.'

'Well, I think I do too. But I would rather avoid these confrontations altogether,' Gareth said softly, in the even tone he had used since we began. 'I find it very difficult to tell any of you that you're rude, or I don't like you picking your nose, or you used the tea towel to wipe the floor.'

'I described life here in a letter as being like a continuous encounter group, where people don't do what they should have been doing,' said Mike, amused by Gareth's seriousness.

'It's not like that,' said Gareth.

'No,' Mike agreed, 'you're supposed to talk to each other in encounter groups.'

'If we were all as reserved as Gareth perhaps we would avoid bust-ups, but the resentments would still be there,' I suggested.

'In the city I can avoid it,' Gareth explained. 'If there are too many things that I don't like about you, I can just change flats. Yet I would not like you to know that I changed flats because I thought you were an asshole. Even though I thought of you as an asshole, it would bother me to know that you thought that I thought you were an asshole.'

Robert tried to return to the original point of the discussion. 'When I contemplate the three of us, Gareth, Roger and me in one small tent, I can't see that we will be safe and happy out there. Communication has got to be open on the Polar journey.'

'How do you think I feel about going out there with you?' I said. 'You're full of hypothetical opinions and romantic ideas, but you've made no attempt to try things out for real. It's like the cable ski-bindings you want to use. I've told you more than once what I think, and in the end you're going to have to come to your own decision, because you're the one who's going to be using them, and when they break you're going to be the one who'll be walking.'

'That's just it,' Robert said. 'It's the *way* you say things. When I ask for your advice, you're often aggressive or won't say anything. One gets into that shell-shocked frame of mind and I don't want to be bothered with it. That's got to stop. I think we need to raise some enthusiasm and get stuck in. A breakdown in the team won't get us through.'

'You won't get through if we break the sextant, or spill the fuel, or burn the tent down,' I said, 'and it will put a greater strain on me if each of us can't look after ourselves.'

'The truth is that I see the preparations as ugly days ahead,' Robert said with an air of finality. 'When I think of being with you and Gareth my heart sinks. When I think of Michael my heart rises up. If Michael were going to the Pole I would have an incentive to learn, rather than saying I'll rely on you and Gareth. I can either tie on to a sledge and start walking – and that's an option I quite like – or alternatively I can apply myself and give everything – and you know I've got a lot – and Michael is the key to that. I can't see there's much going for you, Gareth and me to go out and do anything together.'

'We don't have the time at this stage,' Gareth said defensively.

'We're almost ready to pack the sledges and you're talking of going out to practise,' I said incredulously. 'The time for learning is over.'

'We could still go out for a couple of days here and a couple of days there,' Robert said.

'Yes, we can do that, but you'll learn nothing of value in a two-day trip. The real opportunities have gone. Mike, Gareth and I have made some big journeys, and I have a clear idea of how they perform. I have no idea of how you will fit in with any combination of us three because you have never been out with any of us.'

'That's looking at it in the practical sense,' said Robert confusingly. 'But looking at the results of the Cape Crozier trip, I don't think Gareth and you together would work.'

'That's where you're wrong. On that journey we began to deal with the conflicts. We got through even though there were personal difficulties. It showed we could get to the Pole even if we were not speaking to each other. It wouldn't be very satisfactory, but we could do it even if we each withdrew into ourselves. It's a matter of balancing skills and temperaments. Even enemies perform successfully together if there is a need.'

'They also kill each other,' Mike interjected.

'But so do people who don't know what they are doing and make mistakes,' I said. 'Most deaths in the mountains are not caused by equipment failure or psychological conflicts but come about through personal misjudgments.'

'But most mountain parties don't set off with mutually antagonistic personality problems. They wouldn't dream of it.'

'You'd be surprised.'

'Well, I think it's all so very sad,' Robert said suddenly with great emotion. 'It's the final nail in the coffin.'

'What is?'

'This conversation, it breaks my heart.'

'But it's not this conversation that has created the situation,' I said. 'The conflicts have existed for a long time. This is one of the most open discussions we have had since the expedition began. If your heart was going to break, it should have done so long ago.'

The talk ended abruptly, with an unexpected knocking at the door. Three large, heavily clad figures waddled in and filled the already congested space. The atmosphere of intense seriousness was punctured by the arrival of these smiling visitors from McMurdo, and each of us did our best to conceal, like a guilty secret, all evidence that life at Cape Evans was ever anything but harmonious.

The Americans brought with them a breath of relaxed good humour, and that evening after a meal of lobster tails and steak we proceeded to get merry on cocktails made with schnapps and tinned fruit and a bottle of vodka that the cold had turned to slush. We had met these biologists earlier in McMurdo. Like us they enjoyed a contact with the Antarctic from which the majority of McMurdo's base-bound personnel were excluded. They had come to Cape Evans to dive and the next day they would blast a hole in the sea-ice in North Bay and empty the fish traps they had set earlier in the year.

The lumbering Baldo, who dwarfed us all, would have been more appropriately dressed in the long black coat and wide-brimmed hat of a New England Pilgrim Father. 'What's he on?' he enquired as the evening's bust progressed and Robert became steadily less coherent. Ron Brittain's bright blue eyes sparkled as, through a mass of flame-red hair and bushing beard, he answered quickly, 'Borrowed time'.

The question of who was to go to the Pole was not raised again until the following evening, after the Americans had departed. Robert wanted a decision. There could be no more stalling. His eyes flashed a warning that I should not cross him on this. He threw back at me my statement of twelve months before: 'This journey will only be successful if it is made with love.' But he could see that I would not change my mind, and said coldly, 'If that's Mear's decision, then so be it,' and he stomped out of the hut to wander the dark windy beach. Mike found it hard to comprehend that I could be so unyielding.

'Without me between you two, it will end in disaster,' he said. 'I fear for your sanity.'

'You have no idea about me,' I replied. 'Robert needs the Pole and he needs me to get it.'

John, however, had revised his opinion after hearing all sides of the argument. Later he confided in his diary, 'I hope that by offering a totally impartial view I will at least help strengthen Roger's already strong belief in his own judgment. I went through 180 degrees and stated that I was in support of Gareth. It has no doubt soured Rob towards me, but this is more important. He was very aggressive when I ventured to say something about my change of mind and said he did not want to hear. I don't believe we've heard the end of this unfortunate business. I just hope that all expeditions don't set their standards and play their games in this manner.'

John's support was a great help to me at that moment. Mike, who had tried so hard not to let his desire to go to the Pole influence his judgment, found that 'not going to the Pole is hurting, hurting like hell.' On 23 August he packed his rucksack in preparation for a solo ascent of Erebus. What better way was there to welcome the returning sun than in lonely meditation on the top of a volcano? For a time that day the summit snows turned pink while all of Ross Island and the continent beyond remained locked in a blue twilight. On two previous occasions Mike had been turned back by blizzards, and though he was again hampered by high winds, this time he was successful and was rewarded with the sight of the great hollow disc edging slowly above the northern horizon for the first time in four months. The sun's return heralded the new Antarctic year and suddenly our departure for the Pole seemed very close indeed.

That same day, far away in Santa Barbara, California, a decision was made which began a chain of events that would culminate in the sinking of the *Southern Quest*. Polar Research

Laboratories, the owners of the Tri-turbo aircraft that was to return us from the Pole, informed our pilot Giles Kershaw that they were no longer prepared to allow it to be used in the Antarctic that season. It was a serious blow to our plans, for unless an alternative aircraft was found we could not begin the Polar journey. Giles thought it 'the most extraordinary change of heart, totally out of character and totally without warning.'

The Tri-turbo was to have been used to fly mountaineering expeditions into the Antarctic in conjunction with the Chilean Government's own programme, as it had been during the two previous summers. There was no reason to suppose that this year the aircraft would not be available. Giles was to fly climbers to the Ellsworth Mountains and from there make the short flight to the Pole to meet us at the end of our walk. The Chileans had long ago agreed to this, and the aircraft's owners did not object. Then, as a Chilean general prepared to go to Santa Barbara to sign the contract, the aircraft was suddenly withdrawn.

On the face of it, the reasons given for the cancellation made sound commercial sense. During the northern summer the Tri-turbo was used by the United States Navy in the Arctic and a very lucrative contract would be in jeopardy if the aircraft were damaged beforehand in the Antarctic. It was a risk of which, in previous years, the owners were presumably unaware. What now prompted them to change their minds? Did the State Department remind Polar Research Laboratories of the value of their Arctic contract? What else but American displeasure with the Footsteps of Scott Expedition could have caused the Tri-turbo to become unavailable?

Fortunately Giles also had access to another plane for his work with the Chileans in the Ellsworth Mountains. Despite only six weeks in which to reorganize before the start of the season, none of his planned operations was curtailed. It would be simple for Giles to fly the replacement Twin Otter from the Elsworth Mountains to pick us up from the South Pole. Even so, he suggested a third option.

He saw that the expedition could not afford to risk being thwarted again. Fuel from the Chileans could still be cut off, or permission to take off from Punta Arenas or Christchurch refused. The flight to the Pole had to be completely self-sufficient and beyond the reach of any outside interference. His suspicions were confirmed when later, though he had not told the Chileans he wanted to take the Twin Otter to the Pole, he was informed that on no account was he to do so. The third plan enabled him to respond genuinely that he had no intention of making such a flight.

Early in September Richard Down, who managed the expedition's affairs in London, arranged to meet Giles to discuss the new plan over breakfast at the Holiday Inn in Chelsea. Their table beside the swimming pool and the palm trees made it seem an inappropriate setting for talk of the Antarctic. An elderly American couple came and sat at the next table. They were the only other people there, and it must have presented an absurd scene to the waiter who brought their eggs and bacon to see the two men whispering conspiratorially as they manoeuvred salt-cellar and place mats and glanced suspiciously at the two innocent Americans.

Giles unfolded his plan. He proposed that the expedition should buy a tiny single-engine Cessna 1-85. Though the normal range of the plane was only 800 miles, this could be greatly extended by installing extra fuel tanks. By also carrying drums of fuel in the fuselage it would be possible to fly the 1,800 miles from Ross Island to the Pole and back. If the aircraft were dismantled, it could be loaded on to the deck of *Southern Quest* and shipped to the Antarctic. To have the Cessna on the ice, ready to collect us from the Pole in the second week of January, would entail the ship sailing from Australia much earlier than originally intended. At that time of year McMurdo Sound would probably still be choked with pack-ice, and it was unlikely that *Southern Quest* would be able to reach Cape Evans. Instead, she would go south to the northern limit of the sea-ice. The aircraft would be off-loaded and reassembled on an icefloe, on which a runway would be levelled. From there the Cessna could ferry fuel to the Ross Ice Shelf in preparation for the flight to the South Pole. Giles later wrote:

By taking our own aircraft on our own boat, and operating it from the sea-ice, there was no stage at which anything other than the forces of nature could prevent us flying to the Pole. We would be exactly what the Treaty Nations said we should be – a private expedition that was totally self-sufficient.

After the loss of the Tri-turbo it was clear to those in London that somebody, somewhere, did not want the expedition to succeed. Indeed it looked as if failure might be used to discourage future private expeditions from going to the Antarctic. Secrecy would be the only sure weapon of defence. Richard Down told only his secretary, Amanda Lovejoy, and Giles wrote earnestly to Captain Graham Phippen in Sydney. 'I must ask you to treat this letter in the strictest confidence and mention it to no one.' Though it went against the grain for the Captain to withhold the plan from the crew, he did not tell them until the crated aircraft was safely stowed and the ship was ready to leave.

At Cape Evans we knew nothing of these cloak and dagger operations.

The returning sun lifted by small degrees the heavy weight of darkness from the Cape. It was not a dramatic event. Gradually, as the hours of twilight lengthened, I began to realize how oppressive the darkness had been. It had imprisoned me without my knowing it, and now there was a feeling of release. Now, if you turned your face towards the yellow disc as it crept from behind Mount Erebus and moved from right to left across the northern sky you could feel its gentle warmth.

Preparations for the Pole were under way, and each day brought us a little closer to readiness. The three sledges waited to receive their loads. We began decanting the freeze-dried food into plastic bags and removed the paper wrappings from 480 Yorkie bars, so saving 26 ounces. Weight was everything, and everything was weighed. Remembering that Scott on his return from the Pole had found unopened containers mysteriously short of fuel, Gareth filled and sealed our cans with nervous attention. Open boxes of sledging rations littered the hut. I commandeered the favourite parlour game and turned the board into a Polar chart and used its box, printed with the word 'Risk' in bold red letters, to hold the maps and navigation tables. John taught us the rudiments of astral navigation that we would need to find the Pole and Mike took to cooking the majority of our meals, leaving us free to concentrate on our preparations.

September sped past, punctuated by regular visits from the McMurdo people. It was good to be able to return some of the hospitality they had shown us over the winter. Yet their visits became wearing, for they greatly outnumbered us and no sooner did one group depart than the next arrived, their calls disrupting our work. Mike wrote in his diary:

More enormous orange 'Delta' vehicles arrived with tyres as big as a man – one yesterday, two today. Each disgorged more than a dozen people who descended on the beach and Scott's hut like brightly coloured insects wearing huge white boots and sporting frozen and functionless cameras. Many headed straight for the warmth of our hut and the others soon followed. We stood like sardines in our tiny space with too few cups to go round. There were faces we recognized in the crowd, but it was impossible to give them the attention they deserved. I felt guilty that I should resent their intrusion and annoyed at having to answer the same questions over and over again. Gareth took them on a tour of our home and Robert guided parties round Scott's hut.

Mind you, they came bearing gifts. Now the hut is stocked with oranges, grapefruit, apples and even the odd banana.

Winds blew almost continually. There was more snow surrounding the hut than ever before, snow that was first deposited on the sea-ice between Cape Evans and Hut Point, for it was strongly contaminated with the taste of salt. The weather remained far too unsettled for us to consider beginning the walk. We were waiting, as Scott did, wanting to be away but forced to mark time.

One afternoon, having eaten lunch, we sat quietly around the table, Mike reading *Women in Love*, John listening to some recordings he had made of the sounds of moving sea-ice. Suddenly, a large tin of strawberries exploded spontaneously. A thunderous bang hurled the entire contents of a 12 lb tin from a shelf over walls, doors and ceiling. Upon examination the tin was found to be empty. The door to the Elsan was stained a delicate pink. Fortunately no one was hurt. How unjust life would have been if, after surviving the ravages of the 'Worst Journey in the World', we had all been killed by a can of strawberries.

Slowly Robert began to accept Gareth's inclusion in the Polar party. On 11 August he had written: 'I think I am doomed to GW. Oh, well! I'll just have to live with it.' Four days later he wrote: 'I am being very silly in not liking GW. He is such a nice guy.'

Then he admitted: 'GW is OK. I am now beginning to feel confident in Gareth again. I need these people and they need me. I'm not sure how but I will prove that to them.'

On the day of our departure from Cape Evans Robert wrote:

The weather looks grimish, but we have to go. I feel nervous but now I want to complete the job. I leave in fine company on a great journey. I hardly know what to expect, but I leave with 'a lion's heart' that will roar with everything he has when he sees the Pole, the South Pole, think of that. I want it now.

I could never have contemplated setting out towards the Pole on the terms Robert had accepted. I did not have the trust he was able to give. He had only an unshakeable belief in his own strength, and he needed the Pole as only someone who had committed his dreams for the future on one throw of the dice could need it. And it was only because his need to succeed was so great that I could contemplate setting out with him. Months before I had written: 'He knows nothing of the reality that awaits us, only the heroic tales of History. Perhaps he can carry his History with him, it could sustain him, for he has in his mind no other model of the sanity of the action we take. When we step out on to the Barrier we will enter the unknown. No one knows if it is possible to make this journey unassisted, and we will not find out until it is too late to turn back.'

12
The Silent World

The poor weather that delayed our departure for the Pole had put down a soft covering of snow over the sea-ice. It was the first precipitation we had experienced at Cape Evans in all the months we had been there, and it removed our concern lest the precious 'Fluon' sledge runners be damaged in the first few miles by the particles of black grit, blown from the shore and the rocky islands, that seeded the ice.

Just after noon on Friday, 25 October we were ready. It was still overcast. A low, featureless ceiling of cloud diffused the light and produced a drab, white world devoid of shadow or colour. It was not the hoped-for day of sparkling snows that John had wanted for his filming, but at least the weather was kind enough for him to be able to operate the camera and record something of our departure. We could wait no longer.

The sledges pulled with remarkable ease, despite all the little extras we were taking for the first leg to Hut Point which brought the weight of each load to more than 360 lbs. John and Mike together pulled one sledge, leap-frogging ahead in order to film the passage of the little cavalcade as we made our way between the islands. It was not a time of great excitement, for we knew the real departure lay ahead on the edge of the Great Ice Barrier beyond the town of McMurdo. At Razorback Island, Mike collected the sledge he had deposited under its rocky prow and we continued in sunshine as the clouds rolled back. There was a moment of hilarity when it was realized that Mike had fitted his sledge-wheel upside down, and it was subtracting rather than adding the miles. A steep pull in soft snow brought us on to the icy crest of the Glacier Tongue, where we stopped and melted enough ice to fill all the containers we had with fresh water in anticipation of a night encamped on the salty sea-ice.

We continued for another two hours before halting beside a large plaque of snow that eased the otherwise difficult task of pitching tents on bare ice. Camping on sea-ice is generally not advisable because of the risk of waking up to find yourself adrift. The cross on Wind Vane Hill behind Scott's hut was an ever present reminder, for it commemorates the loss of three members of Shackleton's Ross Sea Party, two of whom, Mackintosh and Hayward, disappeared in this vicinity on 8 May 1915, when a blizzard blew out to sea the ice on which they were travelling. We felt the possibility of a recurrence was unlikely, with more than thirty miles between us and open water and the ice in Erebus Bay held by a glacier tongue that had grown several miles in length since it last broke away in 1911. We spent a relaxed and merry evening warm in the comfort of our large tent. Mike cooked a meal of tinned stew, peas and potatoes. With Dundee cake to follow and a bottle of Glenlivet to aid digestion we were far from the deprivations normally associated with Polar travel. We had, however, covered only 9.04 miles of the 900-mile journey from Cape Evans to the South Pole.

Next morning was again overcast and a blustery wind poured over Hut Point Peninsula carrying with it the snow that had fallen during the last days. We delayed our start in the hope that the weather would improve, and it was 11.25 A.M. before we were under way. With John Tolson leading, we set off towards Hut Point. On the horizon to the west we could see a tractor-train leaving McMurdo on its way to Butter Point, each machine pulling two or more cargo sledges. Later we learned that it unaccountably missed its way and was found many miles from its destination heading north towards the ice edge and open water.

The increasing wind had blown away the dull canopy of stratus cloud, revealing high above a sky streaked with long lines of altocumulus. About a mile from Hut Point we stopped to regroup. Near the ground visibility was reduced at times by the blowing snow to a few score yards, although 20 miles away Mount Erebus remained sunlit and clear.

It was a wild and spectacular scene, with heavily shadowed figures battling into the gale, the air thick with dry particles of snow, straps on the canopies of sledges and on rucksacks streaming to one side, our tracks immediately filled with drift, like white sand. It is not necessarily uncomfortable travelling in such conditions, but care has to be taken to prevent exposed skin becoming frostbitten. John, who was having to pay more attention to the way ahead because he was leading, developed a large white patch on his left cheek, but once it was noticed the circulation was soon restored under a protecting glove.

The dark slopes of Arrival Heights and Hut Point itself hove into view. Robert forged on ahead until he came upon the first of many marker flags that guard the environs of McMurdo. Here he stopped and fixed to his sledge a madly flapping Union Jack before continuing to lead round the point, past Scott's Discovery Hut and into the bay in which nestles McMurdo Station.

We had intended to establish a base on the ice-shelf in the area of Scott's Safety Camp, to enable John to film details of the daily routine we expected to employ on the Polar walk. Although we were to take with us a small super 8 movie camera, weight restricted the amount of film we could carry. Besides, I was unsure that I would have the energy necessary to film as well as haul a sledge. To this end Robert, on one of his many earlier training runs to McMurdo, had dragged a sledge with 475 lbs of fuel and provisions to a cache at Willy Field. With this we stocked Ciné Camp One as it was grandly called, which was set up a few yards from the flagged road and about 4 miles from Willy Field, much to the amusement of the passengers on the shuttle bus which plies its way every half-hour between McMurdo and the airfield.

McMurdo was thronging with people. The winter complement of eighty-seven had expanded to several hundred and more continued to arrive by Hercules from Christchurch, until well over 1,000 military and civilian personnel filled the station. Many of the winterers had departed, their tour of duty finished, and we recognized only a few faces. Our relationship with McMurdo officialdom was cool. It was obvious that the new military commander, Captain Shrite, only tolerated our presence because a number of the senior scientific staff championed our cause. We were granted the use of two rooms in McMurdo and, so attractive was the opportunity to socialize with people other than ourselves, few nights were spent at our camp, despite the growing animosity of the command towards the expedition.

There was little urgency on our part to be gone. The weather was still unstable and I did not want to begin our journey only to be stopped by a blizzard in the first few days, as were both Shackleton and Scott. Robert wanted to leave on the anniversary of their departure from Hut Point, 3 November. Gareth seemed indifferent. John required a little more time to complete his filming and the fickle weather was not making his task easy. Only Mike expressed any need for haste for he had plans for his own summer journey which he was eager to begin. He had, however, been laid low with a high temperature. The threat of infection, by contact with viruses brought in by the newly arrived population and to which we had no immunity, was something we could do little to avoid. I just hoped that once we began the journey south none of us would be incubating an illness that would cause delay.

There was one other reason for our reluctance to be off. We had given the British Foreign Office an undertaking that we would not depart without confirmation that our own aircraft was available to fly us out from the South Pole. We received from Richard Down in London a series of cryptic radio messages, more akin to a James Bond novel than a Polar walk. He had given Robert a copy of John Campbell's weighty biography of F. E. Smith as a parting present, and using words and phrases numbered from its many pages, he had constructed a code. In this way we learned of the loss of the Tri-turbo, and now we waited anxiously, not knowing what, if anything, was to take its place.

I spent some time in the Bergfield Center, the building in McMurdo from which all the many scientific parties draw their equipment and provisions before venturing into the field, helping to repair some of the broken sledges and replace lashings. Robert went over to Scott Base to collect the long-awaited Telex from Richard. It read:

ALL WELL HERE.
MESSAGE PROMISED IS AS FOLLOWS:

SOUTHERN QUEST WILL TAKE CESSNA 185 TO CAPE EVANS WITH KERSHAW.
ESTIMATED TIME OF ARRIVAL CAPE EVANS 14 JANUARY POLE 16 JANUARY.
THEN AIRCRAFT RETURNS TO SOUTHERN QUEST.
FOREIGN OFFICE HAPPY.
EVERYTHING UNDER CONTROL.

It was an audacious plan. Having flown in ski-equipped Cessnas in Alaska I had no illusions about the adventurous nature of what was proposed, but if Giles Kershaw had devised the plan, then I felt justified in accepting its practicality. More than that, the idea of flying a Cessna back along our route, and down the Beardmore Glacier, had tremendous appeal and was much in keeping with the spirit of the expedition; it was also more appropriate that the expedition should be reunited at Cape Evans and leave the Antarctic together.

That evening I met Bob Harler, who in his days as a pilot flying fighters from the bucking decks of American aircraft carriers was inexplicably known as 'Rotten'. He was now the commander of the massive air operations on which the United States Antarctic Program depends and had more than a theoretical understanding of risk. Through his initiative we were able to talk openly without recourse to rhetoric and unhindered by hidebound statements of official policy. Furthermore, he kept good Bourbon in his quarters. Here was a senior American whom I felt I could trust and who respected our right to be in the Antarctic. I understood as well as he that, though we did not wish it, if the worst happened he was morally obliged to come looking for us. I explained in detail our plans for the Polar Journey. That we were not taking any form of radio or satellite communications and that we would not therefore be making any request for assistance. He was, I think, surprised by this, even a little shocked, but all he said was, 'I understand your reasons, but it wouldn't be my choice.' He knew that finding us out there was as likely as finding three canoes in the middle of the Atlantic Ocean. Yet he recognized that we had a perfect right to choose responsibly our own rules for the game, and that they were valid even if they differed from those by which he or Washington played. I respected him for that. I was concerned about the possibility of an unrequested rescue being mounted, and of unverified information of our whereabouts and conditions causing rumour. Harler assured me that he would keep tight rein on the passengers and crew of Polar flights that might by chance spot us and he agreed to my request that if we did not arrive at the South Pole on schedule after seventy-five days he would make no attempt to find us before 120 days had passed, a time by which I was sure we would either have made it or be dead. We finished the bottle.

By 2 November we were ready to go. Mike had been nursed back to health, the ciné camp had been packed up, and our five sledges lay waiting at the end of the flagged road at Willy Field. It was Saturday night, and in McMurdo it was also the night of the Hallowe'en fancy-dress ball. First prize was won by the enormous black fin of a killer whale, a willowy Eiffel Tower came a close second. One of the marine biologists gave me some theatrical blood, and, for want of imagination, I went as an accident, hands bandaged. In the hot darkness, amidst the crowd of gyrating bodies, I met the hooded figure of Death, and, though I shook his hand of painted bones to dispel the omen, there was still a chill. I left long before the party ended. Outside, though it was past midnight, it was still light, and snowing.

Sunday, 3 November

It was a day as glorious as ever the Barrier could provide. It seemed right that we should set off on this anniversary. Scott, seventy-four years before, wrote:

It is a sweltering day, the air breathless, the glare intense – one loses sight of the fact that the temperature is low – one's mind seeks comparison in hot sunlit streets and scorching pavements.

On the most southerly of streets, the hard-packed snow dividing Willy Field's two rows of rectangular huts, we gathered for departure. 'It was', Mike remarked later, 'as good a send-off as any of us could have wished.' A throng of people wished us well and expressed considerably more confidence in our success than I could ever have shared. Beneath their fur-lined hoods and woolly hats there were many familiar faces: the cooks from the galley, whose extra-special breakfast we had just eaten; Jane, the hairdresser at McMurdo, whose contribution to last night's festivities was still evident in the sequins and green and red tufts that graced John's head; the Kiwis from Scott Base, who brought us a bottle of Scotch to warm our evenings. There were many strong handshakes and hugs from the people we had grown to love. Then we harnessed up and, with Robert leading the way over the debris left by the snow ploughs, we followed, one by one dragging our sledges away from the tracks of vehicles on to the unmarked snow.

'Hey!' called a voice, stopping me before I had gone 10 yards. 'Don't you think you had better take your skis?' I had left them standing in a bank of drifted snow.

'It probably would be a good idea,' I said sheepishly, greatly embarrassed.

We headed out on a bearing of 356° aiming to skirt the northern tip of White Island by about 3 miles. Shackleton had warily by-passed the Island at a distance of 10 miles, but, despite his caution, he encountered crevasses into which both men and ponies broke. Three years later Scott had shown even greater respect to this area of disturbance, which is caused by the constriction of the outward flow of the ice-shelf. Fifty miles farther south, the long arm of Minna Bluff has a similar but greater effect. By cutting corners at these two points, I hoped to gain some time and reasoned that, because we were on skis, the risk posed by crevassing would not be too great.

We skied out to the edge of the silent world. The sledges slid over the snow with an ease that belied their weight, and I was grateful that the firm surface, warmed by the sun, allowed us to depart with a semblance of dignity. I had imagined that, at worst, after hours of toil, relaying sledges through a morass of soft snow, we would still be so close to Willy Field that people leaving the bar that evening would saunter over to see how we were doing. Even so, it was very warm work and, within a few hundred yards, we had all stripped down to a last layer of thermal underwear, much to the astonishment of those who waved farewell.

We did not travel far that day, 6.85 miles in two sessions of 2.5 hours, but it was far enough to put the last signs of civilization out of sight. For the first week at least, I wanted to go gently, allowing our bodies to adjust to the régime, and there was still filming to be done.

Monday, 4 November

We woke at 7.30. The sky was overcast and the air was alternately calm and then strong, blowing from all directions in a series of indeterminate order. On the surface we were in good spirits, but underneath each of us worried about his own weaknesses and was concerned about the battered state of our relationship after the winter. Gareth knew from Mike's tests that he would probably be the hungriest of us all, and he worried about his feet blistering as they had on other journeys. I doubted the strength of my right knee, torn in a crevasse fall on Mount McKinley, and feared my need to forge all our actions into the machine of my conception. Robert demonstrated his power as he was accustomed, but the reality of the immensity before us was beginning to dawn on him. He identified with Petty Officer Evans, whose Polar Medal he carried sewn into the lining of his jacket. Like Evans, he feared he would be the first to weaken.

During the last third of our six-hour march the cloud thickened, and though we could see for many miles to the horizon, all around was whiteness, 'far' was as far as 'near', and 'near' was as far as 'far'. When we passed the area of disturbance – the crevassing that surrounds Cape Spencer Smith – at a distance of about 1 mile, we could see what appeared to be a boiling overfall in a featureless sea of ice. It was near this place that Smith died, having been dragged on a sledge for 300 miles by his companions, returning from laying the vital depot for Shackleton. His is the first name on the cross on Wind Vane Hill.

We covered over 8 miles that day and 6 on the next. When the sledge-meter said that we had travelled 20 miles, we turned south, through 34°, on to the bearing that pointed to Mount Hope.

Wednesday, 6 November

This was the day we cast off. The smoke from the crater of
Mount Erebus zig-zagged upward in a light blue sky, pulled
this way and that, as it rose through layers of the sluggish air.
The Barrier was opening up. White Island began to slide away
to our right, ahead was Minna Bluff, and the flat line of the
horizon beyond grew to offer the prospect of complete encircle-
ment. It had been agreed that Mike and John would come no
farther. In the morning we pulled down the smaller of the two
tents. Then we enacted the parting several times before John's
camera, shaking hands repeatedly until the real moment was
pushed away, lost in the falseness of the repetition.

    We began to ski, the sledges pulling heavily on our shoulders.
A last wave and the small figures of John and Mike and the
tent beside them became invisible against Ross Island which,
as it too receded, became to us an island for the first time. To
the south-east, towards the heart of the Barrier, in the ever flat
distance, mirages floated. The flatness beyond the horizon
lifted, to appear as white clouds or the gentle summits of winter
hills. Yet all this visual sensation was as decoration to the
tactile world of breathing, sweating effort, fatigue, muscle, heat
and cold which we were entering.

13

The Great Cloud Table

Every morning we would pull down the home we erected at the end of each day, then set off to roll out behind us a straight trail, skiing as far as our energy would allow (a distance that always seemed insignificant). There we would pitch the same blue tent in an unchanged landscape, at the termination of the same silver track, with the same blank expanse before us.

Sunday, 10 November   61.29 miles

Lying warm in my sleeping bag that evening I wrote: 'The blizzard, that raged gently this morning, still blows. We have moved only 3.01 miles today, taking three and a half hours to do so. Visibility was but a few yards in the blowing snow and the wind was southerly and right in our faces. Keeping direction was the chief problem, trying to watch the compass through a jungle of hats, balaclavas, iced goggles and hoods. Twenty paces, then, stop and check direction. The snow blowing over the skis was a useful guide, but progress was just too slow and energy-consuming to justify continuing. Minus 19°C is cold for such winds at this time of the year.'

Each day was hung upon a framework of unchanging repetition, each step, each camp, each sleep the same, and yet, now, when I look back upon them all, it seems that each one was different.

In the first weeks of the walk, there was always the overwhelming knowledge that before us was a distance the scale of which could not be conveyed in miles. The satellite in Polar orbit takes but a few minutes, Hercules aircraft only three hours for the flight from McMurdo to the Pole. For us it was a succession of days, days that became weeks without interruption, as each month slid into the next. Though each day was of predetermined duration, they stretched out ahead of us into a distance that faded, not only from sight but from comprehension. In that distance, dimly discernible in the future, yet so far away that we could at first not bear to think of attaining them, were the mountains, the Beardmore Glacier and the end of the Great Ice Barrier. After 400 miles, when we reached that point at the foot of Mount Hope, we would be less than halfway to completing our journey. To acknowledge the longing for those mountains to arrive, to desire the future, was to condemn yourself to a present of interminable frustration. Better to pretend not to be concerned with tomorrow and to sneak up on the milestones as if surprised by their sudden appearance. Yet each minute of the day raced past, and we knew that they could never be reclaimed. Our allotment of time was measured in food, which, when it was exhausted, could not be replenished. It was the knowledge that the sand running in the hourglass could not be stopped which became the spur that tore our tired bodies from the rest they craved into action, day after day after day.

We built our own landmarks across the featureless plain and placed them within imaginable distance. Significant were the nines clicking over in unison behind the little window in the sledge-meter, our first hundred miles, and then the second, and still the distance before us seemed immeasurable. Periodically, there would arise ahead a date, a distance or a position, that loomed large in history. Robert said that this first half of the journey was like returning in time, day by day following each page in Scott's journal. Yet never on the Barrier was there any feature upon which to hang the memory of those events which are preserved only in the legend that has grown out of the account in Scott's diaries.

Inside the tent space was at a premium. For the first days of the journey, there seemed insufficient room for the three of us, but eventually we organized ourselves so successfully that the tent appeared to grow to accommodate our activities. Gareth, being much the tallest, slept in the middle with his feet towards the main door; Robert, on his right, stretched out in the opposite direction, giving himself easy access to the entrance; I lay shoulder to shoulder with Gareth, on the left. Between us there was no space at all, but we made room for everything we needed for the night around the walls or under our heads to serve as a pillow. Each day we rose at 7 A.M. I wanted to allow our bodies to assimilate the daily régime, for them to learn the appropriate moment to rise from sleep. I hated the dependence upon the pip, pip, pip of the digital alarms that we used during the early part of the journey. Sitting up in my sleeping bag, I would pull the cardboard box that contained the stove from its place behind my feet. These first movements would be the signal for Gareth to begin his frenzied dressing, all knees and elbows in a tent that gave us enough space and no more. I would warm my hands above the flickering yellow flames that pre-heated the stove and then, as they died, open the valve. With a fiery belch or two, the tent would be filled with a comforting roar and, within a few minutes, heat. Into the pot would go water from the Thermos flasks, melted the night before to speed our progress in the morning. Robert would reach behind his head for the blocks of snow piled outside the door, a task he quickly took to be his own, and add them to the pot. At the same time, he would sneak a look through the flap to determine what was in store for us outside. Was it very windy, was the sky overcast and the contrast poor, with the prospect of an uncomfortable and difficult day and little mileage before us? Or was the air still, or the wind gentle and the sun bright, casting deep shadows that would aid our steering on the white ocean?

As the water warmed, we would continue dressing and crumble, each into his plastic mug, three thick round blocks of oatmeal. As the water began to bubble, I would ladle set amounts into the mugs with an empty aluminium butter-tin. Gareth would want his filled to half an inch below the rim. Robert, who always worried about dehydration, to the brim. I wanted a breakfast to eat rather than drink, and so took the mug two-thirds full. More snow was added to the pot and chunks of butter to the mess which we mashed in the mugs with a spoon. Two cups of chocolate followed, each with either a leathery scoop or brittle fragments of butter according to the temperature. What else we ate for breakfast depended upon how much remained uneaten from the night before and what we allowed ourselves for the day's march. Usually this would mean two or three biscuits and slices of butter and a piece of sausage thawed and sometimes even toasted over the stove. Gareth always had a remaining square of chocolate, Robert never. Our daily ration gave us each twelve biscuits, two bars of chocolate and three ounces of pepperoni sausage.

After the first drink, Gareth would take over the management of the stove with polite requests to Robert for more snow, and, while I dressed, he would begin filling the flasks with hot soup and Mazola oil. Gradually, the balaclavas, socks and gloves, hung in the roof of the tent like dark hams, would be reclaimed. Groin and feet would be rubbed with antiperspirant. The inner sock would be smoothed over the foot, followed by the waterproof sock and a thick woollen stocking, and the whole inserted, with great care to avoid any rucks and wrinkles, into the boot. It became customary for Robert to exit first, and he would squeeze past the precariously balanced stove and thrust himself out into the day. If the wind was not too strong, he would be followed by a rain of things thrown after him into a pile before the door – sleeping bags and bulging stuff-sacks – leaving the tent empty but for the purring stove and the waiting flasks.

Whoever was last to leave the tent would brush from the walls and floor the rime-ice that had formed during the night from cooking and the moisture in our breath. Outside there was no incentive to dally, even on the most pleasant days. If the wind was at all strong, it would be a race to collapse the tent, pack the sledges and be gone as soon as possible before we became too chilled and fingers froze.

Upon emerging, the first task for each of us was one which we always did our best to fulfil, for if it was not accomplished, then the need would always strike us down at the most inconvenient moment later in the day, causing delay and sometimes, if there was a blizzard considerable discomfort. Armed with a snow shovel and our meagre allowance of toilet paper, we would walk a few yards from the sledges and dig a hole, then, with backs to the wind, squat and be done with the uttermost speed. If fingers became numbed with cold before dress had been restored, we would dive back into the protection of the tent without regard for decorum. Occasionally, on a morning when a blizzard made such external activities uninviting, then the tent was so designed that the floor could be removed and a pleasant shit enjoyed. In such circumstances, the tent was generally evacuated by all not so engaged.

Once the sledges had been packed, each of us had to make a decision as to what clothing was most appropriate for the prevailing conditions. An incorrect choice always caused delay if it had to be adjusted, and we soon learned that the wrong combination of clothing, whether it was too much or too little, could not be tolerated for very long. Most often, in the relatively warm temperatures on the Barrier (−10°C), we wore only windproofs over long underwear with, perhaps, a pile jacket, and, on the few days that were like the day of our departure, our underwear alone.

It was usually two hours, from the time the stove was lit to the heavy tug that set the sledge moving. When fuel bottles were refilled or some other task needed attention, we would be slower. Later, as we became more practised, this standard was more easily achieved, and once we were away in an hour and fifteen minutes.

I had feared that of all the problems this journey posed, the endless monotony of marching, pushing one ski-tip before the other against the all-pervading resistance of the sledge, would be the most difficult to endure. I feared that the massive weight to which I was tethered would turn the journey into a nightmare, in which I would be running without progress down an endless tunnel of exhaustion, every leaden movement held back by a force many times that of gravity. During the winter I had told Robert that I hoped it would be possible for the mind to break free of the terrible labour of manhauling, and that I would concentrate my thoughts on the horizon. Robert, with the self-assurance born of great physical strength, claimed the sledge as his friend and that he would enter into the labour of pulling so that it consumed him. So each of us built, according to his character, an idea of how we would deal with the problem. Early in the journey Robert wrote:

It was colder last night, the tent filled with rime this morning. The weather, quite nasty; other expeditions would not have marched, but we have to. I am, thank God, starting to think about more than the sledge, my mind is filled with nonsense, but still the weight, still the sledge. The pulling is heavy but we seem to be getting there bit by bit. I know we will look back on these as being halcyon days.

Monday, 11 November   74.5 miles

On our ninth day, we began our strict régime of three three-hour marches, divided by two half-hour rests, during which we ate biscuit and butter, soup, sausage and chocolate. Once each session began, we stopped for no one unless the reason was exceptional. We travelled alone, each in his own world, each with his own problems, each harnessed to his own sledge, and with no one to blame but himself if it did not move. This was very different from the traditional method of manhauling, where all the members of a team pulled a single sledge, and it gave us a number of advantages. If at some point during a march one of us needed to stop to change clothing, urinate or tighten a loose boot, then this could be done without causing everyone to halt, and the lost ground was usually regained when those ahead stopped for their own purposes. Not only did this reduce the time wasted each day, but it removed the reluctance (and I think group pressure would have been great) to make vital adjustments to clothing as they became necessary. More important, it eliminated a ripe breeding ground for antagonisms between us. Imagine the frustration when, returning from the Pole, short of food and time, Scott's party hauled their single sledge across the snows of the Polar Plateau. First, Bowers has to stop and pull up a sock that is causing trouble, then, ten minutes later, Wilson needs to pee, and Scott who is steering their course has to halt repeatedly to check their bearing, and each time their progress is delayed. Imagine the brewing suspicions that the others are not pulling as hard as they might. Wild had written of Marshall, as they pulled towards the Pole with Shackleton in 1908, that he 'does not pull the weight of his food, the big hulking lazy hog.' I know that if we three had been forced to work under conditions that demanded such tolerance we would not have gone a hundred miles. This as much as anything is a measure of the moral strength of Scott's men.

'Another late start to the march,' I wrote, 'due to problems with getting the skins to adhere to the skis. Despite heating them over the stove, using more fuel than we can afford, they were again flapping within a few hours. The weather today has been magnificent, though cold ($-17°/-22°C$). We managed 13.25 miles, despite all of us being reduced to walking on foot for the last five hours. Gareth's feet are giving him trouble, but he is well in control, never rushing. Robert was surprisingly slow today, many minutes behind at the stops. He assures me that he is simply holding back. It's not just that, I'm sure; the bravado has diminished, the "Huh!" as he pulls from a dead start, and the five-minute spurt at the end of the day, have all gone. I was stopped short with a fatigue fracture in the heel plate of my ski-binding, a problem which was later resolved with the spares we were carrying.'

We were making better progress than I had dared to hope for with heavy sledges, but the troubles with the skins, my broken ski-binding and Gareth's feet, which continued to bother him, were all worrying when one considered the prospect of being reduced to walking so early in the journey.

Wednesday, 13 November   93.1 miles

'Great banks of stratocumulus rolling towards us from the south-west,' my diary records. 'By noon, the first of these gigantic ships sailed over us obscuring the sky and turning the snow surface from a complex of interlaid textures to a flat white blankness. The following cloud soon merged with the first and, by the second period, we were walking into a rising wind. The second rest stop saw us sheltering behind the sledges in driving snow, the wind Force 6. Inevitably, we called it a day and pitched the tent, Robert holding it down while we worked to erect it. Robert says that he is beginning to realize the seriousness of our undertaking. We have 780 miles to go and 78 days' food left. Today we covered 6.77 miles. The reality will become more intense when we reach the Beardmore, with fewer miles to go, less food, and many, many more miles behind us preventing us turning back.'

With each day that passed our isolation increased and the fatigue grew. There was a minimal time for sleep in the cramped tent. There was also a gnawing hunger and doubts that perhaps what we were attempting was impossible. No one had ever made such a journey without support, and if things were hard now, soon they would be harder, and all this added to the stress.

Robert thought that, 'RM and GW are odd, they are bickering a bit already,' and, 'he (RM) bites at me a little for no reason in particular.'

A few feet away on the other side of the partition that was Gareth in his sleeping bag, I was writing: 'The only reason that our "power house", as he styles himself, is so much slower than either Gareth or myself must, I think, be due in part to all the undisclosed weight in his sledge, apart from all the items that have already surfaced. It pains me that I should have spent so much time cutting ounces from sledges, removing things that could prove very useful, and then see all that weight replaced by so much unnecessary clutter. But as long as he does not slow us exceedingly, no matter.'

Gareth was more succinct: 'Robert's extra junk is coming to light now: he has an extra pile jacket, extra wind pants, a scarf and kerchiefs. Asshole!'

Just after midnight a total eclipse of the sun brought twilight to our eternal day. I had waited in anticipation for this event, which would transcend the frozen continent and somehow bring us closer to the friends around the world with whom we shared it. When the moment came, however, we were all asleep.

By the end of the fifteenth day of our journey we had travelled 142.32 miles. During the morning we had passed the point where Scott's One Ton Camp had been sited, and we camped that evening 2.5 miles short of where Wilson, Bowers and Scott had erected their tent for the last time, only 11 miles short of the depot.

Monday, 18 November   152.61 miles

A gentle breeze blew from the south-west, dispersing the early morning cloud, and we travelled for most of the day in sunshine. It was good to feel its warmth. The Barrier is the spawning ground of great lenticular clouds, flesh-coloured and immensely long and tapered towards each end. Floating low above the ice-shelf, they drift slowly northwards, accompanied by their shadows, some miles distant, others looming ominously overhead. They spread and fragmented into massive veils of mackerel sky, golden, orange, the sun flickering through the gaps, illuminating alternately near and distant areas of the Barrier. There were clear blue skies to the south and mirages of mountains to the west. As the day drew to a close, the flat horizon to the east was hard black against a sunlit sky.

Robert had always thought that this day would be 'a moment to treasure all my days . . . I half expected to see the tent or at least something, but nothing alters. It is much like the rest of the Barrier,' the same now as it was then and always will be. A timeless place. It was here that Scott wrote:

We took risks, we knew we took them; things have come out against us, and therefore we have no cause for complaint, but bow to the will of Providence, determined still to do our best to the last.

Had we lived I would have had a tale to tell of the hardihood, endurance, and courage of my companions which would have stirred the heart of every Englishman. These rough notes and our dead bodies must tell the tale.

A few minutes before noon, as the sun approached its zenith in the northern sky, the shadow of a man, heavily clothed and hooded, crept across the snow to lead us southwards. With his massively gloved hands curled around ski-sticks, he pounded rhythmically before us. It was a portentous figure. 'When,' I thought, 'did such a shadow last fall upon these snows?' At first, I found his arrival sinister, but later I used to look forward to the sunny days at noon when he would lead the way.

Behind us the summit of Mount Erebus had receded imperceptibly into the distance until today it was gone, and we understood the significance that the peak must have assumed for those returning from the depths of an uncharted world. Would it, I wondered, have made any difference if Scott and his companions had sighted the mountain beckoning in the distance? We were now at the centre of a vast disc of ice, its circumference our horizon. As we moved, it moved with us, so that we remained, seemingly for ever, at its centre.

Once the routine of nine hours' marching was established, I guarded it zealously. Two days before Robert had asked that we cut an hour off the day so that he might complete some maintenance to his skis without depleting the precious time for sleep. It was a precedent we could not afford. If we needed more time in the evenings, we simply had to become more efficient at breaking and setting up camp. Conversely, it was important that we did no more than nine hours each day. We timed each three-hour session to the minute, and there was always much shouting and waving of ski-sticks from those behind if the leader neglected the time. Scott had tried to maintain a schedule based on miles per day. This, I felt, took no account of the dramatic variables of weather and terrain. Some days the surface gave much harder pulling than others, and a rigid target of distance would, in difficult conditions, push us to exhaustion. One good day of many miles was as nothing if it left us weaker for the next.

There was, however, always urgent concern to know how far we had travelled. The announcement of the distance at the end of each session was eagerly awaited, and Robert dutifully recorded the figure in his notebook. Every evening I plotted our course and added the day's mileage to our total and calculated its effect upon the daily mean. Slowly, yard by yard, as the days progressed, our average grew towards the longed-for score of 10. Only when that figure was attained would we be on schedule to reach the Pole before the food ran out.

Tuesday, 19 November   164.25 miles

'Somewhere about here,' I wrote, 'Oates walked to his death, but this place makes no acknowledgement of such events.' I have always wondered how much unspoken pressure there was for him to meet his fate. In those last days, each one must have known that, even without Oates slowing their progress, their chances of surviving were slim, and that knowledge must have weighed terribly on Oates. Yet it is not given to many people to choose the time of their death: not with the despair of the suicide, or clinging to every last vestige of life until the flame gutters and chokes, but, as Mishima did, recognizing that life is a preparation for death, and that to choose the time is an affirmation of the value of life, to which we should aspire.

'The moon appeared today, its friendly face corn gold and transparent in the sunlight. My other binding broke. It was to be expected, each day I have waited for it to happen, but, no matter, in twenty minutes with a hammer, the adze of an ice-axe for an anvil and the stove as a forge, it was repaired. Tonight, upon examination, Robert's sledge runners were found to be terribly scoured and the abraded surface had developed fine hairs.' Perhaps this is the reason for his "dehydration", he is forever eating snow and craves water at night. I have scraped the runners with a Swiss army knife and Robert finished them with emery-cloth. Gareth claims he "could eat a horse". "Have you ever eaten a horse?" I asked. "Not a whole one," he says. Then, I was cruel and talked of apple pie and custard and fresh fruit and cream, and bread and all manner of distant food, but they were not amused.'

Friday, 22 November   198.13 miles

'Last night none of us slept without interruption. Gareth was very restless, tossing and turning and rising to pee. I thought I was the only one disturbed but Robert, who sleeps head to feet with Gareth, was constantly jostled by his jerking legs. It's all of little consequence until one realizes that we are on such a tight schedule that loss of sleep means a hard day to follow.' The sky was covered in 'a dense canopy of stratus without form. On all sides, in the far distance, blue sky could be seen, a thin circle of colour surrounding us. There was absolute zero contrast for the majority of the day making the heading very difficult and demanding to hold. We left a trail like a Devonshire lane. At the first stop, the most perfect single snow-flakes were falling in the whiteness. Tiny stars falling on our dark blue clothing and into my mug of soup, among the bright golden discs of Mazola oil floating on the surface. Poor Gareth is really having a hard time of late. His confidence, at present, must, I think, be very low. Robert soldiers on, as always exclaiming how easy it all is, but it is apparent from his pace and his drawn look at the end of each day that he is finding it harder than he expected.'

Sunday, 24 November   215.0 miles

Since our departure we had lost not a single day to bad weather, and our daily average distance had risen to 9.92 miles.

Scott had been held up for twenty-four hours after turning south at Corner Camp, and Shackleton had lost two days to blizzards while passing White Island. It was inevitable we would be caught eventually.

'During our second session the wind, which was blowing Force 3–4, became southerly, backing from its more normal south-westerly direction,' my diary records. 'The change was accompanied by a sudden rise in temperature, from −12°C at the first stop to −5°C. At the start contrast had been nil, as would be expected with eight octas of stratus, and visibility decreased markedly as the rising wind brought an increasing ground drift and finally large heavy flakes of warm snow. I had hoped, despite the conditions, to continue for the remaining fifteen minutes of the session, but Robert, who was some way behind, was suddenly in danger of losing contact. The air was thick with snow, so we had to stop. Now we are comfortable in the tent, Robert sews and the stove purrs. Though we are still booted I have my doubts that we will leave until tomorrow.'

Two hours later the boots had been removed. 'Needless to say,' I wrote, 'the storm has not abated, the wind is as strong now as when we quit. Snow hisses against the tent walls. Robert is attempting to smoke his pipe, saying, "there must be an art to smoking a pipe, and I ain't got it yet."'

Monday, 25 November

The blizzard continued all night and in the morning it was still blowing. When I looked out the sun was shining and we should perhaps have made a go of it, but there was little enthusiasm for moving, and the wind grew stronger as the day wore on. Robert noted in his diary:

It's rather pleasant to rest here in the middle of the Barrier, but I don't really feel that we are isolated; the routine makes one feel at home. We are not allowed to eat much, the day's rations must be saved. The possibility of hunger is something I had stupidly never thought about. I wonder how hungry we will become?

We had the choice: walk and eat, or rest and abstain. We nibbled at biscuits, chocolate and sausage saved from the day before, and also a little on account from the next day's ration, but there was no breakfast and no evening meal. The day was spent mending and making good our equipment, writing diaries and drifting in and out of sleep.

Tuesday, 26 November   228.0 miles

We emerged to find the tent drifted to the roof and the sledges buried. We were relieved to discover that it was to be 'one of the friendliest days we've had on the Barrier. From the beginning it has been calm and the sun winging around behind us was only partially obscured this evening. Today we have seen the first mountains to the south. It is such a welcome sight, land foretelling of the Beardmore.'

On 25 November 1908, Shackleton wrote:

It is a wonderful place we are in, all new to the world . . . There is an impression of limitless solitude about it all that makes us feel so small as we trudge along, a few dark specks on the snowy plain, and watch the new land appear.

We continued, pushing hard, taking advantage of the long period of kind weather that followed the blizzard. The loss of a day had reduced our daily mean to 9.5 miles, but slowly it crept back up, until eventually by 3 December, we attained the average of 10 miles per day we required. This achievement was not without cost. We were becoming lean, our bodies drawing on their reserves of fat to compensate for the barely adequate daily ration of 5,000 calories. The Trans-Antarctic Mountains to the west grew steadily closer, converging towards the point where we would meet them, Mount Hope and the Beardmore Glacier.

As we neared the end of the Barrier stage of the journey, the closer we came to our point of no return, the point at which we would no longer have sufficient food to retrace our steps. As our commitment increased, so did the tension between us, as private doubts and fears became more intense. During the first weeks we all experienced problems, pains in backs and shoulders from the enormous loads, inflamed joints, wrists and ankles from the continuous repetitive action of skiing, and sore and blistered feet. Out of necessity we had learnt ways of dealing with them by adjustments to equipment, posture and technique. Some problems were eliminated, others eased or simply accepted as part of the price we had to pay. Gareth experienced trouble with his feet which persisted without respite to the end, and only with continual vigilance did he prevent serious damage. When walking, he was invariably in pain, but it was the consequences of becoming lame that became his biggest fear. He wrote:

Feet generally better, but two more blisters. I stopped five times today to remove boots and socks. It must be infuriating for the others. I can take more pain, but I am frightened of doing too much damage. I'm very worried and beginning to feel like a real burden. I'm not sure if I'm just weaker or if it's my feet draining me.

Roger's advice, to change my ration round and eat more during the day I think has helped, but I find his manner unbearable. I need less sarcasm and sulking from him, just because we don't live up to his standard. He bollocked Robert yesterday for offering to take some weight from me to help me make it through the day. Seems like a strange thing to do. Robert, bless him, gave me one of his pieces of sausage. A mighty gesture, not to be forgotten.

Monday, 2 December   298.67 miles

'A demanding day of slow progress,' I wrote, 'but one of our best in terms of general operation. We departed camp by 8.55 A.M. which is as good as we can expect. It has been, blizzards excluded, the most difficult we have experienced for holding a course. Eight octas of stratus for the duration of the march, the sun never glimpsed, nor any distant shining on the surrounding

The decks of *Southern Quest*, encased in ice as she enters Antarctic waters

Wind Vane Hill, Cape Evans

3 The galley in Scott's Hut as it is today

4 Mike Stroud and Gareth Wood crossing
fields of pumice and felspar

5 Mike Stroud
amongst the
Emperors at
Cape Crozier

6 Wave clouds
over McMurdo
Sound

7 *Above left:* The Polar equipment

8 *Left:* Ice grotto in the Erebus Glacier Tongue

9 *Above:* The American geologists at their camp made no move to approach

10 *Right:* Gareth halts in a rising blizzard

11 Another slope of polished rippled ice

12 -17 The sinking

18 The view that greeted Shackleton in search of his road to the south

19 *Right:* First sight of Amundsen-Scott station at the South Pole

20 The Beardmore Glacier

21 The trail of a Hercules, bound for New Zealand, heads out over Cape Evans and Jack Hayward Base

1 Captain Scott's last birthday dinner

2 Shackleton, Wild and Marshall. Farthest South, 9 January 1909

3 Snow cairn erected over the bodies of Scott, Wilson and Bowers

4 Scott's party on the Barrier, manhauling in deep snow

5 Bill Burton, the last surviving member of Scott's
expedition, meets Mear and Swan on the quayside in
Lyttleton

6 Rebecca Ward and Debra Overton aboard *Southern Quest*

7 *Left:* The Tenements, 1911

8 *Above:* The Tenements, 1985

9 *Below left:* Bowers, Wilson and Cherry-Garrard before their winter journey to Cape Crozier

10 *Below:* Wilson, Bowers and Cherry-Garrard after 'the Worst Journey in the World'

11   The ponies head south in 1911

12   At the South Pole, 18 January 1912 - Oates, Bowers, Scott, Wilson, Evans

snow. Contrast for the whole of the day has been zero. The tracks between us rarely visible. It is an interesting experience moving under such conditions. The eye cannot cope with the lack of reference. A faintly discernible form or colour in the clouded horizon cannot be held by the gaze without the head spinning, and the object, static though it may be, appearing to race across the sky. The occasional piece of sastrugi, visible in the whiteness, vanishes if you attempt to hold it for more than a moment in view. Better a furtive glance and then return the gaze to the tips of the skis, where they have information enough, though it appears that you are floating in a white void.

'The main event of the day was a relief but none too pleasant. Gareth's bottled-up frustrations finally surfaced in a heated exchange between us. He holds his anxieties until he is about to burst, but cannot find the key to release them. I, eager and aggressive, needle and bite until the feelings are out. He said that I was too intolerant of others' failings, and that he felt unable to speak since I told him that his continual moaning was a monotonous bore. He had some strong words for me at the end, but I told him to read his own diary, for what he probably expresses in those pages is impossible to hide, living as we do under such pressure. His fears so dominate his thoughts that he is unable to concentrate on what needs to be done to prevent those very fears from being realized.'

Later we skied side by side, as I had with Robert the day before. My hope was that now we could make a new start though as far as Gareth was concerned little had changed, but at least we talked in a less heated and more tolerant way.

Tuesday, 3 December   311.4 miles

'After yesterday's difficulties in keeping on course, our track today runs straight and true to the horizon. To the south now a peak some 2° to the west of our bearing grew steadily from a small white cone to a prominent point on the skyline that was sometimes a brilliant white triangle and sometimes a deep blue shadow, as clouds drifted over it and the sun moved round behind us. It is so much easier now we have something to head for. During our last three hours I looked at my compass only three times. It is a relief and very exciting to have these peaks before us, knowing that, beside our lodestone, is the Gateway.

Wednesday, 4 December   320.36 miles

Gareth had the stove roaring at 6.50 A.M., and though nothing was said at the time, both Robert and I resented the intrusion into these last ten minutes of sleep. It was, however, a welcome change for me to have someone else supplying the motivation. Gareth began the first three-hour session, setting a pace that soon left me trailing and Robert even farther behind, a small black dot on the horizon. Inevitably, problems with his feet forced Gareth to stop, and I broke trail for the last forty minutes. A few minutes before we were due to halt, I turned to see Gareth signalling with his ski-sticks crossed above his head, the gesture that meant 'STOP!'

'Feet again,' he said dejectedly. 'I'm sorry, but we'll have to put the tent up.'

I was annoyed, and so was Robert when he arrived. We were in the tent, Gareth replacing the tape on his battered feet while I began brewing up a cup of hot chocolate, when Robert began his monologue.

'I've got something to say that will blow your heads off.'

14

Golden Gateway

'It's something that's been on my mind for days, and it's very hard for me to say, so I would appreciate your full attention.' Robert was not pleased that Gareth seemed more concerned with his feet. 'We will soon be at our point of no return, and I'm worried that you' – he spoke directly to Gareth – 'will not make it. We're losing so much time with these continual stops. I've dreamt about this journey for years, but over the last few days I've dug deep and realize now that getting to the Pole doesn't mean that much. I would feel worse if someone died because of my ambition. I think we should consider getting out while we can and leave Roger to continue to the Pole.'

Two days before, we had talked about what it would be like to make the journey alone, and I had said, 'It might be possible, but ask me again when we get to the Pole.' I had no idea that the conversation would precipitate this.

'You're right,' I said, 'we can't afford these delays. I know you're in trouble, Gareth, but I think your biggest problem is in your head. I know you're hurting but I can't allow myself to worry about your pain. If there was something I could do then I'd do it, but there isn't. You've just got to get your finger out. But Robert, you also cost us time with your general disorganization. Even if it's only five minutes a day, in two months it adds up to miles. There is no question of splitting the party, we're in this together and we're committed to each other as much as we will be to reaching the Pole once we hit the Beardmore. Look Gareth, if a helicopter landed outside the tent, would you get on it?'

'No way. You bastards would have to carry me out and put me on it. I want this as much as you, and I really don't understand what Robert is on about.'

We talked on for two hours while the sun moved round the tent, and in the end we just packed up and kept going, each with his own load to pull and not much spare energy for sympathy. I told Gareth later that I thought Robert was projecting his own anxiety on to him. That night Robert wrote in his diary:

It's almost too awful to recount, but my sledge has become nearly impossible and when we stopped my fears came out all wrong. I just wanted out for the first time in my life, and that has hurt me very much indeed.

I began the second leg determined to make up for lost time. Gareth remembered that I set off at a hell of a pace, and we did 5.17 miles! 'I felt I had to keep up,' Gareth wrote, 'whatever the cost, but I ran out of steam. I ate my reserve chocolate bar, but I just ground to a halt. Robert was miles behind, and the weather was getting worse.'

The wind was blowing warmly from the north-west, which was very unusual, and then suddenly gusted strongly from the south-west, and then south-south-east. By the time I stopped, there was a lot of ground drift, and I turned my sledge so we might eat our snack in its shelter. Robert was a distant black point, so minute that he was, at first, scarcely discernible. He was farther behind than any of us had ever been. With the weather continuing to deteriorate, the contrast poor and our tracks drifting over, I was both angry with Robert for not keeping up and guilty that I had been so anxious to recover some miles that I had refused to wait.

After drinking some soup, I told Gareth that I would go back for Robert, who was still only a spot on the horizon that was beginning to vanish in the rising blizzard.

'If it clears,' I said, 'go when you're ready, otherwise you'd better wait.'

It was only after I had been skiing for some time that I realized just how far Robert had fallen behind. It could not have been less than a mile. He must be on foot, I thought, searching for a reason for his delay, but no, he was on skis and moving so very slowly. He smiled when I approached glad not just for the assistance but because my return meant there was still some concern for each other. I hitched up to his sledge, and we began to pull together, jerkily and without rhythm. After a while, I suggested it might be better if he skied on to Gareth and had his soup and rest; I would bring the sledge. He collected his Thermos and his down jacket, which nearly blew away in the wind, and left.

Pulling his sledge into the blizzard was nearly impossible. The snow surface was flowing with dry powder and my skis were awash. It took no more than four or five steps to realize that what Robert had been pulling for days felt heavier than the sledge at the beginning of the journey. It was more like hauling a great pine log through soft sand. I could not understand how he had managed to go on pulling it like this, and saw immediately why he was doubting his ability to make it the remaining 560 miles to the Pole. I was doubting if I would make it as far as the rest stop. The storm was worsening by the minute. It was now blowing Force 7 and the air was thick with snow. Fortunately, Gareth came and gave a hand to lug the sledge the last hundred yards.

At that moment, I thought Robert must have a muscle for a brain not to have complained more loudly, for I knew I would have been screaming days ago. Yet he could not have known, without the advantage of the direct comparison I had now made, that it was his sledge and not himself that was at fault.

We put up the tent, and I told Robert that I had a surprise for him, but it would cost him dearly in his illicit tobacco. While Gareth cooked a meal of bacon bar and mash, we emptied his sledge and unbolted the traces. Then we hauled the sledge out of the maelstrom of wind and snow into the tent.

It took nearly two hours for us to turn the PTFE runners, whose surfaces had become more akin to suede than the super low friction material from which they had been made. It seems that we had discovered a property it was not known to possess, a grain that the dry abrasive snow had frayed, for once this job was done there was an end to the problem. The runners were reshaped and drilled using only a Swiss army knife.

'I thought you were mad taking just that knife as a tool kit,' Robert said. 'Now I'm seeing its full potential.'

Thursday, 5 December

At its height the wind reached 40 knots. It was our second day of inaction. This time, however, we were too hungry to go without food and ate a full ration. With the delay, our average mileage plunged.

'At our present rate,' I wrote, 'the Pole is now fifty-eight days away and we have food for only fifty-five days. It's enough, but I hope there are no more delays. Our sledges will continue to get lighter and perhaps we will make up some time on the glacier, if, as I hope, the surface is bare ice. In the next few days the prospect of returning will become less appealing and, when we have no choice but to push on, then life will be simpler, but it will not be until we are well established on the Plateau that we will have any real idea of how many days the journey will take us.'

One of Gareth's runners had also deteriorated. Two days later he remembered that he 'had never worked so hard or felt so exhausted.' He got into camp at 8.45 and was up until 1 A.M. turning the runner. Next morning, as he harnessed up, he still felt weak and was apprehensive that his sledge might not be any easier to pull. 'What if my difficulties are not because of the runner, what if it's me?' As soon as he began to pull he knew. 'It was as if my sledge was half the weight. It was such a relief, I felt so much better. I continued to have trouble with my feet, but from then on they were never as bothersome.'

The days that followed the blizzard were warm and friendly. Summer had come to the Barrier. Our excitement grew in proportion to the growth of the mountains before us. Their proximity brought a sense of relief that must be similar to that felt by the yachtsman when, with the deprivations of a great ocean behind him, he makes landfall. During our rest stops we lay on our sledges and basked in temperatures that rose to 4°C above freezing. The lure of Mount Hope and the relative ease with which the sledges, now 80 lbs lighter than when we began, slid on the sun-baked surfaces enabled us to cover more than 60 miles in four days, and brought us to the area of pressure and crevasses that guard the entrance to the pass Shackleton called the Golden Gateway.

Monday, 9 December   387.77 miles

'The mountains around us are more beautiful than I expected,'
I wrote. 'The sight of the warm red granite pillars that form the
west side of the col, and the sun, and the earthy-coloured screes
of Mount Hope are a great comfort after the terrible and sterile
world of the Great Ice Barrier. Though it is an illusion, there is
a feeling of security brought by the approaching land. We have
been descending all day, over a succession of rolling waves,
their peaks separated by a distance of about a mile.'

To the east of Mount Hope where the Beardmore Glacier
flows out into the ice-shelf, we could see a turbulent sea of ice
in torment, like surf breaking on a distant reef.

We slept that night near the site of Scott's Depression Camp.
It was here that Scott's party was halted by a blizzard which
lasted four days and turned his plans into a recipe for disaster.
It was here that the delay forced them to begin, prematurely,
the 'summit rations' with which the peak of their pyramid of
provisions was to be built. In addition, the blizzard deposited
feet of soft snow which, scoured by the wind from the length of
the glacier, accumulated in its lower reaches and caused their
first days of manhauling to be a terrible labour.

For us it was different: 'the tent door is open, the first time
we have left it so. Outside it is calm, silent and sunny. I have a
piece of chocolate and a biscuit to eat, such a treat, then bed.'

Tuesday, 10 December   397.38 miles

In the morning, on looking out to see the welcome sight of
sunlight on the snow and good contrast, Robert remarked that
he was glad we had not been caught like Scott, and that it
would make for an easy passage through the crevassing.

'Don't tempt fate,' I warned.

By the time we began pulling, the sky had become overcast.
A heavy bank of stratus drifted in from the south-east and a
wind sprang up, blowing over the col. The cloud ceiling lowered
and, as we skied towards the area of pressure, all signs of the
crevasses before us vanished.

We reached the first disturbance in the ice after an hour and a half. Just as the urge to rope-up became pressing, the sun broke through the cloud and removed the necessity for such a precaution. We took a course to the west, and then, as we passed the first line of crevasses that swirl in an eddy around Mount Hope, we turned south-east and found our way on to a causeway that zig-zags through the turmoil.

There was no obvious demarcation between the ice-shelf and land ice. Before us a snow slope rose steeply to the col which gave access to the Beardmore Glacier. Symbolically, if not physically, this was our point of commitment. On each side, granite cliffs and buttresses gave substance to the name of 'The Golden Gateway to the South'. It was from this point that Scott, having shot the last of his exhausted ponies, began manhauling, though Lashly and Lieutenant Evans had been doing so since the breakdown of the second motor at Corner Camp. Three four-man teams, each pulling 500 lbs, and two dog teams, carrying 800 lbs, continued south.

I asked Gareth and Robert to wait at the bottom of the slope so that I could go ahead and film their ascent to the col. In anticipation of a hard pull to the top, I consumed all my daily ration of chocolate, two whole Yorkie bars. The ascent was easier than expected, once I had dealt with the mouthfuls of chocolate and was able to breathe properly. I was drawn on by the prospect of the first view of the Beardmore, the glacier of which I had dreamed for so long. Nearing the top, the slope lessened and I looked back to see the tiny figures of Robert and Gareth sitting astride their sledges, 800 feet below. The snow was matt and featureless and ahead the crest of the broad slope merged with the cloud-covered sky. With each step my anticipation brought disappointment, until a line of deep blue appeared between the skyline and the cloud and grew at a rate only slower than my mounting excitement. The point of a granite spire began to emerge and I knew that, at any moment, the sight that had greeted Shackleton would burst into view. I paused, and then ambled on with a feeling of calm satisfaction. As I approached the col, Mount Kyffin's Gothic peak continued to rise, and then my eye was attracted to an unexpected movement at the base of the red cliffs on my left. It was – I was sure, there was no doubt – a figure, 800 yards away, and its significance exploded into our isolation. It disappeared from sight over the horizon, and I was left alone again to wonder if I had imagined it. Yet I knew it was not a fancy and, as I continued, I pondered what this awful event might mean.

It was during our meeting with Dr Edward Todd of the National Science Foundation in Washington in 1984 that we first learned of a proposed field camp on the far side of the Queen Alexandra Range. Even that had been a blow to the isolation we sought. Now to have the isolation destroyed by this unexpected encounter made the 400 miles we had walked an exercise without point or reward. Isolation is Antarctica's most fragile resource; only Shackleton had savoured it untarnished, for Scott had carried with him the knowledge that he was not the first to set foot upon the Beardmore Glacier. Our journey too, we knew, added to man's encroachment upon this last great wilderness, and we were selfish in our desire to experience something of what remains of the continent's remoteness. In an instant, the presence of that figure had caused the sense of isolation I had felt to evaporate, as if it had never existed.

I imagined that the figure might be a geologist visiting the area to collect rock samples, and, beyond the rise, a helicopter would be waiting, and perhaps I could persuade him to leave without the meeting ever coming to the knowledge of my companions. Then I knew that would be impossible, for there, on the summit of the pass, were five yellow tents and beside them three attentive figures. It took me fifteen minutes to reach them. They just stood there and waited, making no move to approach. That they were apprehensive I could not doubt. Perhaps they had been briefed by Commander Harler not to instigate any contact with us. What should I have done? Walk past, as though they were not there?

We shook hands. I must have appeared reticent, for at that moment I was more concerned to film the ascent of Robert and Gareth. I left my sledge and skied back the way I had come. They were climbing side by side, eager to reach the top, as I had been, and oblivious of the meeting ahead. I positioned myself a little beyond the point where the American camp came into view and I waited to capture the moment of comprehension on their faces.

Gareth was first to see the tents. He shouted and I made as if not to hear or understand, but watched with cold detachment, through the lens, close in on a private grief, feeling callous that I had tricked them. Both were on the verge of tears, Robert falling to his knees. 'I saw something on the horizon,' recalled Gareth, 'and shortly recognized it as a person. Shocked, I said to Roger, "There's someone out there!" but he ignored me. Then the tents came into view, and I found myself cussing and in tears. I had worked too hard for this.'

Once they had come to terms with the shock, we approached the camp.

'Hi chaps, I'm Robert Swan, so-called expedition leader,' Robert announced.

'Howdy. Jim Mattison. We're very pleased to meet you. Welcome to the Gateway.'

'You're a geological party?' Gareth asked.

'Yeah,' replied the tall man whose white-eyed face was tanned a deep red and who had introduced himself as John Goodge. 'The granite that you see exposed around here is what we're taking a look at.'

'There are just the three of you?'

'Well, actually, there are five of us. Two fellas are off to the south today. Eugene Mikhalsky, who is a Russian working with us, and Scott Borg have gone to the Granite Pillars.'

'I hope you chaps have got some spare food, 'cause we're powerful hungry,' Robert said.

'We'd be delighted if you would join us,' said the third geologist, whose name was Don Depaolo.

'Join us,' repeated Robert, 'you won't be delighted by how hungry we are.'

'Spare food is one of our most abundant commodities.'

'Well, it won't be spare very much longer,' said Gareth.

'You mean the 5,200 calories a day is turning out a bit short?' asked Goodge, revealing a knowledge of our logistics.

'No, it's OK,' said Gareth, 'but we still dream of food and talk a lot about it.'

'Listen, we're being very poor hosts. Can we invite you in for something hot?'

'I was just going to offer you the same,' I said, trying to improve the impression we were making. 'Would you like some soup?'

That evening we were invited to dinner. Eight us gathered in the large cook-tent that we christened The Gateway Inn. We had agreed to make the most of the hospitality that was offered and planned to rest here for a couple of days. During that time, we would not have to use any of our precious sledging rations, and once the need for self discipline was removed and our appetites unleashed, we indulged ourselves like pigs on steak, lobster tails and broccoli, excellent coffee, Earl Grey tea and Amaretto. Our greed was an embarrassment which did nothing to convey to our hosts the tight control we had exercised during the previous forty days.

We spent the following day in dazed idleness, washing our bodies and clothes for the first time in six weeks. The geologists continued their work, travelling to various rock outcrops in the area. They had spent the summer working from a series of temporary camps set up by helicopter. We were fated to meet, for they had planned to be at the Gateway for only five days, and our paths would not have crossed if they had not been behind schedule and we one day ahead. They were probably the first people to visit the Gateway since Dr Charles Swithinbank's party in December 1960, and Borg thought it unlikely that anyone would return in the next decade.

Our second day at the Gateway also slid by in slow torpidity. At four o'clock, I left the camp and climbed alone to the ridge that descends in a great curve from the summit of Mount Hope, walking the length of the precipitous cliffs that form the eastern wall of the pass. The views were stupendous. To the north and east, the flat white plain stretched to infinity, and on both its western and southern shores the Trans-Antarctic Mountains led the eye over a succession of peaks and glaciers to the horizon. I remembered the time I had stood on the summit of Mount Erebus, 400 miles to the north, where those same mountains meet the sea, and had gazed with awe and trepidation at the incomprehensible magnitude of the Barrier. Now I understood, in a way that is only possible when your own body is the unit of measure, the scale of the landscape. Now I could see the thread of our trail, winding its way from where it appeared among the maze of crevasses at the edge of the ice-shelf, to its junction with the encampment in the centre of the col below me.

From the south ran the Beardmore Glacier. At its narrowest point, it was as wide as the Aletsch Glacier, the largest in Europe, is long. Down its 124-mile length flows a stream of ice at a rate of a yard a day. On either side tumble steep glaciers that divide mountains of the most dramatic kind. Mount Kyffin, 14 miles away on the opposite bank of the stream, displayed a 3,000 foot wall of unbroken granite; and Mount Elizabeth, the highest point of the Queen Alexandra Range, of which Mount Hope is a diminutive, rounded satellite, rose majestically more than 12,000 feet above the glacier.

Shackleton climbed Mount Hope to confirm that he had found the road to the South and to determine what might be the surest route. What he found was a glacier, far bigger than could be conceived and of an order that was appropriate to the momentous journey he was making.

John Goodge cooked hamburgers for our last evening at the Gateway Inn and Eugene Mikhalsky gave us a bar of Russian chocolate for the coming Christmas.

It was well after noon by the time we finally resumed our journey. Though we had planned an early start, Robert had been up until 3 A.M. searching high and low for his lost Teddy Bear, given to him by his girlfriend Rebecca Ward. The Americans were bemused by his distress, which was not relieved until a last frantic search revealed its whereabouts shortly before departure. It was during Robert's morning visit to the latrine that he found the bear in the one place he had not thought to look for it, and retrieved the rather soiled Teddy from beneath several days of frozen excrement.

Our departure felt like a second beginning. We had eaten to excess of the Americans' food, and Robert and I had not reacted well to the sudden change of diet, both of us suffering from acute stomach upsets and vomiting. Even so, after the two days of rest, we felt physically restored, but the encounter had destroyed the mystery and doubt that had hung over the remaining 480 miles. Gone was the knowledge that we were engaged upon an unsupported journey of a magnitude that was unique, and the loss removed a good deal of the purpose that, for me, justified our undertaking.

Friday, 13 December   409.08 miles

The descent on to the glacier went gently downhill. We followed the corrugated tracks of a skidoo away from the camp. Patches of smooth blue ice made an appearance through the snow, and as we rounded Cape Allen, the slope steepened and the ice became predominant. Robert sat astride his sledge and tobogganed down. Gareth cautiously removed his skis and donned crampons. Not wanting to waste the only section of downhill skiing of the journey, I snow-ploughed in and out of the isolated waves of sastrugi with the steel edges of my skis scouring the hard ice as the sledge rumbled on behind.

Shackleton had kept to the very edge of the glacier, following a narrow band of neve, passing close under the dramatic pillars of granite that stand there like tall sentinels. The way out on to the centre of the glacier was barred by what he described as 'fantastically shaped and split masses of pressure across which it would have been impossible for us to have gone'. At first, their progress was unimpeded by crevasses, but their second day on the Beardmore took them away from the protection of the Granite Pillars into an area where the ice was disturbed by the convergence of a small secondary glacier. They were forced to relay their two sledges through the crevassing with 'every step a venture'. Wild followed, tentatively leading the one remaining pony over numerous cracks. On their third day, they 'passed several crevasses on our right and could see more to the left . . . and as we marched along we were congratulating ourselves upon it when suddenly we heard a shout of help from Wild.' The pony had broken through and plunged to its death in a hidden crevasse. Then Shackleton recounted that 'we lay on our stomachs and looked over into the gulf, but no sound or sign came to us; a black bottomless pit it seemed to be.' Wild was fortunate not to have been pulled after the pony, and they were also lucky not to have lost the sledge, loaded with food and equipment, to which the pony was harnessed. They named the tributary glacier after the pony, the Socks Glacier.

It was perhaps because of this incident that Scott, having passed through the Gateway, made directly towards Mount Kyffin, out into the centre of the glacier. The lateral crevassing that forced Shackleton close under the Granite Pillars was invisible under feet of snow, and he was able to cross without accident.

15

The Great Glacier

I had no fixed plans for our route up the glacier. We had maps of the area but they were of a scale that gave too little information for practical use in charting a course through the crevassing. The reconnaissance from Mount Hope had served only to reinforce my opinion that, so enormous was the glacier, even large areas of disturbance were lost in its vastness. My one intention was that our path should be as straight as the glacier would allow. I hoped that we would be able to make some savings on the meandering route taken by Scott, as we did in passing White Island.

Once on the Beardmore, we headed straight for the mountain named by Shackleton, the Cloudmaker. It was visible on the horizon, 50 miles distant, at the point where the glacier turns south-west. Almost immediately, we plunged into the region of crevasses that had forced Shackleton under the Granite Pillars and Scott into the centre of the stream. We roped up, linking ourselves and each sledge in succession with the 160 feet of Beal we carried for the purpose. After forty minutes of nervous progress, in and out of great standing waves of ice, we were through. The glacier stretched flat and wide before us and we felt confident that we could continue safely without the precaution of the rope.

After the establishment of Lower Glacier Depot, Scott's two supporting dog teams, led by Meares and Dimitri, were sent back on 11 December. 'With a whirl and a rush,' wrote Cherry-Garrard, 'they were off on the homeward trail.' The three teams of manhaulers continued, pulling slightly less than 200 lbs per man. Shackleton's four-man party, reduced to manhauling with the loss of the pony, Socks, pulled 250 lbs per man; our own sledges, lightened of forty days' food and fuel, were only a little heavier. Now we could begin to make direct comparisons between our own progress and that of our predecessors. The end of our first day on the glacier saw us two days behind Scott and five behind Shackleton.

We camped that evening a little before the mouth of the Socks Glacier, opposite a pointed scarp of black, frost-shattered rock that looked, from some angles, like the leaning headstone of a grave on a steep snow-covered hill. Scott had named it, portentously, The Monument Rock. It was here that Edgar Evans, frostbitten, concussed and terribly exhausted, died of hypothermia. I filmed and photographed Robert holding the silver Polar Medal that was awarded posthumously to Evans, and it did feel that we had returned it, for a time, to where it rightfully belonged.

Saturday, 14 December   425.01 miles

After the endlessly unchanging landscape of the Barrier, where the ever distant mountains to the west crept by with a demoralizing slowness measured in weeks, the landmarks on the Beardmore Glacier sped past at an amazing rate. We were soon abreast of Mount Kyffin and, before us, the rearing bulk of the Cloudmaker drew us on. There was great drama in the sky. The high summit of Mount Elizabeth was capped with a constantly changing, multi-layered crown of lenticular clouds, nacreous in the sun, and, above us, drawn to a distant perspective, long lines of alto-stratus raced. The Beardmore Glacier rose in a series of steps which marked the entrance of a succession of steep tributary glaciers and tumbling ice-falls, which appeared small only because they were dwarfed by the enormous river of ice into which they fell. The level ground that followed each shelving rise seemed to us downhill. As the crusty snow gave way to neve, then to opaque white ice, and finally to ice with the deep green hue of leaden glass, we became excited by the mounting speed of our progress. The sledges rumbled and purred and left no trail behind us.

Sunday, 15 December   444.85 miles

It was the day that Amundsen reached the Pole. We covered l9.84 miles in our nine hours and drew ahead of Scott who had

had to contend with a morass of soft snow on the lower glacier. We slept on the ice, free from the claustrophobic confines of the tent, which we neglected to erect, more because of the attraction of a bivouac rather than for any great saving of time or energy. Towering above was the Cloudmaker. For the whole of the next day the mountain hung over us, the ferrous red cliffs rising for 5,000 feet in an ever-steepening curve from the screes. Only at one place was this wall, which ran for 10 miles, breached. A blue-tinted glacier perched like a curl of thick cream on the lip of a jug. Here we skirted the very edge of the Beardmore, sometimes traversing the crest of a steep whale-back, with grey moraines a hundred feet below, or going along the bottom of a deep trough, scattered with angular boulders and the sledge skirring between them on mirror ice. Though we had replaced our skis with crampons, we retained the poles which tic-tacked across the ice. Robert did not favour these tools of the mountaineer, and the unfamiliar gait that crampons demanded caused him some painful days with an inflamed knee, until we reverted to skis.

Towards the end of the Cloudmaker scarp, we were forced away from the land by a band of pressure. Against a background of crevassing, we made our way up and over giant switchbacks, until the once benevolent ice gave way to acres of deep furrows from which we could see no escape. I had begun to think that our Kevlar sledges were extravagantly strong, but here they were tested to the full. For the next hour, we crashed from knife-edged peak to knife-edged peak, across ground riven and fissured. Ice tinkled into the dark cracks as we leapt from crest to crest with the sledges banging and creaking in our wake. We slept at the base of a steep rise, rolled in our sleeping bags against the sledges which, pulled across the slope, stopped us sliding back from whence we came.

Tuesday, 17 December   480.85 miles

We had climbed to an altitude of 5,000 feet. As the last minutes of our day's march ticked by, I raced, heel to toe on steel points, breathing hard, sweat in my eyes under dark glasses, to top the rise that would disclose not just more of the Beardmore but the first view of its source. We entered the upper glacier. On both sides, the peaks fell back until the stream was more than 30 miles across, a broad flat basin, circled on all sides by island mountains. Behind us stood the sharp pointed prow of Wedge Face, and Cloudmaker, undramatic from this view. On our right, the stratified peaks of the Adams and the Marshall mountains reminded me of the Canadian Rockies. Far to our left the truncated, snow-capped plateau of the Dominion Range marked the junction of the Mill Glacier, an ice source almost the equal of the Beardmore. The top of the rise revealed yet another slope of polished rippled ice, and to climb that I stole some extra minutes, knowing that this sin would infuriate the others, but wanting the reward that I knew was close.

Eventually, the brown cones of Buckley Island bobbed into view, still more than a day distant. Running behind it, almost as high as the island's summits, was the flat white horizon. Like the waters banked up behind a dam, the ice of the Polar Plateau, many thousands of feet deep, presses against the mountains, and where the dam is breached, it pours in a frozen flood into the valley it has carved. From afar, the cataract appears as a bright, white line; in reality it is a mayhem of ice and abyss, stretching for 50 miles, in which a city would be lost, impossible to cross and barring direct access to the Plateau. This was the view that greeted Shackleton in search of his road to the South, and all he could do was to walk towards it, with its impregnability growing like the roar of Niagara in his ears.

The interminable ice took its toll of our crampons as one by one they shed points. Mine were first to go, much to Robert's delight, for on this journey he was determined not to live up to his reputation for breaking equipment. The diaries of Scott and Shackleton are full of accounts of slips and falls. 'We are a mass of bruises where we have fallen on the sharp ice,' wrote Shackleton, whose party, shod in nailed boots, seems to have suffered greatly in this respect, while Scott remarked: 'We have worn our crampons all day and are delighted with them. P. O. Evans the inventor . . . is greatly pleased and certainly we owe him much.'

Our days on the glacier were some of the most pleasant of the journey. The stress we felt on the Barrier was perhaps due as much to the deprivation of the landscape as it was to the uncertainty of what lay ahead. Now we were past half-way and making excellent progress. The sledge loads were no longer monstrous. Though each day we crossed innumerable crevasses, we experienced none of the troubles encountered by Scott and Shackleton. There was only the threat of injury, for without a radio, we were as alone as it is possible to be.

At midnight we were woken by the sound of an aircraft. An American Hercules bound for the Pole flew directly over us at 24,000 feet, another reminder of the smallness of the modern world. It thundered into our world and then was gone. If we had been in trouble, those aboard would not have known, and it served only to reinforce our sense of isolation.

Again we bivouacked on the ice. While Gareth cooked our meal of freeze-dried rice and chicken, I wrote in the diary: 'Snug in my bag. The sun shines through the clouds over Buckley Island. It is snowing, but only the smallest trace. Silver dust sparkles in the air and collects like the finest down on ice that looks like a softly rippled sea of mercury. Robert is slowed by his strained knee and, though I took the tent and Gareth the poles, he was over an hour behind us tonight. He is too pleased to be in this wonderful place to be despondent, though what he really feels I know not.'
Robert wrote:

A terrible day for the leg. My knee is not happy in crampons, but we are camped in a magnificent spot. No tent again, and writing the diary is not so easy, but the camping out has been a great break for us. I have enjoyed it, makes me feel closer to the job in hand. I just hope my knee does not crack up.

A wind picked up during the night, blowing straight down the glacier. By chance, I slept on the windward side of my sledge. Gareth had pulled his parallel to mine and he lay between them. Robert's sledge was to one side, with him sleeping in its lee. The result was that while the drift blew around me, it built up on Robert, and more so on Gareth, who eventually moved, pulling his sledge out from behind mine and in front of Robert's, with predictable effect. In the morning, there were some strong words from a snow-covered Robert, and I lay amused at the bickering, glad that, for once, I was uninvolved. Earlier Gareth recorded:

Logged watches tonight. Have missed two checks and Roger hit the roof and gave me a bollocking. Took first sextant sight, as Roger worried that I should practise before we reached the Plateau and lose sight of land. I had thought about it and perhaps I should have done something sooner, but his attitude just makes me want to rebel.

Thursday, 19 December   517.37 miles

We headed towards Buckley Island, making obliquely for the rocks at the base of a spur that descends to the south-east of Mount Buckley. Shackleton would have been slightly farther east and Scott on a parallel course 6 miles towards the centre of the glacier. Bowers's account records that:

We did not go quite so close to the land as Shackleton did, and therefore, as had been the case with us all the way up the glacier, found fewer difficulties than he met with. Scott is quite wonderful in his selections of route, as we have escaped excessive dangers and difficulties all along.

Then, unaccountably considering the last statement, they 'got into a perfect mass of crevasses into which we all continually fell; mostly one foot, but often two, and occasionally we went down all together, some to the length of their harness to be hauled out by the alpine rope.'

   Fortunately, we did not become involved in such dramas, though we crossed a number of long, crescent-shaped crevasses in the polished ice, each well bridged with snow. Reading Scott's diary each night prevented us from becoming complacent. Our three routes converged upon a narrow crevasse-free passage, half-a-mile wide, that ascended a slope of blue ice, steeper than anything we had previously encountered on the glacier. It curved up between the rocks and seracs of the island and the unimaginable chaos of what is now called the Shackleton Ice Falls. Shackleton recorded his ascent:

We had to take one sledge at a time up the icy slope, and even then we had to cut steps with our ice axes as we went along. The second sledge we hauled up the rise by means of the alpine rope. We made it fast to the sledge, went on with the first sledge till the rope was stretched out to its full length, then cut a place to stand, and by our united efforts hauled the sledge up to where we stood. We repeated this until we had managed to reach a fairly level spot.

For us it was a strenuous and exhilarating pull, especially with the sledges threatening to haul us off backwards and the prospect of a 1,000-foot slide as the price for a stumble. For we, unlike Shackleton, were shod in broken but still functioning crampons. At last, we had encountered an obstacle upon which Robert could unleash the dynamic force which normally carries him through life, and which was so inappropriate in combating the slow attrition of this journey. Suddenly, he was groaning and yelling in exaltation, for he had found the one place in 900 miles of self-restraint where he could, with every justification, let himself go.

We came out on a level area where the blue shadow of Mount Bowers fell across the ice. It was a magnificent view below us, the striated glacier receding for a hundred miles, narrowing to the constriction between Wedge Face and The Cloudmaker. Beyond that was a veil of white incandescent mist. In strict geographical terms, we still had some miles to go before we reached the Polar Plateau, and there would be several days of crevassed terrain ahead before we would be free of the influence of the glacier. Nevertheless it was this place, with the steepest slope below us, high above the mountains under which we had passed, that felt like the top of the Beardmore. Shackleton had camped here on 17 December and laid a depot amongst the rocks. 'Wild went up the hill-side . . . He came down with the news that the Plateau is in sight at last, and some very interesting geological specimens, some of which certainly look like coal.'

With the rise in altitude, we were again beginning to feel the constraints that the cold placed on all our actions. The warm days on the glacier, with degrees of frost in single figures, were replaced with temperatures hovering around the minus twenties.

In the evening, the tent was erected without hesitation, though for the previous four nights we had slept in the open.

We were at an altitude of 6,500 feet, sandwiched between the south-west spur of Mount Bowers and the Shackleton Ice Falls. Before us was a small summit that stood facing the Plateau; beyond it there were undulations and crevasses, and then only white horizons. Shackleton named the peak Mount Darwin, perhaps because, like the zoologist, it stood at the frontier of a world that was then unknown to science.

From the bottom of the glacier to this point we had travelled 102.24 miles in seven days. Shackleton had covered 113.85 miles in thirteen days to reach his camp under Mount Bowers, 1.5 miles away, while Scott had taken twelve days to this point, but had covered 126 miles in his desire to find a safe passage for his party. South of Mount Darwin, 5.5 miles to the south-west of our camp, Scott had placed his Upper Glacier Depot. From there he continued south with eight men, while four, including Cherry-Garrard, returned disappointed.

Friday, 20 December   532.75 miles

We continued to climb, hoping that each steep rise would be the last, only to be greeted on each crest by another long hill. We were all feeling the effects of the altitude: at these latitudes, even a lowly 7,000 feet takes its toll. There were no extreme symptoms of mountain sickness, not even headaches and certainly no loss of appetite, but any dynamic exertion left us weak and breathless. All day we headed south-west, parallel to a long snowy ridge that descended from Mount Darwin, skirting the edge of the Shackleton Ice Falls, which seemed unrelenting. It was very frustrating not to be able to turn south, but a glance to our left at the chaos of ice soon removed the temptation.

At the end of the day we camped opposite a break in the turmoil where a broad snow road offered the possibility of a route south. This was most probably where Shackleton had turned, for there had been no other reasonable opportunity, only to become embroiled, within a few miles, in a maze of crevasses that continued for days. 'The ground is so treacherous,' he wrote, 'that many times during the day we are saved only by the rope from falling into fathomless pits.' He found the following day that the terrain worsened:

Today's crevasses have been far more dangerous than any others we have crossed . . . Constantly – one or another of the party has had to be hauled out from a chasm by means of his harness, which had alone saved him from death in the icy vault below.

Sensibly, Scott had wished to avoid such dangers and had attempted to circumnavigate the ice-falls. Even today there are no maps of this area, and like Scott, we heeded the warning of Shackleton's account. On 22 December Scott wrote:

We look down on huge pressure ridges to the south and S.E., and in fact all around except for the direction in which we go, S.W. We seem to be travelling more or less parallel to a ridge that extends from Mount Darwin. Ahead of us tonight is a stiffish incline and it looks as though there might be pressure behind it. It is very difficult to judge how matters stand, however, in such a confusion of elevations and depressions. This course doesn't work wonders in change of latitude, but I think it is the right track to clear the pressure – at any rate I shall hold it for the present.

The South Pole is 340 miles due south of Mount Darwin. Scott continued south-west for two days, travelling 29 miles from his Upper Glacier Depot and not turning south until they reached longitude 159°31′E., having reduced his distance to the Pole by only 8.5 miles.

After some discussion, we agreed to carry all our litter with us to the Pole. On the Barrier, Robert had burned our wrappers and buried the remains. I had added my empty fuel tin to the American trash, which they would fly out. Now that our sledges were lighter, I felt that it was reasonable for us to make this small gesture. Though as Gareth said, 'it will mean very little to people in the end,' it made a difference to me.

Saturday, 21 December   549.49 miles

It was a taxing day for me, as exhausting as any on the journey. The concentration involved in leading over mile after mile of crevasses was intense. I did not want to resort to the rope because of the delay it would cause. Assessing the strength of a snowbridge with the prod of a ski-stick is not an exact science, and skiing with a heavy sledge in tow out on to a concave band

of snow twenty feet wide, a mile long and concealing a gulf of
unsounded depth, is a tense pastime.

Towards the end of the day, it seemed that the pressure we
had flanked was diminishing, and we turned a little and headed
into it. We climbed a rise and found a passage through bursting
ice. In a mile or two, we came upon a broad shallow valley into
which we descended. There at last we turned south. We were
at Lat. 85°21' Long. 159°29'E.; Scott had turned south at Lat.
85°21', Long. 159°31'E.

16
The Plateau

'Barrier, done. Glacier, done. Plateau ahead.' Robert quoted the line spoken by John Mills in Scott of the Antarctic, the film that had first inspired him to make this journey.

We stood at the top of a rise which, for the first time, gave us an unhindered view of the Plateau. Behind us and on our left, were the ice-falls which divided us from the now distant mountains. We continued to climb, ascending a succession of long rolling hills, snow-covered on the northern inclines and in the valleys between, and icy on their summits and upper southern slopes.

I had thought that the Plateau would be a second Barrier, and in some respects so it is – flat, unlimited horizons, feature-less except for isolated banks of sastrugi and an inexhaustible variety of snow texture. It is like being on the calm smooth waters above a weir, with the overfall invisible from the boat. The bright thin light from the circling sun gave it all a unique quality. To the west, the peaks of the Dominion Range carried white puffs of cumulus on their summits, and to the south, the sky was always a clear blue. Above us, abnormally low swathes of cirrus gave the impression that we were at a great altitude and, with the sun behind them, they shone red and green in a watery light.

We were now in a very strong position. On the glacier we had maintained an average of more than 17 miles a day, and our daily average since leaving Ross Island had risen to 11.2 miles. It seemed that only some unforeseen accident could stop us. Robert admitted to a growing complacency since our 'holiday' on the Beardmore. Yet I felt we could not afford to relax. There were still more than 300 miles to go, and at the end we had to find one small station. It would be like searching for a single house in the middle of a barren plain as large as Europe.

The going was unpleasant, with the temperature in the −20s and the 'searching wind' (as Scott had called it) Force 3–4 from the south-south-east. The wind coloured our day, preventing a detachment from the drudgery that was possible in more comfortable conditions. It was necessary to keep our hoods tightly drawn, which restricted the view of changing landscape or sky. There could be no drifting off into thought. A continual diligence was required to combat the worrying wind and frost nip in the cheeks, and to steer a straight course.

The atmosphere between us had become tense once more after the interlude of the Beardmore. Closeness and antipathy floated around the three sides of the triangle but never settled. Perhaps it was inevitable in a group of three – the drawing together of two which isolates the third. A state of flux which never found equilibrium was reflected in our diaries:

(Robert) I had to say something about GW's relationship with RM. It hurt Gareth, but RM is the man to back and follow now. I suppose it has to be this way? A great paradox, when you think it was because of my poor relationship with RM that Gareth is here at all.

(Gareth) What is he talking about? It's an about-face from earlier conversations with him. I always have the feeling that Robert is not telling the whole truth when speaking in private to me; he often contradicts himself. Oh, well, it doesn't surprise me, but I don't know what he expects, as I refuse to bend, it takes too much energy. He's being extra specially kind to RM tonight. Roger says he expects more from me, and I am capable of more, but he needs to be in front and will not tolerate any deviation from his plans. He has always been in front right from the start, and he won't have it any other way. He can't accept even the smallest error.

(Roger) Robert and I are, astoundingly, getting on well. Each making room for the other. Robert indeed seems very concerned in this respect, though, at times, he does overdo it, making the cynic in me wonder at the truth of the revived friendship. After the battle on the Barrier, he now accepts that all I need him to do is pull his sledge and keep himself together, and though it must be frustrating for him not to take a major part in the daily running of the machine, this is not the place for him to learn how to use a compass.

Gareth demonstrated a lack of concentration and forethought. He left the sextant strapped to the outside of his sledge, though we were crossing crevasses all day. The loss of the sextant in a crevasse fall would be very serious. It is frustrating in the extreme to see this. It all takes more attention and energy from me.

Yesterday I made a gross cock-up with my arithmetic and gave our longitude on dead reckoning as 161°31′E. We were therefore using the wrong magnetic bearing, 166° instead of 169°. Today, to compensate, I moved early to 170° and we therefore head south on a bearing of 10°.

Later, as some sort of peace offering, Gareth gave a square of chocolate to Robert and me, no small gift. As it happened, I already had an abundance of chocolate – a whole bar unconsumed from the day. I was unwilling to accept such an offer so easily and gave the square to Robert. Callous and unfeeling it must have seemed to Gareth.

Monday, 23 December   580.22 miles

The first three-hour session seemed interminable, sighting through the Silva prismatic compass and walking towards some distant sastrugi, light or shadow. I would turn occasionally to check that the trail was straight and then lose the undistinguished, ephemeral object in a change of light or through inattention, and so have to sight again. We climbed the ridge we had begun ascending yesterday at a slow regular pace because the altitude prevented any other. At the end of the session we drew level with the summit, a circular boiling of crevasses on our left. The soft undulating ice-scape resembled a snow-covered Dartmoor, isolated areas of pressure that burst from the white skin looking like distant tors.

On each ridge crest we encountered the familiar, wind-scoured white ice, crazed and cracked like the angular pieces of a giant egg shell. Over them crept patches of dry granules with the texture of coarse chalk dust, whiter than other forms of snow, yet each grain, each crystal had its own dark shadow. Scurrying over the surface was a thin drift, like smoke, flowing close to the ground, snaking over skis and filling our tracks in seconds, yet almost unseen in its passage, less visible than its shadow.

We approached each ridge crest wondering what it would disclose of the way ahead. Always the horizon was limited by the next ridge, the next far rise, until the last. I knew it was the last before we reached the top. Robert sensed it too. With a burst of speed from behind, he caught up, overtook Gareth and pulled up as we gained the crest. Suddenly the hard encircling line of the distant horizon burst upon us.

We stood all three side by side. It felt like an important moment, the last stage of the journey now visible before us. Here was our last chance to resolve the difficulties between us before we reached the Pole. I shook hands with Robert and apologized to Gareth for my harsh treatment of him on previous days. I said, 'I meant what I said, only I wish I had tempered it with a little more kindness.' It was a growing contempt that I felt, and I did not wish to carry it all the way to the Pole, but my clumsy attempt at reconciliation came out all wrong. It did nothing to mend matters between us.

Christmas Day   611.1 miles

The second ice circle began to close in around us and the monotony of the Plateau grew. Unlike the Barrier, where the sky had been a constantly changing stage of clouds and light, the coldness and lack of humidity made the Plateau sky a constant blue. The sun was the only changing factor, as it wheeled around us, traversing a little lower to the south, a little higher to the north. The shadow, the wraith of Scott, was with us again, leading the way at noon with that steady, tireless rhythm, pounding on.

It was one of my rules throughout this journey to try always to centre my thoughts in the present. Hankering after the promise of a future event, the food at the end of each session, the view from the next rise, our arrival at the Pole, stretched time and produced a terrible, unfulfillable longing. On Christmas Day my resolve failed. We had agreed to celebrate the season with double rations. The prospect of a feast at the end of the march made our nine hours seem like a child's interminable wait for Santa Claus to arrive on Christmas Eve.

'I am so replete I can hardly write,' Scott noted on Christmas night, and like him we were full to bursting. It was wonderful to lie in the tropical heat of the tent after prolonged use of the stove. I wrote:

We began with two chocolate drinks, along with extra biscuits. RS is now into his second packet tonight. The main course was a double ration of macaroni-cheese, two full cups each, and bacon bars, Gareth eating two, while Robert and I only managed one. Up to this moment, the score on pepperoni stands at: RS and I, one; Gareth, two. Gareth has also eaten six biscuits with butter, but is falling behind on the chocolate having eaten only one bar, but I think this will increase shortly.

We are dozy and warm. Our bodies responded almost instantly to the food, and we all felt very hot and satiated. I have a surprise for the lads later, when I will make tea with two tea bags I have brought for this day. Periodically, Robert and I fill the tent with blue smoke from Christmas cigars.

Sunday, 29 December   679.11 miles

It had snowed while we slept, just a dusting on the red sledge covers. It could be heard sliding down the taut fabric of the tent. Fine needles of ice floated like silver dust, twinkling as it fell. In the morning it was clear, the air as still as a mill pond, and the sun beautifully warm. We broke camp and packed the sledges in comfort, working gloveless, despite a temperature of $-21°C$.

Towards the end of the first three hours of the march, a band of alto-cumulus formed in the east and gradually spread as the sun moved around to the north. Ice particles filled the air. When Gareth began leading the second session the contrast was good, but as the cloud spread over us the white flashes of sastrugi vanished and cloud masked the horizon to the south. Soon he was having trouble steering, and we left a zig-zag trail. There were numerous stops for sightings and corrections of course. Robert and I shuffled on behind in a halting convoy.

Gareth's increasing difficulty and frustration became more and more evident, for he could always feel my mounting discontent champing impatiently on his heels, and he knew that eventually I would come forward and take over. He later wrote:

Navigation-wise, he feels I'm just plain incompetent. I know the intricacies of navigation as well as he, but I just can't walk in a straight line in such conditions, and I take too long to sight the next mark. I am wasting time and it is costing us hours, even days. Roger is very disappointed with me, not just in this, but, in the back-up and support he counted on for this trip. Robert contributes nothing and is a passenger. He's only led one session since the Gateway, and Roger accepts it.

All Robert had to do was pull his sledge, and that was how he and I wanted it to be. Each of us had our roles on this expedition – his, to provide the drive to get us to Antarctica, and mine, to get him to the Pole. My expectations of Gareth were somehow greater.

I led for an hour, until the cloud dispersed and the sastrugi became evident. As the sun moved to the meridian and the shadow marched in front, I stopped to record the sun's azimuth, and so check the magnetic variation. Behind us, through the cloud and the floating ice particles, the most wonderful parhelion appeared. At first, it was a simple ring around the sun, but as the sun rose to its zenith, the circle's intensity increased. Its spectrum colours became as saturated as a rainbow. Poised on the horizon, on the lower vertical axis, was a bright golden orb. At the top of the halo and on both of its horizontal axes, short arcs grew tangential to the ring, like horns, and all around this glorious display a secondary circle formed, fainter than the first, and the air was filled with a glittering silver dust.

It was humbling to see such a display. Though in the days ahead they became familiar, it was impossible to escape the unscientific notion that the phenomenon was more than light reflected and refracted by the facets of ice crystals in the atmosphere, but a portent of enigmatic meaning.

Robert and Gareth were finishing their break when I caught them up. They departed and I sat astride my sledge in the sunshine watching them grow small as I drank my soup and tore at a frozen slice of pepperoni.

When there is no wind there is a great silence, but only when you are alone and absolutely still do you become aware of it. The silence is so intense that it seems to have a physical presence, yet it is filled instantly by a breath or the movement of an arm. Even in the quietest of places it seems as if silence is something that can never be experienced, for our own bodies are full of sounds, the blood's deep pulsing and the constant soft ringing tone, like the sound that is called by physicians 'tinnitus'.

I enjoyed this short time of contemplation. I was tired, not physically, though the effect of two months of manhauling was readily apparent in the gauntness of our bodies. Rather, I was tired emotionally, drained by the turmoil of our relationships, and exhausted by what I saw as a continual need to motivate and lead. There had been few days since the beginning when I had spent an uninterrupted session at the rear of our procession, able to drift in my thoughts, out and away from Antarctica. Many had been the days when I had marched in front for six or seven hours, and not infrequently for every minute of nine. Yet this was how I wanted it. I could never have made this journey as Robert did, trusting to others. That was beyond me.

The evening was strained. We sat in our sleeping bags under the thin fabric of the tent, a microcosm of human pettiness, hidden inside the small blue dome.

Days before, Gareth and Robert had discussed between them the possibility of an increase in our daily ration. Both of them, it seemed, were beginning to think constantly about food. In his day-dreams during the march, Robert would drift away into thoughts of his mother at home in Barnard Castle, only to find himself opening the refrigerator in her kitchen, or of Rebecca sitting opposite him in a chic London restaurant.

At our present rate of progress, we would reach the Pole with a surfeit of food, and it was not unreasonable to consider whether we should eat more rather than carry it as ballast. Both of them were looking forward to a little indulgence, but I was adamant that we should continue as we were, with the exception of double rations on New Year's Eve and on our last night before the Pole. I wanted to retain a reserve in case of some unexpected delay. Even more, I wanted to arrive at Amundsen-Scott Station with sufficient food to enable us, if necessary, to remain independent of the American base while we waited for Giles to collect us in the Cessna. I wanted to demonstrate beyond conjecture that the journey could be made without outside assistance – especially after the meeting at the Gateway.

It became a heated discussion. As the evening's cooking ended with a round of hot chocolate drinks, the whole dammed-up business, the irritations and resentments, came flooding out. Gareth said that he hated my presence. He found me arrogant, unbearably moody, rude, ill-mannered, selfish, inconsiderate, and totally unsympathetic. Robert was only contradictory and manipulative.

'I don't believe a word you say,' Gareth accused him. 'You denied you had anything extra and at the Gateway you had a lemon.'

Robert defended himself. 'It was in case of scurvy.'

'And what about the cigarettes?' I put in.

'How can you complain when you've smoked half of them?'

Gareth made it quite clear that there was no more to say. 'I just want to make an end to it, get to the Pole and finish.'

They both hid in their sleeping bags, and I too lay back and tried to sleep. Outside it was still, silent and calm, the bright sunlight filtered, green, through the fabric. Inside it was silent and stony.

I thought of the horror of the next days, with such a mood of ill-feeling and contempt between us. It was thirty minutes past midnight. I sat in my sleeping bag, full of dejection. I was angry at Gareth's refusal to make an attempt to deal with the situation in any other way than to grit his teeth until it was over. I could not bear his acceptance, though he was obviously hurt. So I badgered and probed until I raised him, unwillingly, from his bed. Then I told him that beneath his thin veneer of polite manners he was equally selfish, that his gentlemanly exterior was a sham. He was unimaginative and uncommunicative, and always sat on the fence, never showing any enthusiasm. His fastidiousness was exasperating. God, I went on and on, until eventually he rose to the bait and, with trembling voice, talked for thirty minutes, exposing the feelings and concerns that he usually hid.

'This journey has been terrible. I have closed up to avoid confrontation. I just want to get through,' he said. Later he wrote:

My attitude at first last night was that it was all going to be a waste of time, yet another encounter session. It went on until 2 A.M., and included assorted drinks, one extra thick hot chocolate and an extra packet of biscuits. We got down to the nitty-gritty and what we find irritating about each other.

We have all been under a great deal of stress since the expedition began, living in that rat-infested warehouse, and never having any time or money. My relationship with Roger began to break down then. At first, I identified with his ideals and his concern that the expedition should not become a platform for Robert. He was under a lot of pressure, and I began to see a side of his character that I did not like. It bothered me a great deal, and though I still agreed with his ideals, I found myself not being able to support him. Roger was very upset at my desertion and it made things worse between us. The Antarctic only heightened the problem. During the winter he went through turmoil, refusing to accept Robert for what he is, as well as dealing with the obvious problems between us. In spite of all he still supported me. He asked me to join the expedition and defended my place on the Polar team.

I explained how this trip, the whole expedition, had been a disappointment to me. I know I have not participated in the way I would have liked, but, worst of all, how can I look upon it as a great accomplishment, when to recall it brings back the sour taste . . . ?

During our talk, I think we both began to accept that we had traits that were difficult for others to live with, but agreed that we must either accept them or discuss our differences. They should not be a foundation for hatred. Gareth said he had opened himself for the first time. I said that a friendship was shallow if the anger and the turmoil were not shared along with the like and love. Robert, hidden in his bag, stayed quiet and listened. Later Gareth wrote: 'I went to sleep feeling very disturbed. We actually shook hands. I hope there is something there.'

Monday, 30 December   696.01 miles

It was a markedly different beginning to the day. The tension had dispersed. Gareth appeared more relaxed than ever before on this journey. He sat quietly for a while and sipped his chocolate, an act that was unheard of until that morning. I said how pleased I was about last night, and how much friendlier I felt towards him. I thought it could be a new beginning and the salvation of the expedition depended on the three of us completing the journey as friends. We were away without fuss, in the shortest time ever.

The Pole was drawing near. There was an impatience which I had to accept for the journey to be over, as well as a mounting excitement that we were almost there. Most of all, I looked forward to a return of privacy. We had been too close and seen too deeply into each other for too long. At the same time, we all felt an apprehension about our reception at Amundsen-Scott Base. How would we cope with the return to civilization, and what would we find to replace an adventure which had consumed so much of our lives?

17

The Order of Life

The ship had spent the southern winter moored under the Sydney Harbour bridge. Graham Phippen, Peter Malcolm and the crew had organized an exhibition in the Opera House and from odd jobs, selling expedition t-shirts and lectures they earned enough for the ship's upkeep and raised sponsorship for an overhaul of her engine. Then, in December 1985, *Southern Quest* was chartered to carry the Australian expedition, Project Blizzard, to Commonwealth Bay, where it began the restoration of Sir Douglas Mawson's hut. Having been the first ship to penetrate the Antarctic Circle that summer, she returned to Tasmania where six Austrian mountaineers, led by Bruno Klausbruckner, and our pilot Giles Kershaw and his two Alaskan mechanics joined the ship's company. The little Cessna aircraft which was to return us from the Pole was dismantled and loaded on board. On 28 December, a month earlier than she had sailed south the previous year, *Southern Quest* began her last voyage to the Antarctic.

South of the Antarctic Convergence the ship encountered an area of loose brash ice which persisted for 200 miles, until, as they entered the Ross Sea, the waters suddenly cleared.

Wednesday, 8 January 1986

Through an open, calm and lazy sea *Southern Quest* kept course towards Franklin Island. There was not a trace of pack-ice, and even from the barrel at the masthead no icebergs were visible. In the galley a long and unhurried breakfast followed the end of the 4 to 8 watch. Work on board continued placidly until mid-morning, when a great excitement swept the ship. The cry of 'whale' came from the bridge, and soon the galley was deserted save for Alaskan Rick Mason, whose movements that morning were tempered by a delicate constitution.

A pod of some twenty Minke whales broke surface close off the bows. The engines were stopped, and the suddenly silent *Southern Quest* slid into their midst. On each side of the ship the whales were blowing and plunging, first the pointed upper jaw pushing into the air, then the great black curve of the back, with its miniature rounded fin, arching gracefully through the water. The Minke is the smallest of the krill-feeding whales, and was generally ignored by whalers until the 1970s when stocks of the much larger fin whale reached economic extinction. In 1911 members of the crew of the *Terra Nova* found sport in throwing pieces of coal at several Piked whales that surfaced near the ship. Today such a game would have been regarded as irreverent, but then the Ross Sea teemed with whales and the sighting of a few Minkes was not so special.

The summit of Mount Erebus became visible at a distance of 121 miles. Six miles to the north of Franklin Island and extending all around it, the ship encountered dense pack-ice, which she skirted to the east before a course was set for Beaufort Island.

Ross Island was now clearly visible, with the sun lighting up the lower slopes of Mount Erebus beneath an overcast sky that hid the upper 8,000 feet of the mountain. At midnight the ship entered open pack, but the ice was rotten and melting and it was unnecessary to reduce speed. The sun, low on the horizon to the south, cast long shadows over the ice, which took on a purple hue. Adélie penguins ran helter-skelter in all directions and plopped into the water, or looked around in bewilderment at the sight of the bright red Grimsby trawler nudging its way from lead to lead between the floes.

Thursday, 9 January

Through the early hours of the morning the hull rang with the sound of the pack-ice grumbling along the waterline. The throb of the engine would drop a tone as the bows met resistance, and the alternating but irregular breaking and release could be felt by all aboard, especially by those attempting to sleep.

By 4 A.M. it became apparent that progress past Beaufort Island would be unlikely. Skipper Graham Phippen later recalled:

We met a line of dense pack that seemed to stretch over the horizon. From the ship you can't see very far, but you have an idea of how far the pack extends because you can see in the sky ice or water reflected from the clouds. You can see what is called 'water sky' which is an indication of open water, or 'ice blink' a white glare which is an indication of sea-ice. So you could see that it was hopeless to go further south.

The ship cruised the pack-ice in search of an icefloe on which it would be possible to assemble the aircraft and build a runway. The three aviators were woken at 6 A.M. Graham had selected a suitable floe into which he had parked the ship, the bows pressed into the ice, the engine running slow ahead. Peter Malcolm's diary records:

We clambered down a rope ladder thrown over the bows to take a closer look. We were walking on a patch of frozen sea, half a mile wide and under two miles long, its edges curved and angular, like a sliver from a broken mirror. It was slushy near the edge but crisp underfoot in the centre. There was hardly a breath of wind.

Giles Kershaw agreed that it would be possible to take off from the floe, but he did not want to rush into action, and everyone returned to the ship for breakfast. The two Alaskans, Ed Saunier and Rick Mason, reckoned that they would need twelve to fourteen hours to assemble the aircraft, the weather was stable, the barometer steady, and so the decision was taken to go ahead with all haste.

Giles considered that flying to the Pole was the easy part of the operation. They would be at their most vulnerable once they began assembling the plane on the icefloe. When the unloading of the aircraft was begun, it was essential that the job be completed before the fair weather changed or the pack-ice broke up.

After breakfast the entire crew set to work. Australian Lynn

Davis recounted, 'It was my watch. I asked Skippy if I had to remain on the bridge, because I wanted to work on deck. I was excused and went to haul on mooring lines, which we made fast to timbers buried in the ice, to unlash the plane, man the derrick and help offload the fuselage and wings.'

As soon as the plane was lowered on to the ice, the skis were fitted, and the Cessna, still without its wings, was pushed to a safer position away from the edge of the floe before assembly continued. Slowly the aircraft took shape. 'It was a fabulous spectacle and all the penguins agreed. They are so inquisitive, or very short sighted, they waddle right up to us and our equipment, and squawk indignantly when shooed out of the way.'

It was a long day. Ed and Rick worked out on the ice with an eager team of helpers. Lynn reached into wing cavities with her small hands to tighten bolts inaccessible to the big hands of the Alaskans. The Austrians made tea for the mechanics and laced it with schnapps. The mixture grew stronger as the day wore on. A runway was marked out with green plastic garbage bags filled with snow. By evening a 450-yard strip had been smoothed out with mattocks. The sky remained overcast and the temperature remained high, dropping from −1°C to −5°C at night, but with a light breeze making life less comfortable for those working on the plane. Breaking only for a hasty supper, Rick and Ed continued through the sunlit night until the Cessna was ready to fly.

The close proximity of the ship also infected John Tolson and Mike Stroud at Jack Hayward Base with a fever of activity. They had just returned from Cape Royds, where they had assessed the state of the sea-ice from the hill overlooking Shackleton's hut. Mike wrote:

Things are moving so fast that it's scarcely credible. We got through to *Southern Quest* with no difficulty, to find that instead of being at, or having just left Cape Hallet, she was only 50 miles or so away. The plan had been for her to try and reach the edge of the fast-ice, in which we would ski up to meet them. Imagine our surprise to find Giles asking for a runway to be marked out. They are moored to an icefloe from which he reckons he can take off, if it doesn't break up first. He hopes to be here tomorrow.

Friday, 10 January

As the plane neared completion, control cables were linked up and the exterior washed down. Sarah Robert-Tissot made up some stickers to go over the Australian call sign, which read:

ADMIRABLE BYRD – QUESTAIR

– after the American, Richard Byrd, who in 1929 became the first man to fly to the South Pole.

The engine turned reluctantly at first, but then it sprang to life. It was possible to rev it quite high, for the skis were frozen to the ice. Someone went to fetch Giles, who had been roused by the roar. Everyone waited, tired but expectant, eager to see their work fulfilled by the first flight. At 3 A.M. the machine rattled and bumped its way down the runway, and with a sudden burst of power and a great cheer from the ship's crew, lifted into the air. The tiny plane made a series of low passes just a few feet above the ice, then climbed and banked, and grew small and faint beside the black rock of Beaufort Island before disappearing towards Cape Evans. Lynn recalls:

We stomped on to the ship and drank hot chocolate, and the Austrians produced a huge bowl of gluwein – yum! There was a wonderfully warm, cohesive feeling around the mess table, lots of laughter and a deep set joy in each other's company. I had meant to get to bed right away, but somehow the minutes ticked by and the chatter continued until there was only half an hour before the plane was due back.

Returning from its reconnaissance of Cape Evans a little after 4.30 A.M., the Cessna circled while the runway was cleared of penguins. From the fo'c'sle Steve Broni, penguin lover and ornithologist, who had considerable experience in such matters, gave explicit directions in his Scottish accent to Thea who was having trouble with one particularly obstinate bird.

'Kick the bloody thing!' he shouted.

The aircraft made its approach, coming in low and slow, with full flap, Giles cutting the power so that it dropped on to the end of the runway with a bit of a bounce, and then skidded very fast across the ice.

With skis in place of wheels, the aircraft had no means of

braking, and it soon became apparent that the Admirable Byrd was not going to stop before it reached the end of the icefloe. Giles demonstrated remarkable judgment. Aware of the risk of overturning, and of the water lapping the ice on all sides, he turned off the runway. The plane slewed to the right and immediately hit some very lumpy pressure ridges. The starboard ski could be seen bumping up and down over the ice . . . a last big ridge, and BANG! The crew watched in dismay as the right ski flipped and the aircraft stopped dead, skewed, lame. Was this the end of the whole aerial episode?

Figures hastily converged upon the stricken machine. Remarkably the undercarriage had escaped unscathed: only the glass-fibre ski suffered any damage. The aviators did not seem in the least perturbed by the incident. Giles was already thinking of ways in which he could slow the aircraft on landing, and stoic Rick had resigned himself to whatever work was necessary to get the Cessna airborne again.

Few had slept since the aircraft operation had begun. With the sun circling the sky, the terms 'day' and 'night' become meaningless. Normal diurnal rhythms are disrupted not only by the absence of darkness, but by the need to exploit favourable conditions. In the Antarctic the elements dictate the order of life, and one soon learns that opportunities missed may never be granted again. After breakfast, some retired to bed while the ski was removed and work begun to rectify the damage. Lynn Davis wrote in her diary:

Mike Stroud's crackling voice on the radio rasped into my consciousness. I lay in my bunk, half listening as Graham explained the delay. Thea, who shared a cabin with me, was about to go to bed as I prepared to get up. It was 3 P.M. The ski would not be cured for another six hours, and the Austrians had prepared an evening meal. I was amazed how much the world outside had changed. The pack-ice had begun to move. While I had slept the icefloe to which we were moored had broken in two, and one end of the runway now lay upon another piece of jigsaw. I had missed a leopard seal and whales. The clouds had cleared briefly, revealing Mount Erebus and Mount Terror bathed in bright sunshine; but now, when I rose, the sky had fallen again. We ate a good hot garlicy meal, and after this unusual breakfast I began my watch, waiting on the bridge in eerie suspense for our island to crack.

After the floe broke in two, Giles supervised the construction of a second runway. The new strip ran across and was slightly shorter than the old one, and the approach lay directly in front of the ship's bow, with the touchdown point only thirty yards away. Eventually the repaired ski was fitted, and the first of several drums of aviation fuel, required for the flight to the Pole, was loaded on board. Flying was resumed at 10 P.M. A tense crowd watched as the little Cessna, with Giles and Rick sitting shoulder to shoulder in the confined cockpit, bumped down the runway and into the air.

As soon as the plane had gone the new 'end of runway speed retarders' (as they were grandly called) were set up. Three large tarpaulins were drawn across the ice, providing a less slippery surface which would slow the skis. Three rows of snow-filled dustbin bags gave a last line of defence before the ice ran out. After each landing the 'retarders' would have to be removed to clear the runway for take-off, and be replaced once the plane was in the air. In this manner, four flights were made over the next eight hours without incident, carrying all the necessary fuel to a depot on the Ross Ice Shelf, from where the Polar flight would be launched.

Saturday, 11 January

There was time for yet another breakfast before the aircraft made its final departure from the ship. Rick gathered his tools and the engine spares he would take with him to the Pole. They were to fly now to Jack Hayward Base, where Giles and Rick would rest before the big flight south, and Thea was to go with them, to join Mike whom she had not seen for a year.

The last take-off from the diminished icefloe at 6.50 A.M. drew a few worried breaths, for it was within ten feet of the end of the runway, only twenty yards from the water, that the plane became airborne. It left behind a group of people tired but bonded in friendship, respecting in each other those talents and qualities that had enabled them to become the first to assemble a light aircraft on a small icefloe in the cold southern seas and to launch it safely and repeatedly into the air.

As if in recognition of the achievement, the low cloud lifted revealing Antarctica at its most beautiful. Peter Malcolm's diary records:

The scene was breathtaking. Sunlight bathed the whole area, a patchwork of sea-ice extending to the horizon, now with a few open water leads of deep blue, and pressure ridges, great plates of ice breaking the skyline and emitting from their depths a deep green light.

The icefloe was cleared of tarpaulins and runway-markers, shovels, mattocks and empty fuel drums, leaving only footprints and the wide ski tracks of the Cessna. When the work was done, Graham declared an hour of recreation and Australian deckhand Dibble's Christmas present, a football, was brought on to the ice for those who still had energy to burn. With penguins the only spectators the rough-house continued until the ship's horn signalled the end of the game and the mooring lines were brought in. With engines at slow ahead, the *Southern Quest* left its icefloe which would soon become just another piece of pack-ice. It was almost midnight.

A meal was served on board after which, one by one, the crew stumbled gratefully to their bunks, leaving Graham alone on the bridge, steering the ship through the maze of ice. Tim Lovejoy was up in the barrel, pointing out the direction of open water leads, while Ted Addicott in the engine room, smoking his thin roll-ups, dealt with the commands rung down from the bridge on the telegraph. John Elder was typing in the chart room while Dibble, in the galley, set about the pile of dirty dishes.

The ship turned north. The intention was to return to Cape Hallet and there to land the Austrians for their attempt on Mount Minto. Then it would be a matter of waiting for the sea-ice to break out of McMurdo Sound before an attempt could be made to evacuate the expedition's base at Cape Evans. This was an exceptionally bad year for sea-ice, some said the worst since records began when Scott Base was established by Sir Edmund Hillary in 1957. Indeed, the United States ice-breaker *Polar Star*, which entered the pack-ice on 6 January, failed in its first attempt to reach McMurdo Station and was now on its way out of the Sound, though, it should be said, this was due as much to engine trouble as it was to the state of the sea-ice.

With the aircraft safely positioned, there was now little urgency for *Southern Quest* to reach Cape Evans. It had never been our expectation that the base would be relieved so early in the season. After the polar walkers had been collected, they would be flown to the ship. Another suitable icefloe would be found and a third runway prepared for the final landing. Once dismantled, the aircraft would be loaded aboard *Southern Quest*, which would then return to New Zealand, docking in Lyttleton by the end of January. There she would be refuelled in the port that had befriended the expedition, before returning south to clear the beach at Cape Evans by the end of February.

It is open to conjecture whether this plan could have been fulfilled. At the end of January the fast-ice broke out from Cape Evans, leaving a tantalizing corridor of open water five miles wide stretching north to Cape Royds. Beyond that the entrance to McMurdo Sound was blocked by heavy pack-ice extending up around Cape Bird as far as Beaufort Island. At the end of the first week in February, the second United States ice-breaker, *Polar Queen*, reported that the pack-ice around Cape Bird had dispersed.

While joined to its floating airstrip, the *Southern Quest* had drifted slowly under the influence of local currents clockwise around Beaufort Island. During those two days she had moved some 5 miles from a point 3.8 miles north of the island to a position 3.6 miles to the east.

The pack was beginning to change, a light wind had got up from the south, sufficient to start closing the gaps between the ice. Sometimes, with the engine running full ahead, it was necessary to drive large floes aside in order to clear a passage. Forcing its way north, the ship made slow but steady progress. The floes were becoming larger and the leads that divided them longer but less frequent.

It is not unusual for a captain whose ship is in ice to forego the normal round of four-hour watches and while underway to take sole charge of bridge duties. Graham recalled:

It was about 6 o'clock in the evening that I stopped, by which time I'd put some hours in, and reconsidered the position. There were some large floes around and I didn't feel like going through them because there might be pressure. There wasn't an obvious way to go, so I just put the bows of the ship on to a large floe with the engine running 'slow ahead', and had a rest. I was tired. I had a wash and a shave, a cup of tea and something to eat and felt better. Several times I had been in the barrel to see which might be the best way on, and then I went up again. I could see this narrow lead between two large floes, which led into a series of open leads leading to open water. The floes touched at four points along the lead, the last point being 150 metres from the open water route. I thought I would have a look up there to see if it might lead on. I didn't want to go further to the west, because that was taking me closer to the island, and further to the east the ice was coming from that direction, so I knew there was no way out there. I went up the narrow lead between the two floes. The first three points of contact were very easy, they didn't take any breaking, but the last was tough.

While the crew slept, the ship had bashed its way from one open lead to another, until only one stretch of ice lay between it and open water. Graham had done well. He had been at the helm since they had left the icefloe, and it was now early evening. Ahead, the only feasible way through was blocked by what appeared to be loose chunks of ice frozen together. He decided to ram this section. The first two attempts failed to make any impression, but on the third run the bows cut through the barricade and the ship plunged on into the narrow lead beyond, gaining some thirty yards before momentum was lost.

Those asleep woke to hear the chipping of ice, shouting and the engine surging, sometimes ahead, sometimes astern. The ship was locked in a slight bend in the lead. Graham mustered all hands at 8 P.M. and the loose ice was cleared from around the hull. With a mooring line run aft from the windlass and the engine running full astern, they attempted to pull her free. It was to no avail.

Everyone gathered in the mess to hear of a new plan of action. Two teams were chosen from the heavier members of the crew. The mate David Iggulden, Tim Lovejoy, William Fenton (now an experienced Antarctic hand) and Werner the Austrian set to work on the port side, and Bruno and the other Austrians to starboard. Using axes and mattocks and anything that came to hand, they were to clear as much ice as possible from the sides of the ship. Lynn Davis and Andrew Tissot were dispatched to load a cargo net with fuel barrels and to swing it to and fro, suspended from the derrick, in an attempt to rock the ship. The fire hose would be used to lubricate the ice that gripped the hull and the forward ballast tanks, port and starboard, were blown.

With growing concern they struggled for three hours to free the ship. The situation was becoming desperate, for the lead in which the ship was pinned had begun to close. The floe on the starboard side, which was several acres in area, was slowly rotating, and the pivot on which it turned was the ship. The pressure on the hull increased as the teams exhausted themselves without effect. They were caught in a trap and the outcome looked inevitable. Slowly the ship was being crushed.

The hatch to No. 3 hold on the port side burst open as the foredeck buckled. Inside, the bulkhead could be seen slowly altering shape, the plates at the waterline bulging inwards until the steel ruptured.

In the engine room two frames suddenly split down their length and water gushed in, uncontrollably. Nothing would stop that. The second engineer, Ted Addicott, calmly started both auxiliary engines, setting them to drive the bilge pumps, but the water continued to rise.

'How bad is it, Ted?' shouted William Fenton, who had had a nice job in public relations before the expedition disrupted his life.

'Well, I ain't welding that,' Ted replied as he scrambled past.

Graham came out on deck. He told everyone to stop work, go down to the cabins quickly for warm clothing and then get all the safety gear on to the ice. It was time to abandon ship.

The pontoon was unleashed and the life-rafts and the two inflatables were removed to the ice. The Austrians unloaded tents, sledges, skis and radios from the hold. Sarah Robert-Tissot and Lynn Davis threw cartons of cheese, chocolates, biscuits, cake, fruit and drinks from the OCL container out on to the growing pile of debris on the floe.

Peter Malcolm recalls imagining the prospect of a Shackleton-type saga of weeks on the ice.

I dashed back inside to get the camera cases from Andrew's cabin, managing to save all the movie gear. Then I went back to the aft cabin for the last time, not really believing that I would never see it again. It had been my home since February 1984. As I passed the engine room I saw a fire had started, the alarm bells were ringing. Ted was there with a fire extinguisher, but the rising water put it out. The ship was creaking and groaning. In the cabin, clothes were strewn all over the floor, what a mess! The number of times I have relived this moment . . . Oh God, I left so many personal things on board. My wonderful South American poncho that I've always treasured. The crazy 1985 diary with all the notes on how I searched and found this ship. The two leather bound books of Beethoven Sonatas belonging to Granny Fluff, and the piano, my piano; I almost played a last chord on it, but thought it unwise to be delayed.

Half an hour before midnight the Mate was instructed to advise the Americans at McMurdo of the situation, but radio contact could not be established and a message was relayed via South Pole Station.

At 11.37 P.M. the ship sent out the signal, 'The *Southern Quest* in Latitude 76°/58′S, Longitude 167°/13′E, has ruptured her hull by way of the Engine room.'

Aghast, the crew just stood and watched as the Mate and then the Skipper leapt down on to the ice.

At four minutes past midnight the news came through that at 23.53 the Polar walkers reached the South Pole.

Then the ship went down – slowly at first, the stern dipping under the water, then more quickly the funnel, then the bridge, and the deck at 45° and the railings and the barrel at the masthead. Last of all went the great red prow pointing to the sky, with the words *Southern Quest* in big white letters disappearing one by one in a consuming rush.

She was gone.

Where there had been heavy, hard, red-painted steel, now there was emptiness, distance, a flat white sea of pack-ice beneath a flat white sky. It began to snow.

John Elder blew the 'Last Post' on his trumpet, and the crew raised three cheers for the walkers, and three more for the *Southern Quest*.

18
The Pole

We were 11.27 miles from the Pole, so near after so far. Soon the journey would end, and it was difficult not to make the premature assumption that we were safe. As I lay in my sleeping bag on the evening of 10 January I wrote: 'How impatient RS is to reach the Pole. He is counting the hours, like a prisoner, the days to his parole. He talks of sighting the radio masts and the orange tower today, as though, by such fervent expression, he can bring the event nearer. For me all endings, all "summits" hold a touch of sadness. They mark not the climax of an adventure, but the beginning of its loss, the experience will fade into memory, the images and colours captured in a photograph, until all that is recalled is the memory of the photograph itself. Yet there is no denying that all three of us will be very glad to end this journey.'

With the realization of his dream now so close at hand, Robert became gripped by a superstitious belief in the power of his lucky number, eleven. 'If we can do it tomorrow,' he wrote, 'then we will have all elevens. The eleventh expedition overland to the Pole, and we could make it on the eleventh – Emma said it would be that way.'

Despite our eagerness to finish, we had made a late start that morning. The nearness of the Pole and the virtual certainty of reaching Amundsen-Scott Station ahead of our most optimistic schedule had blunted the spur that made us stir from our sleeping bags each morning. Gareth woke a little after 7 A.M. and lit the stove, the roar of which had signalled the beginning of each and every day of this monstrous journey. He wrote:

Got the stove going and the oatmeal blocks on the way. A leisurely morning for me and Rog, as Rob is making the soup. It's the first time

I can remember not bolting breakfast. Enjoyed oatmeal and lay back fully dressed to eat biscuits and drink my chocolate without having to move. An extra soup as well, which I had with a piece of sausage.

The wind blew incessantly all day, 10 knots from the south-west, backing unusually to the west in the afternoon and periodically rising a little in strength. At such times the horizon would be hidden in the drift, making it difficult to stay on bearing, and yet forty feet above us the sky remained clear and blue, bright sunshine illuminating every particle of airborne snow.

Our breaks were short, as they always were when the wind blew, each of us huddled behind the meagre shelter of his sledge drawn at 90° to the drift. We were always pleased to reach the end of each three-hour session, rewarded as we were with food and soup, but on such days, and they were many, there was little incentive to dally. Beginning again was difficult and uncomfortable, fingers and toes cold and getting colder in the race to put on harness and skis, until exertion restored warmth to the extremities and aching bones.

Robert wrote: 'RM is out front, he is a wonder . . . It seems that he must have a compass in his head . . . GW seems excited that we are almost there.'

'Feet very sore today,' Gareth wrote, 'especially during the stops and getting going again, but who cares now!'

The attrition of the journey had worked slowly, almost imperceptibly on our bodies. Gone long ago were the extravagant bursts of energy that had enlivened the days on the Barrier. It no longer required any discipline on our part not to exceed our slow but immutable pace. Gareth's diary records:

Surface very sandy, the ground drift makes for much harder pulling. The first session not too bad, but feeling much weaker these last few days, just don't seem to have energy. Breathing hard, to pace myself with others. Did 16.21 miles, a very good and pleasing effort.

That evening we indulged ourselves again with a double ration of food and unlimited drinks, in celebration of what we hoped would be our last night in the tent. We still had twenty days of food and three one-gallon tins of fuel that were unopened, enough for more than a month. It was far greater reserve than we could ever have anticipated. In the planning of this journey, I had thought it possible that we would by this stage be labouring on reduced rations, not lying in our sleeping bags as we were, full to bursting on two mugs of macaroni-cheese and bacon bar.

Gareth recalled that Robert was 'just discussing how easy it would have been to go on half rations. He forgets that a week ago he said how very hungry and worried he was.'

Our one remaining concern was to confirm our position as accurately as possible. Using the sextant to obtain sun sights, we could not expect a margin of error of less than 3 miles. Seventeen days ago the mountains of the Dominion Range had disappeared below the horizon, and since then we had travelled 264 miles. It required more optimism than I could have mustered to believe that we might sight the Pole without any correction of our course. Over the last days Gareth had increased the frequency of his sightings, and tonight, at 11.15 P.M., he ventured out again into the blowing drift, 'leaving the warmth of the tent and sleeping bag, poor bloke,' to take another. He returned to find that Robert and I were both asleep. Robert's concerns that evening had been less prosaic. We had joked that he would arrive at the Pole with his clothes in tatters. Now he wanted to ensure he looked his best. Gareth's diary reads:

Robert talking about what he will wear going into the Pole. Seems quite concerned. Tonight he is covering himself with Mitchams' deodorant and wiping sun lotion on himself with a flannel! He has changed his underpants and other bits. Guess he's hoping that someone will smell him. Brand new clean socks on too! He seems very keen to make an impression. Think I'll wait for a cup of tea and a shower.

Saturday, 11 January

By the time he had finished bandaging his feet, it was well into the early hours as Gareth finally laid his head upon his pillow of boots and windproofs. He had grown accustomed to nights interrupted by the need to urinate. Again he awoke and reached for the plastic bottle that was suspended by a cord from the roof of the tent.

Bad night. Up this morning at 5.07 A.M. for a pee. RS, who was awake, thought I was up for an early start. He was anxious to get going. I was dead tired and went back to bed for an hour. Robert made the soup again, but we weren't very quick this morning and didn't get away until 8.10 A.M. Roger off immediately, leaving RS and me to pack up the tent and catch up.

The wind was fresh to strong from the south-west, carrying with it considerable drift. Behind us to the north and east was a distant band of blue sky set between two similarly featureless planes of whiteness, cloud and snow. To the south, floating ice particles obscured the horizon, and contrast was intermittently poor as banks of low stratocumulus drifted over us in alternating waves of light and shadow. Steering in such conditions was greatly slowed by the continual need to stop and sight on some ephemeral flash of snow, distant or near, it was often difficult to tell. Ten minutes before the end of our first session I called a halt. Conditions had deteriorated miserably. I hoped that by the time we had eaten and were ready to move once more there would be some improvement.

I began the second session determined to continue, so close were we to the end of the journey, but after 200 yards it was obviously futile. 'White out, nothing discernible, not even a few feet ahead, and the drift increasing.' We stopped, capitulated, and put up the tent.

We were now only 8.79 miles from the Pole. Frustrating as it was, there was little alternative but to wait for an improvement in the weather. It was not possible to navigate with continual reference to the compass, as one would when steering a ship, or like the walker caught in cloud on the wintry summits of the Scottish Cairngorms, holding the compass before him. Although we tried repeatedly to perform this simple skill, on the Polar Plateau the magnetic needle is so weakly attracted that the least movement of the compass set it spinning.

Once inside the tent we drank soup and ate the biscuits, butter, sausage and chunks of chocolate that were our ration for the day, and then, to the accompaniment of the drift hissing against the fabric of the tent, we sought the oblivion of sleep. The winds that day were the strongest recorded at the South Pole since 1958.

Four hours later the wind had eased sufficiently to tempt me to put a head out of the door. 'Yes, we can go. It is still drifting and the wind is now from the west, but the cloud has reduced to three octas and the contrast is adequate. I tell Gareth to go, lead on, but he is only 100 yards ahead by the time I have brushed out the tent, taken it down, packed my sledge and harnessed up. So slow, but he led well and true on 5°, and Robert and I ramble on behind.'

We had travelled for less than two hours and had covered 3.7 miles, slowly extending our narrow silver trail south to its nearing conclusion at the point where all directions are north, when behind us Robert began yelling and waving his ski-stick to the west. In the golden light of drift and rainbow sun stood an object tall and vertical, looking like a man but straight and still, seeming about a mile distant on a bearing of 40°. 'Robert convinced it's the Pole station.' We ambled side by side, all three.

As we approached the object I was amused to think how like Kubrick's monolith it looked standing in eerie isolation, hard black against a yellow sun made soft by the crystal-filled air. It continued to remain distant, and then grew tall as we gained a rise. Robert was scarcely able to contain his mounting excitement. I could feel him growing. Gareth sensed it too.

How was it really for Scott's party, reaching here, like us, to find another's flag? Was their discipline so strong that they could retain grace and courtesy between one another? Was their fellowship never threatened by differences of temperament, class, culture and intellect?

The object resolved itself into a tower, twenty feet high, supporting a capital of automatic instruments. Nearby was a fence whose purpose was not apparent, unless it was to create the great corniced drift that formed behind it. A line of ragged green flags on bamboo wands ran away to the east, on a bearing of 355° towards the Pole.

It was more than three hours since we had left the tent and I wanted to stop for soup. This surprised both Gareth and

Robert, who assumed that the Pole must be very near. Gareth and I moved across under the tower towards the great drift, looking for a place sheltered from the wind in which to rest, while Robert, impatient to continue, waited by the receding flags. Carelessly I dragged my sledge too close to the deep wind-scoop under the drift's cornice and in it went, breaking both my trace repairs. Rather than spend time re-whipping the fractures, I cut the cords and resorted to a rope trace for the final few miles.

Robert resumed the march, following the flag line, and Gareth, too cold to wait while I removed my broken poles, followed him.

'Following these flags in to the Pole makes me sick,' Robert wrote. 'I long to make a headlong dash as fast as I can, just go flat out. I've had enough of being careful. I never want to hear the word control again.'

After a further mile and a half, the Amundsen-Scott base became discernible as a faint grey shadow on the horizon. The sun, circling toward the Greenwich meridian, bathed this most bleak and desolate landscape in a bright warm light. Streams of snow, like heavy dust driven by a hard breeze, flowed across our skis and filled the tracks of the leading sledge before the next could pass. At eye level, the air was filled with minute particles of ice, glittering silver. The sun's disc was surrounded by a huge golden halo, whose lower arc sat precisely on the encircling horizon. Such a dramatic place, unnatural to men. I became acutely aware of the warmth of my body, of the fragile shell of clothing that protected it. If that were to fail, my warmth would dissipate to nothing without melting a single grain of snow. I was the source of sound in a vacuum of silence. The sound of breathing, and of the wind fluting a deep breathy note across the holes in the hollow tube of a ski-stick, was all that could be heard in this timeless place that has seasons but no days.

'Thinking arrival imminent, Robert donned his dress for the occasion – the scarf Rebecca had given him wrapped round his head like Peter O'Toole's Lawrence, and his compass and sternum bag with Teddy poking from the flap.'

The American station, Amundsen-Scott, is housed in a great

grey metallic geodesic dome, a neat and fitting structure for the point where all lines of longitude meet. It is surrounded by a plethora of masts that support HF antennae, and a web of flag lines, green and red and blue. At one side of the dome stands a rectangular tower, five storeys high and painted orange.

'Robert ploughs on ahead, but when the dome does not grow appreciably closer he stops and waits for us to join him. He asks me how far I think the Station is? I answer thirty to forty minutes. It is 10 P.M.'

'Before the eleventh ends we will be there,' Robert wrote. 'Great. All the journey I have longed to see the shining dome at the end of our road. It will be sad to end.'

If we had continued on our original heading, our sledge-meters would have brought us short of the Pole by 396 yards, our bearing of 5° would have taken us 1,144 yards to the east. I am as amazed now, as I was then, at the accuracy of these simple tools of navigation – compass and sledge wheel – that were, for Scott, the same.

The flag line led around to the left side of the dome which was in shadow. I wanted to film our approach to the building with the sun on our backs, so we circled the structures until the sun was behind us. With the super 8 camera mounted and running on its tripod of ski-sticks, we turned and headed for the dome. Then of course we had to stop, and Gareth and Robert waited in the wind while I, feeling rather foolish, returned for the camera. Our route led us under the orange tower and around the crest of a wind-scoop of forty feet deep that guards the windward side of the base, and then out away from the dome to reach the tunnel that leads down under the snow into which the South Pole station is slowly sinking.

We threaded our way through the rows of bamboo poles linked with hand-lines and flagged with cotton squares of bright colour that stood stiff in the wind. We saw no one until we were within yards of the slope that led into the truck-sized entrance. Then a single figure, heavily wrapped and hooded, crossed our path and stopped, disbelieving. It was the 11th January and we were not expected before the 17th – the day on which, seventy-four years ago, Scott reached this place that differs from any other on the Polar Plateau only because of its position at 90° South.

We were led down the ramp and through the entrance, above which was proclaimed 'THE UNITED STATES WELCOMES YOU TO THE SOUTH POLE' and into the half-light that appeared to our unaccustomed eyes as darkness. Even then we were unsure of the reception that awaited us. We dared to hope that we might be greeted, as Edward Todd had suggested, with 'more than a cup of tea'. Yet we were prepared, if necessary, to pitch our tent and live as we had done for the last seventy days until Giles arrived in the Cessna to fly us back to Cape Evans.

It was seven minutes to midnight as we pulled our sledges down the slope, bewildered, not knowing whether to halt or continue into the gloom. The arched roof of the tunnel was covered in a deep frost, and the ground was a morass of grey dry snow, churned and soiled by the passage of tracked vehicles and countless booted feet. There was an overpowering smell of diesel oil, and the deep throb of big generators could be felt as much as heard. The excited cry – 'the Footsteps are here' – filtered through the hubbub, like one's own name called in a dream. Then there were the firm handshakes from nameless shadowed figures, and the muffled clapping of gloved hands, as we struggled through the gauntlet. The weight of the sledges suddenly eased as those same hands pulled and pushed the load the last few yards.

We emerged into an enormous vaulted space, filled with still, cold air. Rectangular, flat-roofed buildings clustered awkwardly beneath the high curving canopy, illuminated by the orange glow of artificial light and a great vertical shaft of white sunlight that poured down from the zenith of the dome, which remained open to the sky. There were more handshakes and backpats of welcome as people appeared from all directions, and shouts and cheers from a balcony above us, and through it all permeated the knowledge that the journey was at its end. I felt an overwhelming sense of release from the discipline of survival, mixed with sadness as the grace that had been glimpsed in the resounding silence of that immense light-filled world slipped away.

I stepped out of my skis slowly, so very slowly. Later, when

I saw it all on film, I could hardly believe how slow our actions had become. Lee Schoen, Officer in Charge of Amundsen-Scott base, an amiable bear of a man, walked unhurriedly from the radio room towards us. He clasped my gloved hand in a firm and honest grip.

'Welcome, I'm glad you guys made it.' He kept hold of my hand, and though he paused, I knew he had more to say. 'I've some bad news for you. The *Southern Quest* is sunk, crushed by pack-ice. Everyone is safe and well and being evacuated to McMurdo.'

In such circumstances how can one doubt the hand of fate, a power that predetermines events with a synchronicity that speaks of more than coincidence. Like Scott, 'The Pole. Yes, but under very different circumstances from those expected.'

I understood Schoen's words but they provoked no response. I gave him no reply. He had answered my only question before I could ask it – 'everyone is safe'. The fact that the ship had sunk seemed inconsequential, without relevance, like news from a distant land. He walked over to Robert and repeated his message.

'Can I speak to our people at McMurdo?' Robert asked.

'I'm afraid not. We were in touch with the ship during the sinking, but now MacTown has secured all communications.'

'When will we be able to talk to them?'

'I don't know. McMurdo are saying nothing. We can only wait.'

We were led off separately, surrounded by animated people, leaving our sledges in the soiled snow. The dome rattled in a gust of wind and a thin cloud of ice particles fell in the column of light from the circular hole in the roof. We were without purpose, following up iron steps, through a heavy door and into a wall of unaccustomed heat.

There were many simple things to assimilate upon our return to society. I stood before the bathroom mirror and stared at a face that was my own but which wore the mask seen before in sepia images of early Antarctic exploration. It appeared to me 'weatherbeaten beyond belief, skin stained dark and brown, but not at all similar to a suntan, tanned in the sense of leather, beard bleached blond, eyes small but oh so white, nose peeling from cold-burn, the flakes revealing fresh pink skin.'

I removed the clothes which I had worn since the Gateway and was appalled by what they revealed, a body as white as an Englishman's on a Mediterranean beach, and shockingly gaunt. I weighed only 136.25 lbs, some 20 lbs less than at the beginning of the journey. The first shower for seventy days was like warm rain on the back of the neck, the soothing torrents running over chest and limbs. I remember the overpowering fragrance of soap and shampoo – for the sense of smell had lain dormant in the cold – and of clean clothes saved for this moment.

I had not the least desire to sleep. Perhaps it was the coffee, or the sudden intake of food, or an over-active thyroid gland: whatever the reason, I slept no more than an hour in the next five days. I spent the remainder of the night sitting quietly in the deserted messroom thinking over what had happened and writing in my dog-eared diary.

'The news about which I am remarkably calm, unbelievably so, considering the tremendous ramifications: *Southern Quest* trapped in sea-ice off Beaufort Island, a fire in the engine room, or the engine room flooded – it is unclear which, communications were poor – and the ship sunk. All the people were off. The journey shrinks in comparison to this event. Giles and the Cessna already put off, but how much fuel is unclear. Whether he will be able to fly to the Pole is also unclear.'

Robert wrote: 'It has all happened so fast, one minute we were out there and now all hell has broken loose. As I dissolve from one world to another I wonder who is kidding whom when I think of normal life as being real. We sit and wait, hardly daring to voice an opinion. The Pole experts will be rubbing their hands with glee to see our dreams strangled in newspaper headlines. I just want out of here. I hate the heat. I wish Giles would arrive. How can I spring my mind from this cotton-wool and begin "to work again with worn out tools", when I thought it would all be over? This might be when I find my best and turn disaster into something better.'

At 7.30 people began to drift into the mess for a Sunday breakfast of pancakes, crisp bacon, eggs and coffee. 'The friendship and concern of these wonderful people whom we seem to have greatly inspired, has saved us from being plunged into deep despair, a despair that the crew of the *Southern Quest* must now feel.'

19

Icy Grasp

The last notes of the trumpet died away and left silence. For the tired crew, it was the first moment there had been in which to stand back from the drama of the event they had just witnessed. They stood and stared at a vacant hole in the ice that the ship had left. There were cries of disbelief and some tears while they struggled to contain the emotion that welled up. For many the *Southern Quest*, (or the '*Sunken Pest*', as she almost immediately became known) had been both home and the focus of all their endeavours.

'I loved that ship,' Peter Malcolm confided. 'I was the one who found her and I'd put nearly two years of continuous energy into her.'

Bruises of red paint stained, like blood, the edge of the two huge floes that had crushed her. Two empty fuel drums bobbed on the agitated waters. The pontoon suddenly crashed to the surface and drifted without purpose around the empty lead. Then, as the water settled, three Minke whales rose in unison amid plumes of spray.

The shipwrecked crew began to take stock of the situation, restoring order from the turmoil. No one had been killed, no one was injured. Chatter and humour returned as they set to work sorting and distributing survival clothing and equipment – twenty-one tiny black figures alone on a jigsaw of pack-ice at the edge of the Ross Sea.

When the first report that the ship was having problems reached McMurdo, Rick Mason and Giles Kershaw were sitting opposite each other across a table in the galley of building 5 at Willy Field. They drank coffee from plastic cups and chatted to the off-duty aircrews and to the Kiwis employed in the kitchens. Out on the snow, a few hundred yards away, stood the Cessna, loaded with food for eighty days and brimming with fuel, waiting to fly to the Pole. They were astonished to learn that the *Southern Quest* was in difficulties.

They hurried across the hard-packed snow to the edge of the airfield, unloaded the aircraft of its cargo of fuel and food, and fired the engine. In 300 yards they were airborne and flying north. The thin finger of Hut Point Peninsula slid beneath them. Ragged groups of seals lined a tide-crack that cut across the bay towards the Glacier Tongue. They crossed the coast again at Cape Evans, Scott's Hut bone grey and cold on the black beach. John, Mike and Thea waited helplessly in the green hut we had erected almost a year ago. Out in the Sound, the ice-breaker *Polar Star* lay in its channel cut into the ice. The edge of the fast-ice was nine miles to the north of Cape Royds, and a curve of open water, three miles wide, ran round the north of Cape Bird. All the rest was a choke of pack-ice across the Sound as far as they could see in the direction of Beaufort Island. Sooner than expected, they spotted from the Cessna's port window a dark huddle on a big floe, figures walking, carrying, waving; the ship had vanished.

Down on the ice, four tents had been pitched and three canopied ten-man life-rafts had been inflated and stocked with sleeping bags and bedding. The Austrians had erected their radio mast and the portable generator was running. Dave Iggulden was already talking to McMurdo. They estimated that there were full rations for twenty-one people for at least fifteen days. It was hastily packed on to sledges. There were skis and Schermully rocket lines, two HF and eight VHF radios, two rubber inflatables with outboard motors, axes and shovels, buckets and rope, a sextant, almanac and altitude tables. The crew were equipped with a multitude of things for sleeping, floating, climbing, grappling, travelling, sheltering, listening, seeing, signalling, finding, carrying, tying, warming, heating, covering and curling up with (for many were the Teddies and soft cuddly friends that escaped a watery grave).

The Cessna circled and then cleared the area as two red Sikorsky helicopters from *Polar Star* made their approach. From afar, Rick and Giles watched as figures ran, crouching, under the spinning rotors. The crew were flown, first in pairs and then four at a time, to Beaufort Island, where they were landed amidst the stink and commotion of an Adélie penguin rookery. Tens of thousands of birds thronged and jostled over the ochre-stained slopes of black volcanic lavas that rose 1,000 feet above the sea. There they waited, huddled together like the penguins which entertained them until the helicopters returned. Some of the crew were taken to Cape Bird before everyone was finally transferred to McMurdo Station. In all, four United States helicopters were employed for an estimated three hours. The equipment on the ice floe was abandoned, but for small items of personal baggage carried by each crew member. Peter Malcolm, himself a Royal Navy trained helicopter pilot, was impressed by the efficient and skilful manner in which the Americans effected the evacuation. Equally impressed were the flight crews by the collected behaviour of the shipwrecked sailors.

In the circumstances, given the presence of helicopters in McMurdo Sound, there could have been no sensible alternative to accepting the assistance that was so swiftly offered. It must be said, however, that after abandoning ship, the crew were in no immediate danger. In an exposed and unwelcome spot though they were, they were well equipped for a journey over ice or water. The Cessna, flown by a pilot whose Antarctic expertise is undisputed, was circling overhead. There was no panic, and if assistance had been unavailable the expedition could have performed its own evacuation, with or without the use of its aircraft, to the safety of the nearest habitation, which was the expedition's own base at Cape Evans.

Captain Shrite, the Officer in Charge of McMurdo Station, greeted the survivors with stern and humourless formality. Two canvas Nissen huts were made available – J162 for the men and 'Depression' (as it was called) for the women. Everyone was asked immediately to undergo a medical examination. The checks were never completed because of the obvious futility of examining twenty-one extremely healthy people who, given what they had just endured, were in remarkably good spirits.

At 9 A.M. the crew assembled around the coffee machine in the steeply-peaked hall of the beautiful wooden chalet that once served as the MacTown chapel and is now used for lectures and the meetings of civilian personnel. They were dressed in an assortment of foulweather gear, insulated work suits, and Burberrys. The clothes they wore were all they possessed, for most of what had been saved from the ship still lay out on the ice floe. Giles joined them, sporting a battered felt trilby from which he could not bear to be parted. Graham wore his orange Argentinian hat, bleached by the sun of many Antarctic summers, and among the crowd of woolly balaclavas and heads of unkempt hair was a cap of olive green, embroidered with the scarlet star of Communist China. The group was animated and gregarious, their humour in marked contrast to that of the two men who waited for them to take their seats. The chatter died as the disparity of mood was felt. Captain Shrite stood to address the visitors as they settled. He bore a grave resemblance to the late Steve McQueen, with his short-cropped blond hair and blue-grey eyes. Peter Wilkniss, his jaw set and arms tightly folded over his chest, remained firmly seated beside him.

'Unofficially we have nothing against you people,' Shrite began. 'We are sorry about what has happened. But you were warned, time and time again. My Government has said we will not support private expeditions, and I'm here to execute my Government's policy. We discussed it thoroughly before I left the United States to come down this season. We will offer you a humanitarian airlift out of here on a dedicated Herc' to Christchurch. Dr Wilkniss and I have discussed that. It is an unfortunate situation, but my plan right now is to fly you out within forty-eight hours. I request that you do not fly your plane to the South Pole, your three people can be returned here by Hercules. You will not be billed for that flight, but you will be charged at the normal rate for civilian charters of navy aircraft for the lift out of here.'

The Americans claimed in no uncertain terms that the expedition had badly disrupted the United States Antarctic programme, and that the lives of the helicopter crews had been put at risk because they had been forced to fly in conditions less than perfect.

There were some impassioned cries of protest from the gathering, followed by more restrained questioning of the main points of Shrite's statement. In a monotone Wilkniss repeated their wish that Giles Kershaw should not fly to the Pole. Giles agreed to comply, if he could be assured that in no way would it be implied the Polar walkers had been rescued. A request to speak to the three at the Pole was refused.

'It is not our policy to assist private expeditions,' said Shrite, emphatically.

In the circumstances, the excuse seemed fatuous. By withholding radio communications they knew that we would have little alternative but to comply with their wishes.

Peter Malcolm thanked the two Americans and said how much he respected the work of the helicopter crews. He also thanked them for the offer of transportation to New Zealand, and said, 'I quite understand your need for a policy of no assistance, but I suggest that it would be in everyone's interest for us first to secure our base and aircraft properly, if only for environmental reasons.'

'The hut is no concern to us,' interjected Shrite. 'We support Government sponsored agencies, and it is your responsibility.'

'But all we are asking is that you allow us to take that responsibility. It would only require a small group of us to remain behind for a few more days to make the hut good for the winter. They would be self-supporting and need make no demands on your programme. You have kindly offered to fly us to Christchurch, and we have agreed that the expedition will pay for that flight. Couldn't you simply allow, say, six people to fly out later? Forty-eight hours gives us no time to . . .'

'From my standpoint it will not happen,' Shrite cut in abruptly. 'I will watch that flight and that is the only option I am giving you people. You either take that plane or you make some other arrangement.'

The meeting continued for another twenty minutes. Shrite and Wilkniss were adamant, and would make no sort of compromise. They were asked again if one of the expedition could speak over the radio to the walkers at the Pole.

'I am flying to South Pole tomorrow, and I will ask your men to climb aboard,' Wilkniss intoned flatly.

They tumbled out on to the dusty summer streets of McMurdo and dispersed. It was a bright-pin day, with white vapours on the breath and the exhaust of vehicles in the cold still air. Some retired to sleep, others were invited by friends to the mess for Sunday brunch. A small group walked the graded road over the Gap to Scott Base and attempted to contact the outside world by means of the phone in the post office at the New Zealand Station. Fortunately they were successful, for though the Americans had released the news of the sinking, the fact that no one was injured had not reached relatives in Britain. That afternoon Lynn Davis climbed to the rocky summit of Observation Hill. On the cross of jarrah wood erected by the Terra Nova party in memory of its five lost men, the weathered inscription, 'To serve, to strive and not to yield' was scarcely visible. Around its base, like an encroaching flame, climbs an ivy of crudely carved monographs, which as it grows will mark the spread of man's corruption of this last great wilderness.

On the path she met a geologist, an Alaskan whose name was Jurgan. He showed her the evidence of the volcanic processes that had formed the landscape, pointing to the sinter cones, the plugs and the three craters of Mount Erebus, the parallel dyke that intrudes vertically into the hill and great pock-marked teardrops of rock blown from the volcano. In the book that had been placed on the spur overlooking the sprawl of McMurdo Station, Lynn wrote:

It's the latitude, the altitude, the solitude of here,
That makes the attitude of the multitude appear to be so queer.

But that was not quite right, for it was with the people of McMurdo that the shipwrecked crew found sympathy and support. Now many were angry, and later they expressed their disapproval by adding their names to a letter to the expedition that read:

Congratulations on the successful completion of your journey . . . It was a splendid feat. Most of us were proud to share in the spirit of what you did.

Apologies for the reception that you received in McMurdo . . . We cannot accept the shamefully hostile treatment of your group: the failure to extend to you free access to communications facilities, the restrictions placed upon your travel about McMurdo and the attempts to limit the personal interaction among us. Had our people taken the time to know you individually, as many of us did, then perhaps you would have been met with a welcome more befitting those who return from great undertakings, and those who have suffered shipwreck.

It was unworthy of us to have imagined that we would not be well received at the South Pole. The two days we spent there will remain for me some of the most rewarding of the expedition. We were welcomed with a generosity entirely in keeping with the spirit of international co-operation that has long been the great tradition of Antarctica.

The official response, under the directorship of the 'new broom' Dr Peter Wilkniss, stood out in stark contrast. Although we did not realize it at the time, the loss of *Southern Quest* had provided the perfect opportunity to justify the new hardline interpretation of United States Antarctic policy, an opportunity that was about to be exploited to the full. Communications had been secured for the sole purpose of preventing our involvement in decisions that were being made concerning our evacuation and the immediate future of the expedition. And they remained secured until we flew out from the Pole. I felt sorry for Lee Schoen, who as base commander found himself caught up in an intrigue for which he had no taste.

'None of us has any idea what is going on,' said Schoen apologetically. 'Communication with your people at McMurdo is strictly withheld. We've been told only that you will be flown out from here in a C130.'

'Why is Giles not flying? Was the plane damaged or did the fuel go down with the ship?' I asked. The last thing any of us wanted was to fly out in an American Hercules.

'I don't know the reasons. The Cessna's at Willy Field but they won't tell us why it won't fly.'

'The National Science Foundation is now well in control of the situation,' I wrote, 'and is poised to make the most mileage out of the sinking. We won't hear the full story until we reach McMurdo, but there is no doubt that it will be of greater political value if we do not return from the Pole in our own aircraft.'

Even messages of congratulations were turned back. One from Sir Vivian Fuchs that never reached us read:

MANY CONGRATULATIONS ON YOUR SUCCESS AND SYMPATHY IN THE LOSS OF SHIP. BE NOT DISMAYED BY OBSTRUCTIONS BUT REJOICE IN YOUR FINE ACHIEVEMENTS.

A more sinister development was that personnel at both South Pole and McMurdo were informed that fraternization with members of the expedition could be detrimental to future employment, and that open co-operation could result in disciplinary action or even premature termination of contracts. Despite these threats, of which at the time we were unaware, we met no one at South Pole, apart from NSF officials, who resented our presence or who expressed anything but admiration for the achievements of the expedition.

The results of this policy could have been foreseen by anyone with even the most rudimentary of managerial skills. A Telex sent from McMurdo Station, dated 17 January 1986, and addressed to the NSF Division of Polar Programs, Washington DC, states:

PERHAPS ONE OF THE MOST SIGNIFICANT EFFECTS TO THE US ANTARCTIC PROGRAM IS THAT THE INCIDENT HAS AFFECTED MORALE AT MCMURDO AND SOUTH POLE STATIONS. WITH EMOTIONS RUNNING HIGH, BOTH COMMUNITIES HAVE EXPERIENCED DEBATES AMONG THOSE SUPPORTING THE EXPEDITION AND THOSE SUPPORTING US POLICY.

A memo circulated to the relevant officials, including Dr Wilkniss and Captain Shrite, the military Officer in Charge at McMurdo, also dated 17 January, the day that Robert and I arrived back in London, and signed by Dr Brad Craig, reads:

Immediately upon their arrival I was asked by our station manager, Lee Schoen, and our senior NSF person, Dr John Lynch, to perform a brief physical examination on each member of the party. At this time I found that all three men were in strikingly *good* physical condition and suffering no significant ill effects from their journey requiring medical attention.

Following this examination, I was clearly informed by my station manager that, according to NSF policy, I was to have absolutely no other official dealings or involvement with the expedition.

After some discussion with those involved, however, I discovered that the Footsteps of Scott Expedition was in fact in keeping with the spirit and goals of our Antarctic endeavours, and was in the process of conducting a very valuable and significant medical study. Under the guidance of their team physician, Dr Mike Stroud, the three polar walkers were involved in a very well designed and medically important study involving the basal metabolic rate and its response to strenuous physical exercise under highly controlled conditions. The members of the team painstakingly recorded and filed important medical data relevant to this study throughout their polar walk.

After learning of their efforts to make a significant contribution to medical science through their experiences, I felt it my obligation as a physician, scientist, and *friend*, to assist them in whatever way possible. Let me emphasize at this time that at no point did they demand, or even request assistance.

On my own time and initiative (and without the knowledge of my station manager or NSF representative), I worked with Mssr's Swan, Mear and Wood, gathering some very simple baseline data to add to their collection of information.

The gathering of this data consumed minimal time, effort and energy, and in no way adversely affected the running of the station or the provision of health care to other members of the South Pole crew.

It was indeed a pleasure to meet, visit and work with these three admirable men. My contribution to their scientific endeavors was minimal, however I am proud to have played a small part in their efforts. They were pleasant, friendly, co-operative and undemanding during their brief visit here and generated a great deal of respect from all of us here who had the good fortune to meet them.

Our return to the world of men had brought with it the bitter pill of lost independence, and independence was fundamental to the expedition's purpose. For Shackleton, in 1915, the loss of *Endurance*, crushed by pack-ice in the Weddel Sea, had been an unplanned change in the choreography of an adventure which led to a triumph no less remarkable than his intended crossing of the Antarctic continent would have been. The pioneers of Antarctic exploration, from Amundsen to Fuchs, conducted themselves in accordance with the rules imposed by the Antarctic alone. If they made mistakes then it remained their responsibility to atone, and it was in search of this basic freedom – to live by one's own judgment, wit and skill – that our expedition had been devised. It had been our proclaimed intention 'to restore the feelings of adventure, isolation, and commitment that have been lost through the employment of the paraphernalia of modern times'. To this end we had pulled our sledges, weighing more than both experts and history said it was possible to pull, nearly 900 miles. We had not taken radio or any other means of communicating with the outside world. We had wanted to play the game by the old rules, and now, just when it seemed we had come through, the game was called off, not because *Southern Quest* was lost, but because it was no longer reasonable to remain isolated from the arbitrary set of rules imposed by the presence of American helicopters in McMurdo Sound. In an earlier age the adventure would then have only just begun. The American machine had taken control of the expedition, and the three of us at the Pole could not find the strength required to wrestle from its bureaucratic grasp the right to remain responsible for the expedition's future and, to prevent the expedition from being used as a means to erode further the unique status of this continent, with its total absence of formal government.

That afternoon, we were invited to climb the steps inside the orange tower, known as the Space Lab, to a lounge where we sat in soft, cushioned chairs and listened to the gentle melody of Fauré's 'Pavane'. We gazed in warm comfort through wide, smoked-glass windows at a panorama of the light-filled world of which, but a few hours before, we had been a part. In the subdued light, we noticed for the first time the effect of the high level of ultra-violet radiation that penetrates the atmosphere at these latitudes. White clothing shone with a luminosity that combined with the tranquillity of the music to produce a sense of unreality in which it was easy to forget the fatigue that saturated our bodies.

The following morning, Lee Schoen informed us that we would be flown to McMurdo aboard one of the two aircraft that were scheduled to arrive at South Pole that day. The first flight would bring Peter Wilkniss and a number of Senators and Congressmen engaged in a public relations tour of US Antarctic bases, who would spend two or three hours at the South Pole viewing the facilities, having lunch and buying souvenirs from the trinket store. We were asked to remain incognito should our paths cross during their visit, and to hide our sledges and equipment from their sight. The second flight, carrying fuel from McMurdo, was scheduled to return empty, like the majority of aircraft returning from Amundsen-Scott base. The orders sent by Telex from McMurdo were succinct:

ALL MEMBERS OF FOOTSTEPS EXPEDITION NOW LOCATED AT S. POLE ARE TO BE MANIFESTED ABOARD THE SECOND FLIGHT FOR RETURN TO MCMURDO. FOOTSTEPS CESSNA 185 WILL NOT REPEAT NOT CONDUCT FLIGHT TO S. POLE STATION.

The aircraft arrived at midday. After saying goodbye to our new friends, we made our way along the tunnel to the dome entrance. There we met for the first time the director of the NSF Polar Program, Peter Wilkniss. He emerged out of the drifting snow amidst billows of tiny ice particles that were settling in the shelter of the entrance. He had rushed ahead of his VIP charges to ensure that they did not encounter the subversives, and he quickly ushered us to one side.

Wilkniss is a big, barrel-chested bull of a man and his sense of humour was on this occasion absent. He was unexpectedly nervous as we stood before him gazing into the face of a man who could not bring himself to look into the eyes of those he was addressing. There seemed to be something of unaccountable interest on the frost-covered corrugated wall behind my left shoulder. He rocked continually from foot to foot, to an extent that made me wonder if he was having trouble with his bladder. We were treated to a rehearsed monologue, which he asked us not to interrupt even before he began. It was apparent that he was expecting a major confrontation.

'I have nothing against you people personally, but you were warned. We made it clear before, and I want to tell you now, that we have a policy of no assistance to private expeditions which it is my business to enforce. There is no place in the Antarctic for adventures such as yours any more, and we are going to make that point. You will be flown to McMurdo now, where you will join the rest of your people. Arrangements will be made for your immediate evacuation to Christchurch.'

We listened as he made his halting statement. I discovered later that Wilkniss thought he would need to use persuasion in order to get us to board his aircraft. Knowing nothing of the concession that Giles Kershaw had made in grounding the Cessna, we had already accepted the arrangement as inevitable.

Wilkniss also maintained that their plan for resupplying Siple Station at the southern end of the Antarctic Peninsula had been put in jeopardy by our evacuation. We made no reply to this absurd claim. The freezing of communications had denied us the possibility of knowing anything of the events of the last two days.

We made our way out into the sunlit drift, passing the flags of the twelve signatory nations of the Antarctic Treaty, arranged in an arc around a chromium sphere that tops a stunted barber's pole. This crude edifice marks the ceremonial South Pole. Beyond that is the point to which yesterday Robert had pulled his sledge. Then he had stood on the ice that had covered the earth's axis in 1912 and since drifted. Approaching the spot where the flag planted by Scott now lies buried, he passed the true South Pole. He later wrote: 'A single Stars and Stripes flew there . . . What about the Norwegian flag? What about the Union Jack?' We walked into the wind and the great noise of the waiting C130. Here aircraft do not shut down their engines while on the ground. We climbed aboard for the three-hour flight back to Ross Island. It made a mockery of the seventy days of toil that had taken us to the South Geographic Pole.

20

A Matter of Principle

The ski-equipped Hercules is a military aircraft designed to carry paratroops and cargo into battle. Along the flimsy rows of nylon-lattice benches lining the fuselage were a number of American personnel who at the last minute had been bundled aboard, to be returned with the three of us to McMurdo. It was impossible to talk; only words which were shouted a few inches from the ear could be heard above the din. We were enveloped in a tube of sound that tore its way through the fabric of the vast silent landscape that we had pulled past us on our overland journey. It was as though all the experiences of the past months were being played back to us in reverse, condensed into a scream of meaningless white noise.

I slept for an hour on one of the casualty stretchers in the aircraft. It was the first time I had closed my eyes since arriving at the Pole.

When we landed on the snow at Willy Field, we expected to see a group of dejected strangers and a few sad familiar faces. Only seven of the members of the expedition gathered at the airfield had known the Polar walkers. Perhaps it was their excitement that the others shared, as they waited in the warm sunshine. The pilot crouched in the hatch-way that led to the flight deck as we left the aircraft. In a glance I recognized that he, who had flown across that ice countless times, understood the magnitude of what we had done and regretted as much as we did that our return from the Pole should be like this. Rebecca wrote:

. . . and off got the boys. To see Robert – what can one say? – Roger and Gareth . . . we all hugged and kissed. I felt quite strange, but I do love him dearly. It was so sad that the sinking should overshadow the incredible fact that they had done it, and Robert had fulfilled his ambition.

My first impression was that it was so warm. It is an experience peculiar to air travel which allows you to leave London or New York on a cold and windy March morning and know with the first contact of hot humid air on your face that you have emerged in a tropical climate, Delhi or Honolulu. McMurdo basked in sunshine beneath a gently smoking Mount Erebus. The familiar landmarks of Castle Rock and Observation Hill appeared like old friends after the stark immensity of the Polar Plateau. Peter Malcolm had dreamt that this meeting would take place alongside the *Southern Quest* as we stepped from the Cessna on to the icefloe. The dream had been crushed. He hugged me around the shoulders and said in his breathy excuse for a Geordie accent, 'Wal 'ow are ya?'

'Everything's fine, no problems,' I said, knowing that it was true because we were alive and false because of the mess we were in.

He hurried us off for a meeting of the Talkers, the expedition spokesmen. For the first time we heard details of the events which led to the sinking, the refusal of the Americans to give our pilot or the ship weather information (a ridiculous situation which lasted for just one day), the crushing and the incredibly fast response of McMurdo in mounting an evacuation.

Giles Kershaw told us why he had agreed not to fly the Cessna to the Pole, when the Americans insisted on returning the Polar walkers on a routine Hercules flight. All aircraft, big or small, flying in the Antarctic face a similar degree of risk. Mere size does not guarantee safety. In 1979, a DC10 with 257 people on board crashed into the slopes of Mount Erebus. Several American Hercules aircraft have broken into crevasses and others have been stranded and abandoned on the Antarctic ice – a grim witness to the dangers. Giles had consulted the Foreign Office in London over the public telephone at the New Zealand base about what to do and recognized that it was unnecessary in the circumstances to continue with his own flight. It was a bitter disappointment to him. Now Giles was beginning to doubt the decision. His sense of responsibility and fairness was not being reciprocated by the uncompromising Wilkniss. About one thing he was emphatic: he was not going to see the Cessna destroyed. If necessary he would fly it out across the continent to the Antarctic Peninsula where the British Antarctic Survey has its bases, and from there to South America. He too wanted us to take back some control of the expedition's future.

Yet it seemed ungrateful and ungracious to sit there castigating the people who had provided the frozen yoghurt I was eating. Defeated armies forfeit their right to make decisions, but we were not a military force. We were a private expedition whose misfortune on losing its ship was being exploited behind a cloak of humanitarian concern, and whose achievement was being denigrated in an attempt to prove our helpless inability to cope with the demands of the Antarctic. It seemed that we were providing the opportunity they wanted, to persuade other nations to adopt their position, that all non-government expeditions should be barred from Antarctica.

There is a fundamental hypocrisy in the American condemnation of the expedition. The National Science Foundation of Washington contended that it was irresponsible of us to have come south without the scale of logistic support that only the Americans can command. No country operating in Antarctica is in a position to remain utterly independent, regardless of any emergency that might have to be faced, and emergencies are not infrequent in this inhospitable land. Even the NSF recognizes that risks have to be accepted in the Antarctic. After hearing of the destruction of the space shuttle *Challenger*, Walt Seelig, Director of NSF operations in Christchurch, said:

I couldn't help relating it to Antarctica. Everything may be going smoothly when Bang – out of nowhere – something goes wrong. There are things you can't control no matter how excellent the safety precautions you take.

In the previous spring a man at the Australian station had been terribly burned. He was spraying the inside of a water-storage tank with a volatile water-proofing agent, when the gases ignited and exploded. He was thrown clear, but sustained severe burns through inhalation and to 70 per cent of his body.

There is not a medical facility anywhere in the Antarctic continent that could have offered him any hope of survival. His one chance was immediate evacuation by air to New Zealand, and the only people with the capacity to give him that chance were the Americans. I saw how very much Bob Harler, who commanded that evacuation, wanted to save the Australian's life and how upset he was when the man died during the long flight. Without the great umbrella which the United States Navy squadron VXE-6 has erected over the Antarctic that man would have died at the Australian base. If the accident had happened before the advent of radio, he would have died months before any request for help could have been carried.

The Americans do not consider that nations whose official Antarctic programmes are supported by smaller resources than theirs act irresponsibly, or that all those people who sailed the seas or travelled the ice of this frozen continent before radio was invented were taking unjustifiable risks. Our enterprise was equal in skill and experience to most and better than a good many government-backed operations. It was just smaller, not less competent. We understood as well as anyone the extent of our power over the elements and how easily control can be snatched away. Bigger ships than *Southern Quest* have got into trouble in Antarctic waters. That summer the British Antarctic Survey's *John Biscoe* was abandoned, presumed lost, when northerly winds closed the leads in the pack-ice and trapped the ship off Adelaide Island on the Antarctic Peninsula. In December 1981 the West German ship *Gotland II* sank when it was pushed by pack-ice against a permanent ice edge and crushed.

In 1985 *Southern Quest* was in McMurdo Sound establishing our base long after the last American ice-breaker with its helicopters had left the continent for the winter. If that had been the case in 1986, when the ship sank, we would have had no choice but to perform our own evacuation. We were equipped for such an eventuality and were not incapable of dealing with the emergency.

It is presumptuous of the National Science Foundation to suppose that an expedition such as ours, which had undergone the most careful scrutiny by its patrons, and had been given the blessing of both the Foreign Office and the Prime Minister, was ill-conceived and would only have been attempted under the protection of the American umbrella. We based ourselves at Cape Evans not on account of the proximity of McMurdo Station but despite it. We were there simply because that was where Scott began his journey. We declined to take radio with us to the Pole because we wished to demonstrate that while we could not remove the American presence we did not depend on it, or expect to be rescued if things went wrong. Antarctica, like the high seas, is still international territory and we felt we had as much right to be there on our own terms as anyone else. The single-handed yachtsman sailing round Cape Horn would not be expected to provide himself with a massive naval escort, nor would any attempt to control or regulate such shipping on the high seas be condoned simply because one nation has, for its own purposes, set itself up as a power in a particular area.

It is the great size of the American programme that enables it to be a potential support to others in virtually every corner of Antarctica. With that potential goes a moral obligation to offer assistance in emergencies. The two things are inseparable. In fact the obligation applies to everyone in Antarctica. It applied to ourselves as much as to the Americans, just as every ship at sea, yacht or supertanker, is expected to give aid in an emergency to any other vessel in need. If the United States cannot bear the responsibility that goes with a massive presence in Antarctica, then perhaps the National Science Foundation should reduce its compass. Such a reduction would certainly not prevent expeditions like ours going to the Antarctic. It would, however, remove the threat that the enormous American operation imposes upon a continent as yet free of any national sovereignty.

Of course, we were not naïve enough to suppose that we might decline outside help in an emergency if it were expedient, or that anyone with the capability of offering assistance would fail to exercise their moral obligation in such circumstances. We had therefore covered the expedition by taking out extensive insurance, and this would not have been possible if the Institute of London Underwriters had thought we were foolhardy or working towards inevitable disaster.

Before a final meeting with Captain Shrite the expedition met to discuss its options, if indeed we had any. Robert asked Giles to represent him, for he felt too angry to be diplomatic. It was the first time that so many expedition members had been gathered together in one place, and it was an emotional occasion. Despite the haze of fatigue which enveloped everyone, we found a new spirit of unity and a determination not to accept meekly the dictate of the NSF.

What could we do? The Americans would give us no time in which to prevent the littering of Cape Evans that the abandonment of our base and aircraft would inevitably cause. Were there alternatives to leaving the Antarctic on an American Hercules? On the icefloe, the ship-wrecked crew could have been evacuated by the Cessna if the helicopters had not arrived, or boats could have been hauled across the 15 miles of sea-ice to Ross Island, as Shackleton had done after the loss of *Endurance* in 1916. Evacuation from Antarctica itself was not so simple. Our people in London could have chartered another ship, but that would have taken time which our immediate deportation denied us, and though there was enough food at Cape Evans for us all to survive if we had decided to make a stand, we did not have the resolve to turn down the easy option of a quick flight home.

To the astonishment of everyone it was Gareth Wood who provided the expedition with a new possibility.

'It is my base,' Gareth said. 'I put that place together, and I am not going to stand by and see it destroyed. We have enough provisions there to enable us to rewinter. We have provided against the possibility that it might be necessary to spend another year at Cape Evans, and that I am willing to do.'

Suddenly we were in awe of this man who had just walked to the South Pole and was now, on a matter of principle, contemplating a second year in the Antarctic. Others immediately offered to complete the team of three that he said he needed, and it was left to Gareth to choose his companions. My respect for him was all the greater for the fact that I knew in my heart I was unwilling to match his sacrifice. At that moment I dreaded his call for me to join him.

Armed with Gareth's resolve, five of us went for one last

attempt to gain from Captain Shrite the small concession we required.

'We're just looking for some time,' began Graham Phippen. 'The expedition is not going to disband, not to the four corners of the world. We are going to stay together to take care of our responsibilities. We're not looking for your support. Anybody who stays behind doesn't need to live on your base. All we're asking is that you allow a very small number to remain behind for a few days to tidy up our affairs here, while the rest fly out. I think that is the best . . .'

'Well, I guess I sort of figured it would be some sort of compromise that you'd like to propose to me,' Shrite interrupted with an air of self-righteous confidence. 'Now, as we said yesterday, we will provide a humanitarian airlift out of here, and that is it. There will be no other exceptions or options or anything else, nor will I do it later on. There has been a great deal of concern about private expeditions, tourist groups and folks like you. We cannot afford to get involved any longer. We want to make that point. Unfortunately you are the ones that are here now, and it's a sad situation, but I feel I don't have any other option on it.'

'If our plane stays at Williams Field, what in your opinion will happen to it?' Giles Kershaw asked, knowing full well the answer.

'It will be destroyed by 90 knot winds,' Shrite replied with a shrug. 'Some time every season, the wind will hit 90 knots and that plane will be destroyed. There's no doubt in my mind.'

'The same applies to our base,' I put in. 'We have external stores that were placed with the intention of being there for a limited period. If they're abandoned, it will eventually make a devastating mess on the beach. There are outbuildings, tents and wind-generators that wouldn't survive the winter unattended, things that given a few days we could secure and make safe.'

'The environment will suffer,' Giles added, 'and that will reflect badly on not only the expedition but yourselves.'

'Those are issues all right,' Shrite said, unable to deny the point, 'but we don't support your endeavour. We have no respect for . . .' He stopped himself in mid-sentence. 'We're in scientific support down here. It was an adventure you guys did, and it didn't come out quite right, and we don't want any more of them. That is it, cut and dry.'

'It's one of the stated aims of the expedition that it is concerned about pollution in the Antarctic,' said Giles, 'and what you're asking us to do goes against that. I would have thought that you'd be against pollution too. I would have . . .'

'There is another option,' Shrite interrupted again. 'You could taxi your airplane over to the sea-ice, where the ice island is, and it will be gone in two months.'

'Yes, yes, yes, I know that,' – Giles was becoming more impassioned – 'but think about what you've just said.'

Shrite stabbed the air with his finger. 'I am not going to haul your aircraft out of here, so whatever you do with it is something you are going to have to arrange on your own, either now, later, or what have you.'

'That's exactly what we're asking for,' I said, 'time to make the necessary arrangements for the . . .'

'We told you not to come. You chose to come. You chose this too I think,' said Shrite, unwilling to listen to any reason. 'My plane leaves tomorrow evening. That's what I'm trying to tell you. I hope you all get on it. And if you don't, then you must vacate my base and do your thing, because there won't be another ride later, or anything else.'

There was no point in arguing. If we abandoned our base to the elements then the resulting mess would add further to the ammunition drawn against the right of small expeditions to visit the Antarctic. We had carried our litter with us to the Pole, when every ounce we pulled on our sledges added to the risk. We wanted to demonstrate that it was possible 'to leave only footprints and take only memories' – an objective that is evidently of very low priority amongst those who administer McMurdo Station.

I rose and announced in an absurdly formal manner: 'We are grateful for your offer to fly the expedition to Christchurch, which we accept. However, we have no alternative but for a small group of us to rewinter. Those of us who will be leaving will present themselves tomorrow at whatever time you require.'

Perhaps Captain Shrite did not think that the expedition had within it people who were committed enough to carry this intention through, for if he was surprised, he did not show it.

I caught the shuttle bus with Giles and our two Alaskan bush pilots, Rick Mason and Ed Saunier, out along the flagged road which runs in a great curve on the sea-ice around Cape Armitage, bumping up the steep ramp on to the ice-shelf before terminating its seven-mile journey at Williams Field. Giles had agreed to fly me out to Jack Hayward base in the Cessna. I wanted to spend one last night in our own hut away from the turmoil of McMurdo. There were diaries among my possessions there that I wanted to collect. I looked forward to seeing John Tolson and Mike Stroud again, and was sure that they would have a multitude of questions to ask about events from which they had remained isolated.

The Cessna stood small and forlorn on the edge of the airfield, in marked contrast to several matt-grey Hercules aircraft that sat, massively ponderous, on the snow a few hundred yards away. I crawled into the cramped space behind Giles, who had clambered into the only seat on our stripped-down machine. He handed me the in-flight reading, a butchered copy of *Playboy*, the cover of which now declared it to be a 'Quest Air Publication'. Beside my right elbow was the plastic fuel line and the lever of the small hand pump which was to have been used during the flight to the Pole to transfer fuel from storage barrels into the plane's tanks.

Giles sat and patiently followed the shouted instructions of Ed and Rick standing outside. It was interesting to watch these two very different men as they worked to get the cold and reticent engine to fire. Ed was leggy, swashbuckling and mercurial but methodical, while Rick's inscrutable manner hid a compassionate and generous nature. They were having to swing the propeller by hand because the cold battery was not providing enough power for the electric starter. Periodically Ed would rush round to the cockpit and, leaning across Giles, adjust the choke and throttle controls. Once back at the nose he would shout, 'ignition off?' Giles would check the switch and confirm 'ignition off'. Only then would Ed rotate the stubborn blade and turn the engine towards compression.

'Ignition on,' he would shout, and back would come the reply, 'Ignition on'. Then, grasping the propeller with arms outstretched above his head, he would pull down hard and step quickly back. He went through this routine several times, always moving clear in case the engine fired. Then Rick quietly took over.

'Let's try it with the ignition on.'

I did not understand the significance of what he was about to do, but I could tell from Giles's silent reaction that it was not something about which one could ever become complacent. Rick pulled the propeller through its viscous resistance. With each slow consecutive rotation, I could sense the tension grow in Giles as he gazed through the perspex screen into the concentrated face of the man before him. And then the engine exploded into life. Rick was standing with his head back and the palms of his hands held up in mock astonishment, but without the slightest betrayal of emotion on his face, the transparent disc of the invisible blades spinning inches from his fingers.

'He's a rum character,' said Giles, as Rick strolled off without a word, hands in pockets. Ed climbed in and we took off. It was midnight and the shadows were long.

Robert and Rebecca had walked arm in arm in the cold evening sunlight down the dusty hill out of McMurdo, past the barren hut of Scott's *Discovery* expedition and the iron pipes that lead from the pumping station to the silver fuel tanks that deface this historic point. Looking north from the top of the black volcanic spit, out across the white, frozen, waveless sea, it is possible to forget the ugly town and imagine how it was before man brought time to this place. There beside the wooden Celtic cross, Robert asked Rebecca to marry him, and produced the ring he had worn around his neck throughout the long haul to the Pole.

Later, he tried to get our story out to the world, to balance the negative reports that we knew would now be pouring forth. At 2 A.M., carrying a fistful of dollars donated by friends in McMurdo to pay for phone calls, Robert entered the United States satellite communications office. Before he had time to request the use of the telephone, Peter Wilkniss, who, it seemed, had been watching the building even at this late hour, stormed in and informed the operator that he would lose his job if Robert made as much as a single call. Robert asked Wilkniss why the expedition was being treated in a manner that suggested we were criminals. The American retorted that if there were any more such comments he would remove the entire expedition from his station. Afterwards Robert confided that this was the nearest he had come to assaulting physically anyone in all the years of the expedition, but instead he turned his back and left. He would have to wait until morning, when the public phones at Scott Base could be used to ensure that our side of the story was heard by the world's Press.

The Cessna slid to a halt a few yards from the beach after a bone-jarring trundle across the improvised landing strip on the hard, blue sea-ice. A beaming John Tolson gave us a warm welcome, and there were sincere congratulations from Mike Stroud, who wished for all the world that he had been with us on the Polar journey.

The sun had loosened the frozen grip of winter that had held the beach at Cape Evans unchanged through the long dark months. Now the chalky banks of snow, formed in the lee of the hut and behind the lines of boxes that lay in rows among the rocks, were being slowly etched by the process of ablation. The matt white drifts had metamorphosed into heavy beds of aerated cup-crystals and between them were eroded deep channels that cut through the snow to the black sand. Icicles hanging from the underside of the thick plates of rafted ice overhung the shoreline and dripped into the water that lapped beneath the glassy, pockmarked sea-ice. In the last two weeks the temperature at Cape Evans had risen to within a few degrees of zero and, once, the maximum thermometer had soared to +2°C. It was no longer inconsiderate to leave the door of the hut ajar.

Since our departure for the Pole John and Mike had found their own adventures. They had hauled sledges across 30 miles of sea-ice to the far side of McMurdo Sound and toured the Dry Valleys to the edge of the Polar Plateau. It was a magnificent journey of 240 miles, covered in twenty-two days. It was then John found that humping rucksacks up mountains had its rewards. Later, alone, Mike had tried to force a route up the Blue Glacier to the summit of Mount Lister, but he had to abandon the attempt when poor weather and reduced visibility made wandering about the crevassed glaciers inadvisable.

We sat round the table drinking tea, and talked into the early hours of the morning. Giles and Ed visited Scott's hut and then returned to McMurdo. After a breakfast of tinned kippers and thick slices of bread, we finally went to bed.

The weather deteriorated. Dense white cloud sank lower and lower over the Cape as the morning progressed. Just before noon, when Giles was due to return and begin ferrying us to McMurdo to meet our flight out of the Antarctic, it began to snow. Were we, I thought, to be the ones who would spend another winter in this place? It was then, with a blizzard threatening to maroon us at Cape Evans while Captain Shrite refused to delay evacuation of the expedition, that I began to comprehend the magnitude of Gareth's selfless action. For Steve Broni and Tim Lovejoy, who were to be his companions, it was an opportunity that many would have accepted without hesitation. Antarctica is a unique continent where the seasons and the elements are primeval in their rawness, and to live a year under their authority is an experience of immense power that cannot be gained in a fleeting visit to its shores. In their position I would have done the same. Gareth's decision I could only gauge through my own need to return to normal life. His sacrifice required infinitely more courage than our little adventure following in the footsteps of Scott.

Fortunately the cloud lifted by mid-afternoon and we were drawn from the hut by the drone of the Cessna. Unexpectedly Giles was alone. The Americans had decided to return us to McMurdo by helicopter, and so Giles took the opportunity to leave the aircraft at Cape Evans rather than abandon it on the ice-shelf. Rick Mason had given brief details on how to dismantle the plane and Gareth, armed with a book of instructions and a few spanners, would remove the wings and tail so that the machine could be stored through the year without risk of damage in high winds.

The helicopter arrived with Gareth, Steve Broni and Tim

Lovejoy, but the mood was dominated by the funereal presence of Dr Wilkniss, who stepped into our hut for a brief assessment. He refused an offer of tea, and with a brusque announcement that 'the chopper leaves in twenty minutes', left to wait outside.

There was no time. No time for John and Mike to convey even the briefest summary of the status of the base, no time for Gareth to discuss with Mike, our doctor, the prospect of a year without medical supervision, no time to consider the continuance of the scientific work, or to be sure that Steve and Tim had sufficient clothing for their stay. There was no time to talk to Gareth about the reasons for his choice or to say how much I respected what he was about to do.

One by one we climbed on board the waiting helicopter and into an oppressive atmosphere ruled over by a silent Wilkniss. The crew had often, on their summer flights around Ross Island, dropped in for coffee and a chat; now they spoke only to indicate how the seat belt was fastened. The door slid shut, and through the milky perspex screen I watched the three standing in the drab light of an obscured sky, waiting as the whine of the engines increased to a scream. Tim and Steve were smiling, excited by the prospect of the year ahead; Gareth looked resolute but tired, unrecovered from the walk that was beginning to seem like a dream. We held each other's gaze as the helicopter rose vertically into the air. Then, as the figures grew small beneath us, I saw Gareth turn and begin to take stock of the stores around the hut.

Epilogue
by Robert Swan

It was December 1986, less than two weeks from Christmas, and more than ten months since we had said goodbye to the three who stayed behind for another winter in the Antarctic, and had boarded the American Hercules on the first stage of the journey home in a mood of both triumph and dismay. Most of this book was now written, and while expedition members read and mulled over the proofs, I found myself heading south again, into the perpetual light of the Antarctic summer.

The Twin Otter taxied along the windswept runway at Punta Arenas, at the southernmost tip of South America, and turned its nose into the wind. All around us lay a rugged hostile landscape of snow-capped mountains and deep fjords. As I watched Giles Kershaw and his co-pilot Ron Kerr going through their pre-flight checks, the plane shuddered alarmingly, buffeted by squalls driven by the fierce winds. Giles sensed my concern and stretched round in his seat to offer me some assurance.

'Don't worry, we won't be turning back.' He smiled, and I grinned weakly back.

Ahead was a daunting journey, a flight that would take us across some of the bleakest and most forbidding territory on this planet. To cover the 3,400 or so miles to Cape Evans on the far side of the Antarctic continent, we would have to land twice on rough ice strips to refuel from barrels deposited earlier by parachute. At the end of it we would pluck Gareth Wood and his two companions from their year of isolation, and return to write the closing chapter of our expedition.

In perfect conditions the mission would take just a few days, but Giles had equipped us to withstand weeks of unpredictable weather, or even disaster. Normally a 17-seater, the aircraft had been adapted to take only six seats and an increased fuel load. Behind me were five drums of extra fuel, tents, sleeping bags and a supply of emergency rations. I hoped they would not be needed.

The flight path would begin by taking us south over Tierra del Fuego, across the Drake Passage then on over the Antarctic peninsula – a spectacular region of soaring peaks and glaciers that tumble into the ocean. At least we were beginning the Antarctic crossing where our own British Antarctic Survey conducted their operations.

'The weather looks grim for the first leg,' Giles said over his shoulder, 'but that's probably just as well. You want to fly through the bad weather to get to the good. You don't want it the other way round.'

Well, it was never going to be easy, I told myself. We could not discount altogether the possibility of an unscheduled forced landing. If we had any sort of mechanical trouble we would have to go down, Giles reminded me cheerfully. His main concerns were clearing the high Darwin Mountains of Tierra del Fuego and getting through the storm that was forecast over the Drake Passage.

'The mountains are a problem because of the weight we have to carry,' he said. 'We'll ice up as we go, which makes us even heavier, and ice will form on the leading edge of the wings, which reduces lift.'

'What about the storm?' I shouted above the engine noise.

'Too big to fly round. We'll just have to punch right through the heart of it.'

I prayed the weather would be kind to us. Storms in Antarctica can spring up from nowhere on even the clearest days, blocking out the sun in minutes, or blowing with enough force to send stationary aircraft skidding across the ice. Temperatures drop to a level where metal becomes brittle, and I wondered what effect that would have on an aircraft. With our march to the Pole, we had not conquered Antarctica: it had let us through. The same would apply to this flight. Giles was certainly not going there to take Antarctica on, as if doing gladiatorial battle; it was a calculated risk. We were going with Giles's experience and my determination, but it was as well to recognize that if Antarctica did not wish to let us through, it would simply clobber us. I suddenly had a vivid image of the fifty-one known abandoned aircraft skeletons in Antarctica.

Giles interrupted my thoughts as the rainstorm passed, opening a large blue hole in the Patagonian sky.

'Okay, let's go!' he said in a raised voice, giving a thumbs up to the co-pilot, before pulling on his favourite beaten-up old baseball cap.

'Giles, this isn't your idea of a weather window, is it?' I yelled over the revving engine.

'What d'you mean? This is high adventure. That's what you wanted, isn't it?'

A few moments later flight X-ray X-ray Bravo lifted from the runway into the blue over the Magellan Strait.

Some days after our departure in the American Hercules last January, Gareth Wood had gone to Scott Base to contact his parents in Canada about his decision to stay on in Antarctica for another year. He took with him a short list of odds and ends of equipment that he wanted the expedition in London to fly down to him before the regular mail flights came to an end at the onset of winter. He was treated to a frosty reception. The New Zealanders would allow him access only to the post office, and then later, after some wry remarks, to the lavatory. He told the officer in charge that he had full sledging gear and a tent pitched just outside the Base, and left.

Although he knew that he would be even more rigorously barred from the American Station at McMurdo a couple of miles away, he decided nevertheless to pay a courtesy call on Commander Harler and Captain Shrite to test the extent of his exclusion there. Bob Harler, who commanded United States air operations in the Antarctic, spoke politely and at length about general meteorological subjects, and Shrite said how pleased he was to see Gareth looking better. When asked for their permission to make a radio check with South Pole Station, they told Gareth to go right ahead and make his check, but there the cordiality ended. If they could not actually bar him from walking the streets of MacTown, they wanted Gareth to be in no doubt about the fact that all buildings there were 'off-limits' to Footsteps expeditioners.

To ensure that there was no relaxation of the official line concerning hospitality, a detailed policy document (which had been read aloud to Gareth) was distributed to all personnel, who were obliged to sign and return it, indicating it was understood that not even a tube of toothpaste was to be sold to the Footsteps people from the stores; no accommodation, or refreshments, or laundry facilities were to be provided.

Staff at McMurdo and Scott Base were obviously upset by the instructions they received, and though concerned about the effect on their jobs, many turned a blind eye to the Footsteps regulations. Even so, hasty conversations with old acquaintances encountered in the street were conducted with furtive glances over the shoulder. But despite the rigid clampdown on freedom of speech and association in this barren territory, where friendship had enjoyed an unbroken tradition, Gareth made it clear to both the American and New Zealand authorities that he had no intention other than to abide by their wishes.

The Footsteps expeditioners stayed well clear of McMurdo until the end of February, when all three men set off to Scott Base to use the radio telephone link and to send mail on the last flight out before winter. They pitched a tent outside the Base perimeter, booked calls at the post office and handed over their mail. Again it was made clear to them that all other facilities were out of bounds, yet nothing could keep back the tide of surreptitious offers that were heaped upon them.

By chance, Gareth ran into the South Pole Station manager, Lee Schoen, who invited him into a bar for a beer. He seemed unaware of any restrictions and was surprised when Gareth politely declined. Gareth mentioned an official Telex which had been sent from McMurdo to Washington concerning charges to the Footsteps expedition for meals and medical facilities at the South Pole and the effect our presence had had on morale. Schoen was taken aback. Morale had never been higher, he said, and the two parted with an arrangement to make radio contact at a later date. Other personnel returning from a spell of duty at the South Pole were equally unaware of the embargo placed on Gareth and the others, and were shocked to discover that they were forbidden to invite them in for so much as a cup of tea.

The three winterers enlivened their lonely vigil in April with a journey to Cape Royds and Shackleton's original Base, an adventure which came a little too close to disaster and nearly cost Gareth his life. In the twilight before three months without sight of the sun, they took a short cut across the old sea-ice trapped in Backdoor Bay where a crack had opened up and then frozen over again with a thin ice covering. Such small cracks can usually be crossed quite easily with a jump. Gareth did not see the leopard seal until the moment it struck.

'Gareth was out ahead,' Steven Broni told us. 'He tapped his boot on the thin sea-ice to test its strength and the next thing I knew he was flat on his back. I just heard him screaming, and then I saw this huge creature had him by the leg.'

The leopard seal is a giant predator that grows to twelve or fourteen feet in length and can weigh anything up to 750 or 1,000 lbs. This one had burst through the veneer of clear blue ice an inch thick covering the crack, shattering it in shards, like plate glass exploding. With its jaws locked round Gareth's lower leg, the long incisors puncturing deep into his calf muscle, the seal began dragging him towards the open water of the crack. Gareth took up the story.

'The seal must have been tracking us for some time. I remember this head with huge jaws, like a giant snake, appearing suddenly in front of me. I fell over backwards because I could feel myself being pulled in. Steve rushed up and I yelled at him to kick it with his cramponed boots. It was like something out of a Japanese horror movie. I knew that if I hadn't had my left crampon dug into the ice, it would have had me in the icy water.'

Tim Lovejoy had witnessed the whole thing from some distance away and raced across the ice to help. Gareth's foot was dragged out over the water before, suddenly, the seal let go, and with blood pouring down the side of its head where Steve had gone for it, sank back into the crack. Steve was in a daze when Tim arrived and Gareth pulled at his trouser leg to inspect the damage. Afraid that the seal might return, Tim began wrestling Gareth away from the water's edge.

'It had a head like a dinosaur,' he said. 'Steve had inflicted a lot of damage and blood was everywhere. It was a gruesome sight.'

Then, without warning, the seal surfaced again and charged towards the three of them, this time flinging itself over on to the ice in a great spray of blood and water. It caught Gareth again, clamping its jaws around his right boot. Steve ran forward.

'I remember aiming for its eye. The thing was actually looking at me with a cold stare. It gave no sign of emotion or that I was hurting it.'

After a moment, the seal released its grip and Tim dragged Gareth to safety. The sudden violence left all three in a state of shock. It was two weeks before they were sleeping properly again.

The bizarre exclusion from McMurdo was lifted momentarily after the accident for the briefest of medical consultations by radio when Gareth got back to our hut. Otherwise he tended to his wounds himself and slowly they healed.

At the end of May, they ventured another journey to Scott Base, this time in winter darkness, to use the post office radio telephone to make contact with London. They knew that there would be one winter mail-drop, without the plane landing, in June, and that would be the last chance for some while to receive news and the few small items of equipment that would be useful to them. Again they camped outside the Base, but the cook invited them to stay to dinner. Jim Rankin, the officer in charge, was asked by one of his men what he thought the political repercussions of this gesture would be.

'What happens at Scott Base while I'm over in McMurdo tonight,' he replied, 'I won't know about.'

Everyone felt awkward during the meal, especially when Rankin returned and ignored their presence. Gareth and the others went back to their tent. It was crammed with parcels of food! The enormous generosity of these gifts was overwhelming, and yet the three Footsteps men cursed the extra weight they would have to drag on their sledges the 17 miles back to Cape Evans. Despite their own food supplies (enough to last for two years), they could hardly leave the donations behind in the snow, to be discovered and so embarrass their unknown well-wishers.

They decided not to tempt fate again by risking another visit to collect the mail in June. Eventually some New Zealanders visited Jack Hayward Base in July, bringing with them airdropped mail and asking Gareth to radio Scott Base. It appeared there was uproar as a result of statements I had made in the New Zealand press. When he got through, Gareth was told by Jim Rankin that there had been a shift in New Zealand policy and he was now authorized to extend normal basic hospitality to the Footsteps winterers. He was urged to telephone Bob Thompson at the New Zealand Antarctic office in Christchurch when next he visited Scott Base.

It was not until 14 August that Gareth spoke on the telephone to New Zealand. Thompson, who had just returned from a meeting in Washington with Dr Wilkniss and John Heap of the British Foreign Office, proposed flying the Footsteps team out of Antarctica as soon as possible, and at no extra cost to the expedition. He was unsure whether London as yet knew of the plan. Gareth repeated his concern about abandoning the Base, the aircraft and our equipment and said that he would make no move without the agreement of the expedition in London.

Rankin's problem over 'basic hospitality', he said, was one of definition: just what was 'basic' or 'normal'? Well, the least he supposed he could do after their long discussion about the new turn of events was to offer a meal and a bed for the night. Damned if he did and damned if he didn't, Gareth accepted.

Meanwhile, American staff were still expressly forbidden to visit Jack Hayward Base, but with the slight thaw in the New Zealand quarter, our team anticipated a few friendly overtures. They put up a sign showing a plate, knife and fork, a bed and a petrol pump on it, and wrote 'Cape Evans Rest Area – 500 yards'. On the back they wrote, 'This sign erected by Private Enterprise'. But though some Americans made visits to Scott's hut 200 yards away, no one approached our hut. Some weeks later, the sign was replaced with another which Gareth, Steven and Tim felt more accurately reflected their status. It read: 'Leper Colony'.

On 11 September, two tracked vehicles appeared suddenly at Jack Hayward Base, bringing mail and a hamper from the officer in charge of Scott Base. The drivers also let slip news of a disturbing rumour they had heard about a forcible removal by the Americans of the three Footsteps men from Antarctica. The idea was laughable; what measure of force could be applied by officers of a supposedly allied power in international territory? This sort of petty psychological warfare was, as far as possible, ignored by Gareth, who refused to allow it to diminish morale at our Base.

More unexpected visitors arrived in an unmistakable VIP vehicle on 5 October. As Dr Peter Wilkniss (head of the US Antarctic Polar Research Program), Stewart Guy (the new officer in charge of New Zealand's Scott Base) and other high-ranking officials climbed out of the Hagland, Tim and Steve went outside to greet them while Gareth switched on the tape recorder. He wanted an undisputable record of what this powerful delegation had come to deliver.

Once seated round the table with tea and coffee, they got down to business. The New Zealanders began by expanding on the terms of their recent change in policy. They said that they had received as much bad publicity back home as we had, and their handling of the Footsteps affair had reached the attention of the Prime Minister himself. Everyone was anxious now to defuse the situation and let the matter cool down. They were willing to open up full facilities to us, and even keep the post office open to us (could they legitimately bar us if postal services were to remain open to everyone else?); they would do all this providing the Footsteps expedition kept them fully informed of all its plans in a new spirit of mutual trust and exchange. They even planned to publish a policy document outlining their fresh approach to all private expeditions along these lines. They wanted there to be full co-operation or none at all.

'I must emphasize that this is not United States policy,' Dr Wilkniss continually interjected.

What he had come to offer was a free flight out. Gareth told the American, as he had earlier the New Zealanders, that he could make no move without the agreement of the expedition

in London. His supplies of food and fuel were more than
enough to see them through.

Soon afterwards, in a story circulated by the Reuters News
Agency, Wilkniss was quoted as saying that the three wintering
Footsteps men 'are principled, capable people, but they are
showing signs of strain. We and the New Zealanders will make
sure no harm comes to their equipment but they should get out
of there.' The offer to fly the men out, 'no strings attached',
Reuters said, did not include moving general expedition equipment. The *Daily Mail* in London reported Wilkniss as saying
'they have run out of proper food and their generator is down',
adding that he had 'begged them to leave by air immediately
for the nearest US base'. *The Times* said the expedition 'denied
claims by US officials that three of its members were showing
signs of strain and had run out of proper food'. When *The Press*
in New Zealand asked Dr Wilkniss why his offer of a free flight
out had been made when the expedition had plans for an
evacuation by sea in February, he said, 'There is a certain
probability that plans don't pan out.'

It was incomprehensible. For all their hostility towards
private expeditions in Antarctica, it was hard to understand
what the Americans hoped to gain from such distorted public
pronouncements. Perhaps, we thought, the unwelcome news
that a glamorous young Norwegian glaciologist, Dr Monica
Kristensen, was on her way south with dogs and a support ship,
to attempt Amundsen's route from the Bay of Whales to the
Pole – an expedition that at one time in their planning might
have run concurrently with ours – had something to do with it.
Whatever the reason, I could not allow these reports to go
unchallenged.

Until now, Richard Down, our expedition co-ordinator,
working closely with John Heap at the Foreign Office, had
always refused to over-react to American hostility, either at the
time of the loss of the *Southern Quest* or in the months of
attrition since McMurdo had been put out of bounds to the
three winterers. Keep to protocol, they had both counselled,
and the terms of the Antarctic Treaty. If the Americans asked
us not to do this or that, then abide by their wishes, and Gareth
had been scrupulous in keeping to this as far as circumstances

allowed him. We were capable of staying in Antarctica to clear up our Base, we had a right to do so, and we were not going to make difficulties for anyone else if it had to be done alone.

At the same time, cut off from Gareth as we were in London, I could not be altogether certain that there was no grain of truth behind what the Americans were reported as saying. Had the boys suddenly come to the end of their tether? It did not seem at all likely that Gareth's professionalism would have deserted him or that his exemplary sense of self-discipline had evaporated, but I had to be sure. We Telexed him via Scott Base and waited for him to get through to us on the radio telephone. Richard took the call when it came and recorded Gareth's very clear replies to the points he raised from the Wilkniss news story. Then he called a press conference at the Royal Geographical Society, where we played back the tape.

It produced the first sign of a thaw in American attitudes, for it was not long before reports reached us that the National Science Foundation had asked the American Alpine Club to produce a paper on what they saw as the proper and reasonable way for the United States government to deal with the presence of private expeditions in Antarctica. If no more, it was a step in the right direction.

Back in the real world, we had for some time been planning our final evacuation – men, hut, aircraft and equipment – leaving no trace behind of our incursion into the frozen wilderness. The original idea had been to arrange for the Norwegian '90° South' expedition to retrieve our team and everything, including the Cessna, on their ship *Aurora*. Yet it had always been in the back of my mind that we might need to collect the men first by air. When, a year earlier, *Southern Quest* had returned to collect us from the Polar walk, the ice conditions had been among the worst ever known. If it was bad again this year, I did not want to risk a second failure. It was unthinkable now to admit defeat by going cap in hand to the National Science Foundation for help in closing down our operation.

When it became clear that the Norwegians were held up by the weather,* I asked Richard Down to investigate alternative

* Bedevilled by bad weather and overstretched resources, Dr Monica

methods of withdrawing. Once more Giles Kershaw came to our rescue. He put us in touch with Bart Lewis of 'Adventure Network', a Canadian company specializing in Antarctic travel. With just two weeks to go to Christmas, we decided to take the plunge, using a Twin Otter from Calgary which was already in Chile, staging flights for mountaineers in Antarctica and available for Giles to fly me in from Punta Arenas. Dick Smith and *Australian Geographic* generously provided most of the finance.

It was to be a marathon round trip of almost 7,000 miles, across Antarctica to the other side of the barren continent, by a route probably never flown before in one piece, all the way to Cape Evans on the Ross Sea. It would entail refuelling by means of a small hand-pump from fifty-gallon drums previously dropped into pre-selected landing spots on the ice. Before we took off from Punta Arenas, Giles assured me that he had calculated everything very carefully so as to avoid calling upon United States satellites for weather briefings or any other sort of assistance, except in the most critical and dire emergency.

'WILL VISIT FLYING FISH IN LATE DECEMBER' was the Telex message to Gareth's parents in Canada, transmitted from Scott Base as soon as we had confirmed our intentions to the team. The coded signal made sense only to Gareth's family; to the unwanted eyes of the NSF it would be meaningless.

'That was Gareth's way of telling us he'd be home for Christmas,' John Wood told a newspaper. '*Flying Fish* is the name of our sailboat. That message wouldn't mean anything to anyone but us.'

If word leaked out, we knew only too well that it was not beyond the power of the Americans to ground the flight even before it took off. As the Twin Otter soared into the Chilean sky, Gareth, Steve and Tim began packing the equipment and dismantling the hut. It seemed some sort of auspicious omen that we were within a few hours of the 75th anniversary of the precise moment when Amundsen had succeeded in becoming the first man to reach the South Pole.

The Twin Otter climbed high over the forbidding waters of

Kristensen's team of four dog sledges was forced to turn back when still 250 miles from the Pole.

Drake Passage and got above the storm. Soon we would be over the Antarctic Peninsula and the area where Roger and I had spent a year with the British Antarctic Survey in 1981. Our course would then take us west across the unclaimed sector of Antarctica, the region where the American, Admiral Byrd, had explored in the 1930s.

Once past the storm we entered the high pressure area which hangs almost permanently over the Antarctic interior, sending turbulent weather systems circling round the edge of the continent. A scene of breathtaking beauty spread to the horizon beneath us, a white desert interrupted here and there with mountainous outcrops of dark rock that penetrated above the sea of snow and ice. For the first time, I think, I comprehended the enormity of our endeavour, setting out to cross this awesome, empty landscape on foot.

After one refuelling on Adelaide Island, Giles again brought the plane down to a much lower altitude as he began to search for the cluster of flags and tents that marked our next refuelling stop, the Base Camp of a mountaineering party in the Ellsworth Mountains. This was surely one of the remotest self-service filling stations in the world. As we touched down in a flurry of disturbed snow, the front wheel drifted down to steady the skimming path of the Twin Otter's skis at the rear. Outside the temperature was −25°C. The engines would have to be kept running in turn for periods to prevent a disastrous icing up that would leave us stranded.

After a total of twenty-four hours in the air and ten on the ground refuelling, we touched down on the sea-ice in front of the hut at Cape Evans. It was an emotional moment. Gareth strode across the ice on those long legs of his, unaware that I was aboard, and greeted Giles at the cockpit window. I jumped down from the rear door and clasped Gareth's hand. It was almost noon on 15 December. Only the bare shell of the hut remained standing, all ready for a quick dismantling. Everyone seemed to be talking at once as we went inside. It was tempting to relax and sit around for an hour or two, catching up on each other's stories, but there was still much to be done and we did not have unlimited time.

While Giles, Ron and I snatched a few hours sleep, the

others kept going with feverish activity. Ron Kerr slept in the plane in case the ice cracked and the Twin Otter began drifting out to sea. By 2 A.M., the sun still shining high in the sky, everything was packed, neatly stacked and secured to withstand the fiercest gale. I wanted to pay a courtesy visit to McMurdo before we left but the Americans told me over the radio that they were too busy to see me. Giles flew me to Scott Base instead for a brief but pleasant reunion with the New Zealanders. Giles was keen to get away while the weather held. The storm over Drake Strait had broken in two and was being pushed north, either side of Tierra del Fuego, by a high pressure system that Chilean weather experts were forecasting to last for the next forty-eight hours at most. If we got airborne now, we could have ideal flying conditions – high winds and clear skies – all the way. After only a short rest in sleeping bags, we left Cape Evans less than thirty-six hours after arriving. Already the weather system was breaking down to the east, and we flew low and fast ahead of the approaching front in deteriorating conditions, over the frozen wastes, a tiny aircraft carrying six men back to civilization. If our luck held, we would be out of Antarctica the next day.

I found myself praying that all this wild loveliness would be left untouched. 'Man, having destroyed the whales, may end by destroying himself,' Cherry-Garrard wrote. 'The penguins may end like the prehistoric reptiles from which they sprang. All may follow the mammoths and dinosaurs into fossilized oblivion, like the ferns which grew at the South Pole two hundred million years ago, found by the Polar Party on the Beardmore and carried on their sledge to the end at Wilson's special request: museum pieces of life in time.'

For me also, Antarctica today is unique in one overriding respect: no one owns it. Every other continent on this earth has seen wars and more recently urban pollution, testimony to the greed that almost overwhelms human history. It is up to us to ensure that Antarctica, the last of the virgin continents, is the exception in this saddening catalogue of human destruction.

As we flew, my mind wandered back over all the years of effort we had put into our expedition, back to the cold, damp warehouse at West India Docks, back to our very first office –

just a few square feet of space, a desk and a battered old typewriter – all those years ago, with just William Fenton, Rebecca and myself. I remembered writing out a personal cheque for the first payment on the warehouse when we had no money and did not know where the next was coming from. It was a bleak time, begging gas cylinders from the local supplier with the promise of payment next week, a time of constant soul-searching about the commitment other people were making to an enterprise that had nothing to show for itself. Even now, when I am asked what was the toughest aspect of the whole expedition, I can truthfully answer that it was receiving letters from schoolboys that said, 'Dear Mr Swan, please don't get cold, here's 10p', or coming home late to the warehouse to find Rebecca's envelope containing her tips from her job as a coat-check girl, or William's very last savings lying on the expedition desk, or the thought of Rebecca cycling home through dockland to the warehouse in pouring rain in the early hours of the morning because I had taken the car to go and pester yet another far-flung person or company for money for the expedition . . . nothing, absolutely nothing, was harder to take than that.

After the joy of reunion with Gareth, Steven and Tim, I had walked the 200 yards from the neat stack comprising all that was left of our Base to take a last look at Scott's hut. It was a beautifully clear day, the air so clean, the light so bright that it seemed I could see all the way to the Pole. I remembered the feeling I had had on my very first visit – the feeling of belonging, almost of coming home. It made me think how closely we had indeed travelled in the footsteps of Scott. Memories flooded back of all the parallels that contrived to bring our story so close to his. I recalled driving down to Sheerness, where Scott's ship *Discovery* was in dry dock. It was cold and raining, and the night watchman let me sleep on board, in Scott's bunk. I thought of Warehouse 34 in West India Dock, where our stores were assembled, so close to Warehouse 13 which had been Scott's, and meeting Stoker Bill Burton, the last surviving member of Scott's expedition. I remembered being guided out of harbour by the tug *Lyttleton*, whose first task afloat had been to do the same for the *Terra Nova* all those years ago.

The atmosphere at Scott's hut at Cape Evans had changed since last I was here, just before setting out on the Polar walk. Gone was the air of eager anticipation. Everything was at peace. The hut was empty. It was as if the team had dispersed, content at last. I was overcome with an intense satisfaction, a quiet elation at what we had accomplished: not simply the Pole, though that in itself was a great prize for us. Perhaps – I dared to think – we had also come close to achieving what Scott had described as 'the height of that fine conception which is realized when a party of men go forth to face hardships, dangers and difficulties with their own unaided efforts.' My own gratitude for the company of such professionals as Roger Mear, Gareth Wood, Mike Stroud, John Tolson, Graham Phippen, Peter Malcolm, Giles Kershaw and Richard Down is inexpressible.

In our race to get to the Pole we had retraced Scott's route in seventy exacting, exhilarating days. Each one of us had stretched himself to his limit. Each one of us had known moments of acute anguish, of personal fulfilment, of self-revelation, and of wonder at the beauty and scale of the bleakest continent on earth.

On 11 February 1987, we received news that the ship *Greenpeace* had safely loaded the hut, the aircraft and all our remaining food and equipment. We had finally removed all trace of ourselves from Antarctica and left the continent as we had found it.

I am left with Cherry-Garrard's closing words in *The Worst Journey in the World* – 'Any age, new or old, wants courage and faith. To me, and perhaps to you, the interest in this story is the men, and it is the spirit of the men, "the response of the spirit", which is interesting rather than what they did or failed to do: except in a superficial sense they never failed. That is how I see it, and I knew them pretty well. It is a story about human minds with all kinds of ideas and questions involved, which stretch beyond the furthest horizons.'

I hope that others may find the inspiration in our story to stretch themselves beyond their own horizons.

What I did was not special. I simply said to myself, 'We'll walk to the Pole', and on 11 January 1986, we arrived there.

I described my adventure to the four-and-a-half-year-old daughter of a friend. She heard me out patiently, fixed me with a searching look, and said, 'Why not?'

Why not indeed?

LETTERS TO THE EDITOR

Obstacles in the steps of Scott

From Lord Shackleton and others
Sir, There have been a number of statements and criticisms of the "In the footsteps of Scott" expedition, both as to the competence of its members and their right to be in the Antarctic. We believe these criticisms are unfair and unjustified

"In the footsteps of Scott" was a unique expedition. Robert Swan, Roger Mear and Gareth Wood set out to walk to the South Pole manhauling their sledges, recalling Captain Scott's epic journey. While it never pretended to be anything but a commemorative adventure retracing Scott's and Shackleton's route, it did have a limited scientific programme.

In view of its exceptional nature, extra care was taken to examine the membership and logistics of the expedition before the Royal Geographical Society decided to support this highly professional venture. On January 11, 1986, the three men reached the South Pole.

Simultaneously with the arrival at the Pole, the support ship Southern Quest was crushed by the ice and sank off McMurdo Sound. Whatever its limitations may have been, the ship had been ice-strengthened and passed to Lloyds Ice Class III. Stronger ships than Southern Quest have encountered serious trouble in Antarctic waters this season.

The Institute of London Underwriters paid the full £100,000 for total loss within four days of her sinking. Arrangements have also been made through the same route to pay the bill rendered by the United States authorities for £21,000, for subsequently flying the expedition from McMurdo to New Zealand.

The captain, Graham Phippen, with eight years' experience with the British Antarctic Survey, was duty-bound, after the loss of his ship, to take up the offer of American helicopter assistance. Had that help not been available, the crew could have made landfall themselves; but the prudent choice was to accept the generous help offered.

Meanwhile the aircraft which had been dismantled in Australia and shipped down on Southern Quest had already been offloaded and flown. Thus Captain Giles Kershaw (one of the most experienced of polar pilots) was fully prepared to take off for the Pole to retrieve Swan, Mear and Wood. But the United States officials, who had already accepted that his flight plan was feasible, asked him not to fly. He agreed to this as a matter of courtesy after the assistance given by the United States to the crew of Southern Quest. Consequently, the US authorities undertook to return the polar party to McMurdo.

Regretfully, we feel bound to comment on the quite extraordinary reaction to the expedition from certain Antarctic authorities arising out of their declared policy that they would not support "private expeditions". A letter signed by 56 members of McMurdo and Scott Base stations we think tells the tale.

After warmly congratulating the expedition the signatories went on to say: "What we cannot accept is the shamefully hostile treatment of your group, the failure to extend to you access to communication facilities and restrictions placed upon personal interaction among us."

Those who have heard the recording or read the transcripts of the official exchanges can only regard them as an aberration in stark contrast to the warm and generous reception of the expedition by those manning the South Pole, McMurdo and Scott Base Antarctic stations.

The expedition has left three men in the Antarctic to care for their hut and aircraft and to make sure that everything is removed next year, so as to leave Antarctica as they found it. These three men have been banned by the authorities from visiting Scott and McMurdo bases, except for the use of the post office at Scott Base. This means that normal Antarctic hospitality cannot be accorded to them without special permission.

The view has also been expressed by certain authorities that only governmental expeditions should participate in Antarctic work. We strongly support the scientific effort of the Government-based expeditions within the Antarctic Treaty, but to exclude properly planned and supported expeditions approved by societies such as ours is something that we cannot accept.

We write with two objectives in mind. One is to set the record straight. The expedition has been called "a group of enthusiastic amateurs"; enthusiastic they are, but amateur certainly not. Secondly, in the light of the unfortunate happenings described above, we wish to see an understanding established that will preclude bureaucratic difficulties in the future.

Then we can expect the time-honoured amity that has always existed among polar explorers and scientists to continue within the Antarctic Treaty.
Yours sincerely,
SHACKLETON,
GEORGE BISHOP,
VIVIAN FUCHS,
JOHN HEMMING,
JOHN HUNT,
PETER SCOTT,
Royal Geographical Society,
Kensington Gore, SW7.

APPENDIX 1   Meteorological Report

by Raymond Chapell

Antarctica's weather is dominated throughout the year by an area of high pressure located over the continent, which in winter extends to much of the seasonal ice that forms out to Latitude 65° South. It can be considered as a stable air mass producing relative good weather and very low temperatures. If this were all that had to be contended with, exploration of the continent would be relatively simple, but the Antarctic weather is caused by the combination of extremely cold air from the continent meeting the relatively warm air from the surrounding areas. Where these two air masses come into contact the cold, dry dense air lifts the warmer, moist, less dense air, leaving an area of low pressure on the surface. It is the great contrast in temperature between these two air masses that causes the violent nature of the weather over Antarctica.

On any given day weather systems can be found that extend from as far south as the upper Polar Plateau and north to the Auckland Islands. With no major land mass around the Antarctic to block them, or slow them down, these extensive systems move as fast as 60 knots clockwise around the continent. They can last for many days and travel great distances. Despite the great number of these storms few actually penetrate on to the 10,000 ft high upper plateau. Most pass over Marie Byrd Land which is approximately 3,000 ft in elevation. Local weather patterns on the continent and the surrounding coastal areas are dominated by the influence of the dramatic changes in topography, especially on the Ross Ice Shelf.

Captain Scott, with the aid of his meteorologist, Dr George Simpson, discovered during the 1910–13 expedition, that the winds on the western side of the Ross Ice Shelf blow predominantly from the south. Little was then understood about the causes of this phenomenon which would later be called a 'mountain barrier wind'. The mechanism is characterized by a stable, cold air mass moving off Marie Byrd Land into the Ross Ice Shelf, which then continues to move east towards the Trans-Antarctic Mountains. The mountains then deflect the wind northwards to Ross Island and the coast.

This was why predominantly southerly headwinds were encountered by both Scott and the 'Footsteps' expedition during their journeys to the foot of the Beardmore Glacier. In comparing the wind-speed data recorded on Scott's Polar journey and that of the 'Footsteps' expedition, it is noticeable that winds of Beaufort Force 4 and above were encountered more frequently by Scott. One reason for this was the presence of a strong low pressure system over the Ross Ice Shelf which gave a steeper pressure gradient and helped to increase the intensity of the southerly wind. A classic example was the storm that delayed Scott from 3 to 8 December.

Phenomena of this sort located at 83° 20′S are evidence of a storm of major proportions over the Ross Ice Shelf. It is an uncommon occurrence in the region at that time of year, and it is unusual for a coastal disturbance with such warm temperatures to penetrate as far inland as the Beardmore Glacier.

It was Scott's misfortune to experience this storm, which increased the pressure field over the Ross Ice Shelf, causing Beaufort Force 9 winds and the depositing of an enormous amount of snow. There is no evidence of an intense storm of this nature during the journey of the 'Footsteps' expedition, despite on several occasions temperatures rising due to the presence of warmer maritime air being transported in from a surface ridge of high pressure near Marie Byrd Land. The chief cause of the winds encountered on the Ross Ice Shelf in 1985 was the mountain barrier wind effect associated occasionally with a weak low pressure system over the Ice Shelf.

Winter weather patterns in the vicinity of Ross Island are dominated by outbreaks of extremely cold air flowing off the high Polar Plateau on to the Ross Ice Shelf. Running parallel to the Trans-Antarctic Mountains they produced a predominantly southerly flow over the western Ross Ice Shelf.

Winds also flow off Marie Byrd Land on to the Ross Ice

Shelf, thus inducing even stronger mountain barrier winds with accompanying blowing snow. As the air moves along the Trans-Antarctic Mountains towards the Ross Sea, it encounters Ross Island which is approximately 40 nautical miles east of the northern portion of the Trans-Antarctic Mountains. There the air flow is diverted round the island, creating a disturbed flow in the region. The winds recorded by Scott's party at Cape Evans blew almost always from the south-east, except for an occasional northerly wind of very little force. The same can be said for the 'Footsteps' expedition. Accompanying the strong south-easterly wind, both parties experienced similar temperature extremes of actual snowfall during strong southerly gales because the very cold air off the continent is incapable of holding moisture in amounts significant enough to produce snow. The snow that does fall as precipitation on Ross Island during the winter months usually occurs when a large migratory low pressure system moves near the Ross Ice Shelf from the Ross Sea, transporting relatively warmer air on to the ice-shelf. This in turn produced a southerly flow over the western Ross Ice Shelf, with a marked increase in temperature, such abnormally high temperatures and falling snow preceding the onset of gale force winds on the island. Conditions like this, infrequent during the winter night, but common when the sun returns in the spring (August to October), caused both expeditions to delay their departures for the Pole until November.

The complexity of the winds and temperatures around Ross Island during the winter can best be illustrated by Wilson's winter journey to Cape Crozier with Bowers and Cherry-Garrard in 1911 and its repeat by three members of the 'Footsteps' expedition during June and July 1985. The temperatures and winds encountered by both parties are classic examples of a winter outbreak of continental air flowing off the Polar Plateau. Both parties experienced extremely cold temperatures on the journey and distinct changes in the prevailing wind direction. At the eastern end of Ross Island the winds were from the south-west, while at Cape Evans they were from the south-east, the island deflecting the predominant southerly wind from the Ice Shelf to south-westerly near Cape Crozier.

Both parties also noted the lack of winds located at Tranquil Bay (Windless Bight), which is located midway along the south side of Ross Island, yet another effect of the deflection of winds around Ross Island. Both expeditions experienced similar meteorological conditions during the winter months at Cape Evans.

APPENDIX 1

Meteorological Log of the Expedition's Walk

Note: the different types of cloud are:

cirrus – Ci	altostratus – As	stratus – St
cirrostratus – CiSt	nimbostratus – Ns	cumulus – Cu
altocumulus – Ac	stratocumulus – Sc	cumulonimbus – Cb
lenticularis – Len, as in AcLen – altocumulus lenticularis.		Scott's Register uses ASt for altostratus

Date	Temperature C				Wind Spd		Wind Dir		Pressure mb		Cloud cover		Comment	
	a.m.	p.m.	max	min	a.m.	p.m.	a.m.	p.m.	a.m.	p.m.	(type)	a.m.	a.m.	p.m.
Nov 4	-13.0	-15.0	-13.0	-17.0	0-1	3-4	SW	SSW	986.5	987.0	StCu	8		blustery squalls force 4-5 ground blizzard all day
Nov 5	-15.0	-18.5	-8.0	-22.0	0	0			982.5	973	AcSt	1	clear sunny	blowing
Nov 6	-9.5	-10.0	-7.0	-25.5	1-2	0	NWN		964	965	CiSt	5	light wind clear	blown snow
Nov 7	-12.0	-11.0	-7.0	-22.0	1	3	SW	S	978	990	St	4	blowing snow vis. 150 yds	zero vis. 10-12 sunny late p.m.
Nov 8	-11.0	-12.0	-8.5	-25.5	0	0			994	994	StCu,St	7-8	poor contrast White Is. vis.	clear at 3 p.m. sunny calm
Nov 9	-16.0	-17.0	-7.5	-22.5	1	1	S	S	989	987	StCu	1	good contrast clear vis.	clear all day v. light S wind
Nov 10	-19.0	-18.0	?	-23.0	4-5	3		S	985	983			blizzard	much snow
Nov 11	-13.5	-22.5	-11.0	-28.5	0-1	0		S	986	982		0	clear, calm	fine, clear
Nov 12	-13.0	-22.5	-11.0	-32.5	0	0			977	967	StCuLen	1	haze, still gentle breeze	light westerly winds SW 12 p.m.
Nov 13	-19.5	-16.5	-12.0	-19.0	5-6	3	SW	SW	963.5	960	StCuLen	1	clear	increasing to 4

Meteorological Log of the Expedition's Walk (*Cont.*)

Date	Temperature C a.m.	p.m.	max	min	Wind Spd a.m.	p.m.	Wind Dir a.m.	p.m.	Pressure mb a.m.	p.m.	Cloud cover a.m.		Comment a.m.	p.m.
Nov 14	−12.5	−17.0	−11.0	−25.0	2–3	3	SW	W	968	970	8	St	cloud at 500' light snow	SW–W wind all day 2–3, some areas of fresh snow dusting
Nov 15	−14.0	−22.0	−10.0	?	0–1	0	SW		970	965	7	StCu,St AcSt	warm front from South	lenticulars drift from South wind E at 4 p.m.
Nov 16	−14.0	−22.0	−15.0	−26.0	0	0			968	974	1	CiSt	good visibility cloud North	surface hoar much altst
Nov 17	−14.5	−22.5	−9.5	−26.5	2–3	0–1	SW	SW	974	971.5	2	AcSt StCuLen	a dense cover	poor contrast cloud increasing
Nov 18	−12.5	−10.0	−7.0	−19.0	1–2	0	SW		967.5	964	7	St 500'	poor contrast	cloud increasing
Nov 19	−11.0	−16.0	−4.5	−20.5	0–1	0	SW		962.5	964	3	CiSt, AcSt	good contrast good vis.	
Nov 20	−9.0	−13.0	−9.0	−17.5	3	0	S		970	973.5	3	AcSt, CiSt,StCu	sunny good contrast	
Nov 21	−9.0	−13.0	−7.0	−13.0	2–3	2	SSW	SW	974	973	8	St	snowing warmish	overcast
Nov 22	−10.5	−10.0	−8.5	−11.5	2–3	3	S	SSW	971	970	8	St	light snow contrast	clear to SE zero all day good contrast sunny
Nov 23	−7.0	−17.0	−7.0	−17.0	2	0–1	S	SW	969	968	6	St,AcSt	poor contrast some drift	sudden rise in temp + snowfall
Nov 24	−12.0	−7.0	−5.0	−11.0	1–2	4	S	S	967	966	6	AcSt,St	poor contrast lents. to S	
Nov 25	−6.0	−9.0	−6.0	−17.0	3	4	S	SSW	970	975	3	CiSt	good contrast & vis. bright	sunny good vis. wind & cloud
Nov 26	−7.0	−11.5	−4.0	−17.5	2	0	S		977	976	2	CiSt	good vis. clear slight wind	calm sunny cloud building

Date											Cloud type		Remarks
Nov 27	−10.5	−10.0	−9.0	−17.5	0	0			973	970	CiSt,St AcSt,Len	3	good contrast & vis. warm sunny calm all day
Nov 28	−9.5	−14.0	−6.0	−17.5	0	0–1	SSW		970	969	AcSt, CiSt	5	good contrast & wind — cloud & wind increasing — excellent surfaces
Nov 29	−9.5	−7.0	−3.5	−14.5	3	1	S	S	972	977	St	7	av. contrast thin cloud — warmest day yet
Nov 30	−7.0	−7.0	−5.0	−14.5	1	2–3	S		977	978	St.StCu	4	good vis. cloud decreasing — cloud all day + sun
Dec 1	−10.0	−11.5	−7.0	−15.0	1	0–1	S	SW	981	978	CiSt,St	4	snow from S — cloud increases from 3 p.m. light
Dec 2	−6.0	−10.0	−6.0	−12.0	1–2	0	SSW		977.5	980	CiSt St,Len	7	good contrast — light wind and snow less cloud
Dec 3	−10.0	−9.5	−7.0	?	1	1	SSW		983	979	CiSt,Len	5	poor contrast cloud breaking — zero contrast
Dec 4	−6.5	−8.5	−6.5	?	3	7–8	SE	S	974	972	StCu	8	good contrast mountains — wind light
Dec 5	−6.5	−5.0	?	−10.0	5–6	3–4	SSE	S	970	970	StCu	7	good vis. — new snow cover sunny
Dec 6	−7.5	−6.0	+0.5	−10.0	3	4	SE	SE	971	974	St.StCu	7	wind rising ground drift mtns vis. — wind rising — to 8 blowing snow ground drift
Dec 7	−7.0	−3.0	0.0	−6.0	2	0	SE	NW	981	977	St.StCu	7	calm till 6 p.m. SE wind rising — less good vis.
Dec 8	−3.0	−6.0	+4.0	−7.0	1	3	NW	SE	975	974	St	8	wind intermittent — warm wind rising
Dec 9	−4.0	−3.0	+2.5	−2.0	1–2	2	SE	SE	977	978	StCu	6	warm wind cloud 1000' — overcast all day less cloud
Dec 10	−1.0	−1.0	+0.5	−5.0	2–3	2	SSE	S	975	965	CiSt, StCu	7	visibility good clear — SSE melt — warm calm cloud forming later on
Dec 11	+3.0	+2.0	+5.0	−5.0	0	0	S		964	962	StCu, CiSt	6	sunny cloud high thin — sunny calm cloud — cloud building later calm — cloud forming wind — radiation very hot

Meteorological Log of the Expedition's Walk (Cont.)

Date	Temp a.m.	Temp p.m.	Temp max	Temp min	Wind Spd a.m.	Wind Spd p.m.	Wind Dir a.m.	Wind Dir p.m.	Pressure a.m.	Pressure p.m.	Cloud type	Cloud cover a.m.	Comment a.m.	Comment p.m.
Dec 12	+2.0	−5.0	+6.0	−7.0	0	1		S	961	967	CiSt	3		wonderful day all day
Dec 13	+1.5	−7.0	+6.0	−7.0	0				971	950	CiSt	4	beau temps!	calm, cloud increasing
Dec 14	−1.0	+0.5	+3.0	−9.0	0–1	0		S	954	927	CiSt	1	beau temps	calm, high radiation
Dec 15	+3.0	+10.0	+1.5	−8.5	0	0			925	893	CiSt	3	cloud building	beau temps
Dec 16	−2.0	−2.5	+3.0	−4.0	0	0			894	869	Ci.AcSt	3	beau temps	Cu. over
Dec 17	+1.0	−5.0	+1.0	−12.0	0	1			869	827	StCu	8	calm	Cloudmaker
Dec 18	−5.0	−6.0	−5.0	−12.0	2	3–4		S	821	792	CiSt,StCu	6	more cloud	v. light snow
Dec 19	−5.0	−17.5	−5.0	−19.0	3	0–1	S	S	793	759	StCu	1	drifting snow	clear bright
Dec 20	−5.0	−18.0	−10.0	−19.5	3				762	743	CiSt,Cu	2	clear sunny	wind off plateau
Dec 21	−16.5	−17.0	−15.5	−24.5	2	2	S		744	727	CiSt,Cu	3	glorious day	more cloud
Dec 22	−17.0	−23.0	−17.0	−25.0	2	2	SE	SSE	725	777.5	0		wind decrease	wind cold
Dec 23	−23.0	−18.5	−17.0	−22.0	3–4	3–4	SSW	S	777	736	0		wind 12pm +	wind no drift
Dec 24	−23.5	−27.0	−23.5	−27.0	3–4	3	SSE	SSE	736	722			wind + drift	cold wind
Dec 25	−27.0	−19.0	−17.0	−25.0	2	1	SSE	SSE	724	697	Ci	1		calm gentle breeze all day
Dec 26	−17.5	−22.5	−17.5	−24.0	1	0	E	SSE	694	687	Ci	5		more cloud + calm all day
Dec 27	−23.0	−21.0	−20.0	−25.0	0	0	S	SE	688	681	CuSt	1	snow + warm	no cloud or wind
Dec 28	−17.0	−20.5	−17.0	−29.0	2	2	E	E	686	681	StCuLen	1	calm + drift; overcast	increased wind + cloud
Dec 29	−21.0	−19.0	−19.0	−23.5	0	1		NE	689	666	CiSt	4	wonderful	calm, snow crystals in light wind
Dec 30	−22.0	−25.0	−22.0	−28.5	1	1–2	NNE	NW	665	650	StCu	6	thin cloud	light wind
Dec 31	−24.0	−23.0	−20.0	−30.0	0–1	1	SW	SW	650	652	0		no sound	no cloud

Date											Cloud			
Jan 1	−21.0	−23.0	−21.0	−24.0	3	3	SE	SSE	662.5	665	StCuLen	1	windy	wind increase
Jan 2	−20.0	−24.0	−19.0	−24.0	3	1	SW	SSW	664	661	Ci	5	cloud	moving cloud / nacreous cloud
Jan 3	−21.5	−25.0	−16.5	?	1	1	SE	SSW	657	649	St,CiSt	3	nacreous cloud + parhelion S	ice particles
Jan 4	−20.0	−22.0	−20.0	−25.0	4	4	SW	SSW	650	656	St,StCu	7	much ground drift poor	blizzard gusty / much drift
Jan 5	−20.0	−23.5	−20.0	−26.5	3	3	SSW	SSW	664.5	674	CiSt,St StCu	5	much drift vis. 3 miles	ice particles to 20' windy
Jan 6	−17.0	−18.5	−17.0	−24.0	1	1	S	SSW	673.5	677	StCu	1	light wind good vis.	cloudless / windless warm
Jan 7	−16.0	−19.5	−16.0	−29.0	1	1	SSE	SSW	678	684	0		clear sunny	warm all day / parhelion halo
Jan 8	−21.0	−21.0	−19.0	−23.0	2	1	SW	SSW	682	696	0			ground drift
Jan 9	−22.5	−16.0	−15.0	−21.0	3	2	SSW	SW	695	703	StCu,St	6	ground drift cloud	cloud snow vis. 1 mile
Jan 10	−14.0	−14.0	−11.5	−15.5	4	4	SW	W	687	699	St	1	clear good vis. warm	wind drift clear
Jan 11	−11.0	−14.0	?	−14.0	4	4-5	SSE	SW	703.5	694	AcSt CiSt	3 2	ground drift clear windy	much ground drift

APPENDIX 1
Meteorological Register of Scott's Polar Party

Date	Temperature C		Wind Spd		Wind Dir		Pressure mb		Cloud cover a.m.		Typ/Amt p.m.		Comment
	max	min	a.m.	p.m.	a.m.	p.m.	a.m.	p.m.					
Nov 3	−6.5	−16.3	1	1−2	NNE	NE	997.27	992.86	Ci	7	Ci	7	Blue sky
Nov 4	−14.2	−23.2	2	0	S	–	989.82	1002.34	Ci	6	CiSt	10	Mirage on Bluff
Nov 5	−10.2	−15.8	2	0	N/E	–	1000.99	999.30	Ci	6	Ci,CiSt	4	Land and peaks clear
Nov 6	−15.7	−19.4	4−5	7	S	S	994.22	992.19	ASt,St	8	St	8	Double corona around sun
Nov 7	−11.9	−16.8	6	3	S/E	S	991.85	995.91	St	6	St	8	All peaks save Bluff obscured
Nov 8	−10.2	−17.8	0−1	0	S	–	995.23	989.48	Ci	5	CiSt	5	Sastrugi S by W
Nov 9	−10.5	−17.5	3	4	S/W	SW	986.09	984.74	Ci,CiSt,	3	CiSt,St	8	Low drift
Nov 10	−16.4	−17.4	4−5	2	S/W	SW	998.80	990.83	ASt,St,	7	CiSt,St	8	Slight drift
Nov 11	−10.3	−17.3	3	4	E/N	NNE	989.14	988.12	CiSt,ASt,	8	CiSt,ASt	8	Blue sky to SE
Nov 12	−11.1	−13.7	3	4	ENE	ENE	989.14	990.49	St	8	St	8	No landmarks visible
Nov 13	−9.2	−16.6	1	0	E	–	992.52	992.52	Ci,ASt, St	8	CiSt,ASt	8	Large snow flakes melting
Nov 14	−14.2	−20.8	0	0	–	–	993.54	991.51	Ci,CiSt, ASt,St	6	CiSt,St	8	
Nov 15	−9.2	−11.6	1	2	SE	S	993.88	995.91	ASt,St	8	CiSt,St	8	Light snowfall
Nov 16	−19.3	−25.9	4−5	3−4	SWS	SW	996.93	995.57	Haze	8	Haze	8	Horizon visible
Nov 17	−24.2	−28.1	3−4	1	SSW	SSW	995.23	993.88	ASt,St	3	CiSt	3	
Nov 18	−19.7	−28.9	1	1	SW	SSW	992.52	994.89	ASt	3	CiSt	3	
Nov 19	−19.1	−25.9	0	0	–	–	993.88	995.57	Ci,CiSt	2	ASt	2	
Nov 20	−16.5	−23.9	2	3	SSW	SW	995.91	1004.04	Ci,CuSt	5	Ci,Ci,St	4	
Nov 21	−14.6	−21.3	2	1	SSW	W	1005.05	1005.39	Ci	4	Ci	1	
Nov 22	−16.8	−23.3	0	1	–	NW	1004.38	1004.72	Ci	2	Ci,CiSt	4	Mirage to S

Date	Temp.	Temp.	Force	Force	Wind	Wind	Bar.	Bar.	Cloud	Amt	Cloud	Amt	Remarks
Nov 23	−13.0	−17.5	4–5	3	S	S/W	1005.39	1011.49	CiSt,ASt	4	CiSt,ASt	5	No drift
Nov 24	−16.6	−20.9	3	2	S	SW	1011.15	1007.42	ASt,St	4	CiSt,ASt	3	Slight drift
Nov 25	−17.4	−22.8	0	0	–	–	1005.73	1004.04	Ci,ASt,St	1	Ci,CiSt	3	
Nov 26	−11.0	−19.6	0	2	–	S	995.23	991.51	Ci,ASt,St	8	St	8	Horizon just visible
Nov 27	−8.4	−12.5	4	3	SW	SE/S	994.89	998.28	St	8	Ci,CiSt	8	Continuous snow
Nov 28	−9.6	−16.7	4–5	6	SE/S	SSE	1000.65	1000.65	CiSt,ASt	8	St	5	
Nov 29	−10.9	−12.8	3	1	SSW	S	1002.34	1002.34	St	8	CiSt,ASt	6	Land just visible under cloud
Nov 30	−12.6	−19.3	2	0	S	–	1003.02	1005.73	Ci,CiSt	4	Ci,CiSt	4	Heavy St over land
Dec 1	−11.7	−18.1	3	2	NNW	NW	1003.36	1002.01	ASt	6	ASt	7	Mirage, land very clear
Dec 2	−8.9	−13.4	3	3	SE	S	1002.68	1000.65	St	8	ASt,St	8	
Dec 3	−8.6	−13.2	5–6	7–8	SE	NNW	997.27	994.22	St	8	St	8	
Dec 4	−7.9	−14.7	6	4–5	SE/S	S	1011.49	1004.38	St	8	Ci,ASt	6	
Dec 5	−0.8	−2.9	8–9	8	SSE	SE/E	997.27	997.60	St	8	St	8	Thick, heavy, driving drift, very wet
Dec 6	+0.1	−17.8	8	7	SE/S	SE/S	996.25	996.93	St	8	St	8	Snow like sleet
Dec 7	−0.6	−0.5	7–8	8	SE/S	SE/S	1003.02	1007.76	St	8	St	8	Phenomenal snow, wet flakes like sleet
Dec 8	+0.7	−3.6	3	2	SSE	N	1007.42	1005.39	St	8	St	8	Much snowfall, squashy snow
Dec 9	−6.9	−9.2	2	0	N	–	1004.04	1003.02	ASt,St	4	ASt,St	5	Fine during night, land clearing
Dec 10	−2.8	−8.2	2	1	–	VAR.	1003.70	981.01	CiSt,ASt	2	CiSt	1	Fine clear
Dec 11	−3.6	−4.6	1	0	–	S	983.38	976.95	–	–	CiSt,ASt	5	Knee deep snow
Dec 12	−0.2	−5.3	3	2	SE	SSW	978.30	967.47	ASt,St	6	CiCu,CiSt	3	Fine clear
Dec 13	−3.9	−9.3	1	0	–	VAR.	967.47	957.98	ASt	4	CiSt	2	
Dec 14	−6.2	−10.4	2	2	SSW	NNE	954.60	934.96	CiSt,ASt	3	ASt,St	7	Tops Mts in St
Dec 15	−5.8	−7.8	3	1	S	NE	931.57	918.36	ASt,St	8	St	8	

Meteorological Register of Scott's Polar Party (*Cont.*)

Date	Temperature C		Wind Spd		Wind Dir		Pressure mb		Cloud cover		Typ/Amt		Comment
	max	min	a.m.	p.m.	a.m.	p.m.	a.m.	p.m.	a.m.	p.m.	a.m.	p.m.	
Dec 16	−6.8	−11.7	2	1	NNE	VAR.	929.54	911.25	8	5	Ast, St	Ci, CiSt	Breeze 4–5 at times
Dec 17	−10.3	−13.1	0	3	–	N/E	910.58	886.53	2	8	CiSt, Cu	ASt, St	Steady N breeze all day
Dec 18	−10.4	−11.7	0	2	–	NNE	885.52	852.33	8	7	St	St	Snow large flakes
Dec 19	−10.0	−13.9	2	3	S	S	853.35	824.90	4	2	CiSt, St	CiSt, StCu	Light, drift, fine clear
Dec 20	−10.3	−14.8	0	1	–	SW	826.26	801.20	6	3	CiSt, Ci	Ci, ASt, StCu	
Dec 21	−14.1	−20.3	3–4	0	S/W	–	801.54	760.22	2	1	StCu	St	Low fog in hollows
Dec 22	−17.9	−20.3	2	0	N	–	760.90	752.77	4	2	ASt, St	StCu, CiSt	
Dec 23	−19.6	−23.3	0	3	–	S/E	752.77	733.13	3	4	Ci, CiSt	Ci, CiSt, ASt	
Dec 24	−18.1	−23.6	3	4	S/E	S	734.15	725.68	0	0	–	–	
Dec 25	−18.3	−23.6	4	4	S	S/E	726.02	718.23	1	0	CiSt	–	Drift
Dec 26	−18.3	−23.8	3	4	S/E	SSE	719.93	714.85	1	2	Ci	Ci	
Dec 27	−18.1	−23.5	3	0	S/E	–	715.19	707.40	3	1	Ci	CiSt	
Dec 28	−21.1	−25.8	0	4–5	–	S/W	708.08	701.64	0	0	–	–	Fine clear, low surface drift
Dec 29	−19.6	−21.4	–	–	–	–	701.64	696.56	–	–	–	–	
Dec 30	−17.8	−24.6	–	–	–	–	696.90	694.53	–	–	–	–	
Dec 31	−23.4	−24.7	3	1–2	S/E	S	692.50	686.74	1	0	Ci	–	
Jan 1	−22.2	−26.0	2–3	–	–	S	683.36	680.31	1	0	Ci, CiSt	–	
Jan 2	−24.4	−27.6	1	3	–	SSE	679.63	674.21	1	6	CiSt	ASt	
Jan 3	−28.3	−28.4	4–5	4	SSE	SSE	672.52	669.47	2	1	ASt	CiSt	Continuous drift, Upper arc of 22° halo
Jan 4	−27.1	−28.3	3	0	SSE	–	669.81	666.42	2	1	CiSt	CiSt	Fine clear
Jan 5	−26.3	−29.4	1	4	N	NW	665.07	662.02	5	6	CiSt	CiSt	

Jan 6	−30.0	−30.6	0	0	–	–	661.01	657.62	ASt	3	CiSt	1	Hazy, with drift, strong breeze
Jan 7	−29.9	−32.7	0–1	3–4	–	S	657.28	655.93	–	0	CiSt	1	
Jan 8	−25.4	−31.7	5–6	6–7	S/E	S/E	655.93	656.94	CiSt	8	–	8	Thick, high drift. Nothing visible
Jan 9	−19.8	−20.3	4	3	SE	E	658.97	660.67	CiSt	8	CiSt,ASt	6	Faint Parhelion
Jan 10	−21.3	−22.1	2	3	SE	ESE	662.02	658.97	Ci,CiSt	6	CiSt,ASt Ast	7	Snow crystals falling constantly.
Jan 11	−25.7	−26.0	3	1	SSE	S	656.26	655.93	Ci,CiSt	4	Ci	5	Crystals falling all day, 22° halo
Jan 12	−27.6	−32.1	0–1	2	–	SW	655.25	656.26	Ci	1	CiSt	5	
Jan 13	−30.0	−30.8	1	3	S	S/SW	656.94	662.02	Ci,CiSt	3	Ci,CiSt	4	Air full of crystals
Jan 14	−26.3	−30.8	0	3	S'	SE	663.71	674.89	Ci	4	CiSt	8	Low surface drift
Jan 15	−30.4	−32.2	0	3	–	NW	675.23	676.24	Ci	4	CiSt	1	Fine clear
Jan 16	−31.1	−33.1	4	5	WNW	SW	674.55	679.29	–	0	Ci	2	
Jan 17	−29.3	−17.8	5	5	SW/S	N,SSW	680.31	683.02	Ci	3	Ci,CiSt, ASt	6	Wind gusty, surface drift
Jan 18	−30.9	−30.9	3–4	4	SSW	SSW	686.06	686.06	Ci,CiSt	4	CiSt,ASt	6	Parhelion with 22° and 45° halo tangent arcs and waved tangent

APPENDIX 2 Daily Log of the 1985 Polar Walk

Day	Date	Hrs March	Dly Miles	Ave mph	Total miles	Ave mpd	Comment
1	Nov 3	5	6.85	1.37	6.85	6.85	
2	Nov 4	6	8.36	1.39	15.21	7.61	
3	Nov 5	4	6.05	1.51	21.22	7.07	Bearing: 356° Mag
4	Nov 6	5	7.17	1.43	28.39	7.10	
5	Nov 7	7	8.39	1.15	36.78	7.36	Bearing: 30° Mag
6	Nov 8	7	10.05	1.38	46.83	7.81	Bearing: 29° Mag
7	Nov 9	7	11.45	1.57	52.28	7.47	
8	Nov 10	3	3.01	0.91	61.29	7.66	Blizzard
9	Nov 11	9	13.25	1.47	74.54	8.28	Bearing: 28° Mag
10	Nov 12	3	11.84	3.59	86.38	8.64	Bearing: 27° Mag
11	Nov 13	5	6.77	1.35	93.15	8.47	Blizzard
12	Nov 14	9	12.75	1.42	105.90	8.82	Wind Force 2–3 SW–W; poor visibility in first five hours
13	Nov 15	9	13.29	1.48	119.19	9.17	Good visibility; good surfaces except last 1hr 30 mins
14	Nov 16	9	11.58	1.29	130.77	9.34	Fresh snow cover blown off after first hour; breakable crust
15	Nov 17	9	11.55	1.28	142.32	9.49	Surface hoar, breakable crust
16	Nov 18	9	10.29	1.14	152.61	9.54	Poor contrast; soft crust
17	Nov 19	9	11.64	1.29	164.25	9.66	Good contrast; soft slab; some settling
18	Nov 20	9	12.22	1.36	176.47	9.80	Wind SE; good contrast; hard pulling on soft slab
19	Nov 21	9	11.47	1.27	187.94	9.89	Poor contrast; soft slab
20	Nov 22	9	10.19	1.13	198.13	9.01	Zero contrast all day; some improvement of surface
21	Nov 23	7	10.12	1.43	208.25	9.92	S wind Force 3; good weather and contrast; Bearing 25° Mag RS blister cut short day
22	Nov 24	5	6.75	1.24	215.00	9.77	Blizzard continues; fresh snow
23	Nov 25	0	0.00	0.00	215.00	9.35	Did not move; no rations consumed
24	Nov 26	9	13.04	1.45	228.04	9.50	Calm sunny day; good contrast; reasonable surface
25	Nov 27	7	11.54	1.55	239.58	9.58	Good weather, visibility & surface; day cut short due to GW's feet. Bearing 24° Mag

Day	Date	Hrs March	Dly Miles	Ave mph	Total miles	Ave mpd	Comment
26	Nov 28	8	12.55	1.57	252.13	9.70	Reasonable contrast; excellent surface; late start 11 a.m. Bearing 23° Mag
27	Nov 29	9	12.66	1.41	264.79	9.81	Good weather; no wind; sun; good contrast; reasonable surface
28	Nov 30	9	12.14	1.35	276.93	9.89	1st session good contrast, warm; 2nd contrast less good; 3rd session contrast zero; snowing
29	Dec 1	7	10.78	1.45	287.71	9.92	Reasonable surface & contrast; time out due to GW's feet
30	Dec 2	9	10.96	1.22	298.67	9.96	Zero contrast all day; direction difficult otherwise trouble-free
31	Dec 3	9	12.73	1.41	311.40	10.05	Bearing 22° Mag
32	Dec 4	5	8.96	1.68	320.36	10.01	GW calls halt + tent up; RS talks 1hr 30 min; 6 p.m. blizzard Force 7–8
33	Dec 5	0	0.00	0.00	320.36	9.71	No movement Wind S Force 5; drifting snow
34	Dec 6	9	16.65	1.85	337.01	9.91	Overcast all day; warm; wind calm; surface best yet; Mt Hope visible
35	Dec 7	9	16.07	1.79	353.08	10.09	Excellent surface again; GW tired; changed runner
36	Dec 8	9	17.94	1.99	371.02	10.31	Calm sunny +4°C; good surface; GW's good day; downhill for last 3 miles
37	Dec 9	9	16.75	1.86	387.77	10.48	Desolation Camp; easy day for all
38	Dec 10	6	9.61	1.54	397.38	10.46	The Gateway: RS & GW wait at base; RM ascends; meet US geologists
39	Dec 11	0	0.00	0.00	397.38	10.19	Rest & recuperation at the Gateway
40	Dec 12	0	0.00	0.00	397.38	9.93	No movement; no rations consumed; climbed Spur of Mt Hope
41	Dec 13	6	11.70	1.86	409.08	9.98	Calm, good visibility, little crevassing; camp opp. Monument Rock
42	Dec 14	9	15.93	1.77	425.01	10.12	Easy going day
43	Dec 15	9	19.84	2.20	444.85	10.35	Blue ice; névé; sastrugi
44	Dec 16	9	18.25	2.03	463.10	10.53	Sledge meters removed to prevent damage
45	Dec 17	9	17.75	1.97	480.85	10.69	Last hour excellent
46	Dec 18	9	20.77	2.31	501.62	10.90	Best day yet; new skins
47	Dec 19	8	15.75	1.90	517.37	11.01	Scott's total Beardmore mileage 142 miles; ours 119.99 miles
48	Dec 20	9	15.38	1.71	532.75	11.10	Two sections of crevassing, no rope used. Bearing 57° Mag
49	Dec 21	9	16.74	1.86	549.49	11.21	Turned South, 6.15 p.m. pressure over? Bearing: 60° & 14°
50	Dec 22	9	15.32	1.70	564.81	11.30	Surface, flat hard, wind-packed
51	Dec 23	9	15.41	1.71	580.22	11.38	Crevassing 2nd session on ridge Bearing: 10° mag
52	Dec 24	9	15.31	1.70	595.53	11.45	More ascent & long low waves

Day	Date	Hrs March	Dly Miles	Ave mph	Total miles	Ave mpd	Comment
53	Dec 25	9	15.57	1.73	611.10	11.53	Calm; good surface; long ascents
54	Dec 26	9	17.00	1.89	628.10	11.63	Calm, warm; good surface; two shallow climbs
55	Dec 27	9	17.28	1.92	645.38	11.73	Calm, warm; good surface; plateau ad infinitum
56	Dec 28	9	17.22	1.91	662.60	11.83	Wind Force 3–4; poor contrast; best session; more level
57	Dec 29	9	16.51	1.83	679.11	11.91	Poor contrast; good surface; flat going. Bearing: 9° Mag
58	Dec 30	9	16.96	1.88	696.07	12.00	Descent all day; last 3 hrs heavy pulling, snow like dry sand
59	Dec 31	9	16.02	1.78	712.09	12.07	No wind, beautiful day; new snow, 2' high sastrugi; 2nd & 3rd sessions very hard
60	Jan 1	9	15.57	1.73	727.66	12.13	Sastrugi some 3.5' high continuing all 15 miles + very extensive & required finding a route through
61	Jan 2	10	15.29	1.61	742.95	12.18	Sastrugi all day. Diminishing in size but not extent RM broken trace GW skins unstuck. Surface hoar
62	Jan 3	9	15.95	1.77	758.90	12.24	Hard day; diminishing sastrugi; better surface; much surface hoar
63	Jan 4	5	8.33	1.63	767.23	12.18	Wind force 4; ground drift; rapid deterioration of visibility – 100m. much ground drift; blizzard
64	Jan 5	9	16.33	1.81	783.53	12.24	Wind Force 3–4 gust 5; contrast poor – airborne snow; sastrugi end; soft drift – very hard pulling, 20° parhelion
65	Jan 6	9	16.22	1.80	799.75	12.30	Beautiful day, no wind, no cloud; heavy pulling in soft wind pack
66	Jan 7	9	16.04	1.78	815.79	12.36	Bearing: 10° Mag
67	Jan 8	9	16.17	1.80	831.96	12.42	1st & 2nd sessions perfect but heavy pulling in soft wind slab; 3rd – SW wind Force 3
68	Jan 9	6	10.79	1.80	842.75	12.39	1st session contrast imtermittent; 2nd zero contrast & light snow; 3rd, abandoned. Bearing 5° Mag
69	Jan 10	9	16.21	1.80	858.96	12.45	W wind Force 4; good contrast & visibility ground drift; deep soft pack, hard pulling 3rd session, waves & 2 long rises, saw aircraft in & out of Pole
70	Jan 11	9	14.03	1.56	872.99	12.47	1st session abandoned – blizzard; 2nd sight flags; 3rd session arrived at Dome/Pole 11.53 p.m.

APPENDIX 3 Equipment and Provisions for the Polar Walk

Rations	Unit weight lbs oz	No.	Total lbs oz	
Service Biscuits; Survival Aids	00.00.57	30024	107.12	
Oatmeal Block; Survival Aids	00.01.1	756	52.00	
Butter; tinned – Butterdane	01.03.1	84	100.04	
Mazola corn oil	02.07	8 Lts	19.08	
Cadbury's Instant Hot Chocolate	04.00	13	52.00	
Maggi Instant Soup; Rich Beef	04.00	2	08.00	
Maggi Instant Soup; Beef & Tomato	04.08	1	04.08	
Maggi Instant Soup; Chicken & Veg	04.00	2	08.00	
Maggi Instant Soup; Vegetable	04.00	1	04.00	
Maggi Instant Soup; Chicken	04.00	1	04.00	
Mountain House Bacon Bar	00.02.6	165	26.13	
Mountain House Macaroni-cheese	00.03	84	15.12	
Mountain House Rice & Chicken	00.03.1	87	16.13.7	
Mountain House Freeze-dried green beans	00.00.5	48	01.08	
Raven Freeze-dried peas	00.01	39	02.07	
Raven Instant Mashed Potato	00.02	81	10.02	
Pepperoni Sausage	00.01	756	47.04	Total
Yorkie Milk Chocolate Bar	00.02.1	504	66.02	545.03.7
Fuel: Lead free Petrol:				
Tin, 15.16 Litres	07.00	4	28.00	Total
Tin, 30.00 litres	08.08	6	51.00	79.00
Equipment:				
Sledge, Gaybo Kevlar	42.00	3	126.00	
Sledge Harness; Troll	01.10	3	04.14	
Tube traces	01.03	6	07.02	
Rope traces	00.10	3	01.14	
Dome Tent, Snowdon Mouldings	18.00	1	18.00	
Tent stakes – Ramer ski poles	00.08	6	03.00	

Equipment	Unit weight lbs oz	No.	Total lbs oz	
Tent brush	00.03	2	00.06	
Metal Snow shovel – Ramer	02.02	1	02.02	
Plastic Snow shovel – Ramer	01.09	1	01.09	
Ski; Ramer Grand Tour	03.01	3pr	18.06	
Ski bindings; Ramer	00.10.5	3pr	03.15	
Ski poles; Ramer	00.12.5	3pr	04.11	
Nylon skins, 55mm; Dynastar	00.06.5	3pr	02.07	
Polypropylene skins, 75mm; Ramer	00.03.5	3pr	01.05	
Snowshoes; Ramer	00.12.4	6	04.10	
Crampons; Salewa	00.15.7	3pr	05.14	
Ice axe; Chouinard	01.13	1	01.13	
Ice hammer; Chouinard	01.11	1	01.11	
Ice screw; Chouinard tubular	00.08.8	3	01.12	
Ice screw; Lowe Snarg	00.10	3	01.14	
Karabiner; Selewa Hollow	00.01.6	12	01.03	
Karabiner mini; Chouinard	00.00.5	9	00.04.5	
Glacier rope; Beal 8.2 mm	02.09	2 × 25m	05.02	
Prussic loops	00.04.5	6	01.11	
Nylon tape sling; Troll 1"	00.04	3	00.12	
Stove; MSR GK	01.07	2	02.14	
Stove kit, spares, pots & box	07.05	1	07.05	
Thermos flask, steel	01.08	3	04.08	
Plastic mug	00.01.6	3	00.04.8	
Down sleeping bag; Mountain Equipment, Everest	05.14	3	17.10	
Outer sleeping bag; Mountain Equipment, Hollowfil	04.00	3	12.00	
Closed-cell foam mat; Karrimat	01.02	3	03.06	
Self-inflating mattress; Thermarest	02.07	3	07.05	
General repair kit	04.00	1	04.00	
First Aid kit	03.00	1	03.00	
Swiss Army knife, Victorinox	00.05.6	3	01.00.8	
Flags; Union Jack, Blue Peter	00.01.5	2	00.03	
Rucksack; Karrimor Silverguard	02.03	3	06.09	
Anometer; Methcheck	00.04.5	1	00.04.5	
Minimum thermometer; Zeal	00.04	1	00.04	
Toilet paper; Andrex	00.05	3	01.00	
Pee bottle	00.05	1	00.05	
Antiperspirant stick; Mitchums	00.04.8	3	00.14	Total
Diaries etc.	02.00	3	06.00	301.02.6

Navigation:

Compass; Silva Type 54 NL	00.01.7	3	00.05.1	
Compass; Silva Type 23	00.00.5	3	00.01.5	

Navigation	Unit weight lbs oz	No.	Total lbs oz	
Sledge wheel; Trumeter	04.11	2	09.06	
Sextant, artificial horizon & box; Zeiss	07.08	1	07.08	
Map box containing: maps, Almanac tables, Ozalith plotting sheet, Rotring drawing instruments	04.04	1	04.04	
Signal mirror	00.02	1	00.02	
Binoculars: Trivor	00.08	1pr	00.08	
Watches; Rolex, clockwork & analogue quartz; Cassio digital alarms	00.03	6	01.02	
				Total
Altimeter; Thommen	00.03.5	1	00.03.5	23.08.1
Clothing:				
Down jacket and salopette; Mountain Equipment, Gortex	05.11	3	16.08	
Windproof jacket and salopette; Mountain Equipment, Gortex	03.01	3	09.03	
Fibre-pile jacket; Helly-Hansen	01.14	3	05.10	
Fibre-pile suit; Helly-Hansen	02.05	3	06.15	
Long-sleeved polo-neck vest; Wild Country	00.06	6	02.04	
Long-sleeved zip-neck vest; Wild Country	00.07	6	02.10	
Long John; Wild Country	00.09.2	6pr	03.07.2	
Underpants	00.02	6pr	00.12	
Longloop-stitch stocking; Europa Sport	00.05	9pr	02.13	
Tube sock; Europa Sport	00.04	9pr	02.04	
Vapour-barrier sock; Chouinard	00.02	6pr	00.12	
Windproof over-mit; Snowdon Mouldings, Gortex	00.07.5	3pr	01.06.5	
Fibre-pile mit; Helly-Hansen	00.04.5	6pr	01.11	
Oiled-wool gloves	00.03.6	3pr	00.10.8	
Polypropylene gloves; Wild Country	00.01.7	9pr	00.15.3	
Peaked cap, Gortex/fibre-pile; A16	00.03.7	3	00.11.1	
Balaclava; Damart	00.03.2	6	01.03.2	
Boots; Koflach Ultra/Aveolite inners	05.06	3pr	16.02	
Overboots; Berghaus Yeti Gaiters	01.09	3pr	04.11	
Goggles; Cebe	00.04.8	3pr	04.14.4	*Total*
Glacier glasses; Rohan	00.03.5	3pr	00.10.5	82.02

	Unit weight lbs oz	No.	Total lbs oz	
Photographic:				
Super-eight camera; Braun 801	03.15	1	03.15	
Tri-pod; Ramer	02.03	1	02.03	
Tape recorder; Sony Walkman	02.03	1	02.03	
Batteries; Vidor Lithium	00.14	4	03.08	
Film; Kodak super-eight (rolls)	00.02	30	03.12	
Sound tape; Sony C90	00.02.8	9	01.09.2	
35mm camera; Leica M4 with 24mm, 70mm & 135mm lens	03.01	1	03.01	
35mm SLR camera; Leica R4 with 35–70 zoom lens	02.05	1	02.05	
35mm SLR camera; Olympus OM1 + 21mm, 35–70 & 75–150 zoom lens	04.10	1	04.10	
Protective cases; Camera Care	Included	3		
Film 35mm; Kodak 25, Kodak 64,				*Total*
Ectachrome 200 & Ilford FP4	00.01.1	69	04.12	31.14.2

Total weight for three men: 1062.14.4 lbs *Each sledge*: 354 lbs

APPENDIX 4 Physiological Report

by Dr Michael Stroud

Hon. Research Fellow, Department of
Physiology, St George's Hospital, London

The research on human physiology that was performed during the expedition took advantage of the unique opportunities offered by both the isolation of five healthy men in a Polar environment and the accomplishment of the Polar walk itself. We were concerned at Base with investigating the mechanisms of human body weight control and metabolic adaptation to cold. Many authorities would deny their existence altogether saying that all adaptation is behavioural, so that, for instance, we dress more warmly or avoid going out of heated areas. Nevertheless, most men, including those on the expedition, would say that after living in the cold for some time they notice it far less and can function outside for much longer periods, wearing far less clothing. This is probably due partly to psychological adjustment and partly to adaptations in the blood vessels to extremities that allow the feet and hands to stay warmer.

There have been a few previous studies suggesting that human beings can increase their resting metabolism to compensate for cold, as has been shown clearly to be the case with smaller mammals. In these experiments animals exposed to the cold not only show increases in their Basal Metabolic Rates (the energy consumed at rest), but also demonstrate an increased dietary and ephedrine induced thermogenesis (DIT and EIT). This increase is very similar to that seen in overeating animals, though the capacity to burn food at rest in this way has not developed in order to dispose of food excess but to increase body temperature to counteract cold conditions. If man can do the same, why has it not been demonstrated clearly? The answer may lie in the same reasoning that leads to the denial of an adaptive mechanism.

The human body is indeed very good at avoiding getting

cold, and particularly so when working in Polar environments where a greater part of cold adaptation research has been performed. Our expedition, however, differed from most groups of Polar residents that had been examined previously. Unlike the average government base of any nation, we were under no restrictions as to when we went out, and when we did so it was on foot rather than by vehicle. Thus we received genuine exposure to cold, and so might show some adaptic changes after our trips, which would be reflected in increased levels of DIT and EIT.

All the men showed a considerable variation in body weight during their stay. Initially, they all lost weight while long hours were spent working to establish the Base, but from March onwards they progressively gained, to reach peaks between 5 and 8 per cent higher in the latter part of the winter and early spring. This seasonal variation has been the noted pattern in nearly all previous Antarctic weight surveys, and it is always attributed to the more sedentary lifestyle of the winter period rather than to any adapative mechanism to cope with the cold. Our data, in conjunction with the activity survey and the dietary intake survey, supports the same conclusion.

Table 1 shows the mean body weights in kilograms for the five men during their time at Cape Evans, with the January weights for the Polar party recorded forty-eight hours after their arrival at the Pole, once they had rehydrated.

1.

Month	Wood	Tolson	Stroud	Swan	Mear
February	79.5	73	68	84	66.4
March	76.4	72.5	65.8	80.8	65.2
April	80.4	74.6	66.8	82.2	66
May	79.8	75.4	66.8	82	70.2
June	80.4	75.2	68.4	81.4	69.4
July		76		83	
August	82	76.2	67.8	84	71.2
September	82.4	76	69	83.2	70
October	82	77.2	71	83	69.8
November		76	67.6		
December		73	66.4		
January	76.3	72.5	66	74	64.9

Although the accumulation of body fat fluctuated slightly, these variations did not follow the changes in body weight, proving that muscle tissues as well as fat play a part in weight control. This has generally been the case in other surveys of Antarctic wintering personnel. The pattern in our case was almost certainly due to our average level of activity in the winter remaining fairly high by comparison with the much more sedentary life that the environment and safety rules usually impose upon the personnel of various national Antarctic bases.

Measurements of metabolic rates, and the changes caused by either food or ephedrine, were made every month, with the rate of metabolism derived from the amount of oxygen that the subject was burning. This was calculated from the volume of air breathed through a portable respiratory monitor supplied by Harvard Instruments in Edenbridge, Kent, and from the concentration of oxygen in the expired air measured on an oxygen analyser from Servomex Ltd in Crowborough, Sussex.

Basal rates were taken after a night's rest and several hours without food. The changes were then recorded after the subjects were given either a test meal of 1,250 calories of Complan or a 75mg dose of ephedrine.

The results give monthly means for the five men as follows: March 1.07; April 1.08; May 1.13; June 1.15; July – ; August 1.1; September 1.06; October 1.09. A 7 per cent increase in these mean Basal Metabolic Rates occurred during the winter months, but this is unlikely to represent an adaptive change to the cold, for resting metabolism is proportionally related to lean body weight, and so the change can be accounted for by the increase in body weight during this period.

With regard to changes in thermogenic responses with food intake, only Wood and Tolson showed a positive correlation, suggesting that they were the only ones in which a dietary induced thermogenic weight control mechanism was attempting to operate. Central adaptation to cold indicates no uniform pattern of changes relating environmental exposure to thermogenic responses. This seems to suggest that no adaptation to cold took place except in the case of Mear, where distinct increases in his levels of DIT are shown after the Ross Island Traverse and the Winter Journey.

All the men were convinced that they could function much

more comfortably in colder conditions and wearing less clothing as the year progressed.

Considerable variations in fitness occurred for all the men at different times of the year. Previous studies have shown a connection between maximal aerobic capacities and thermogenic responses, which is thought to be part of the reason why fit people tend to be thin. In our study such a correlation was not borne out.

For one week of every month the men weighed and recorded every item of food or drink they consumed and recorded the times spent in different classes of activity. The food data was later interpreted as calorific intake, using food composition tables and a specialist computer program provided by *Slimming Magazine*. Nearly all the values of food intake were exceptionally high by normal standards, often far exceeding levels that would be expected for men doing hard physical work in a normal environment. Table 2 shows the kilo-calorific intake of each of the five men as recorded in the monthly dietary surveys.

2.	Month	Wood	Tolson	Stroud	Swan	Mear
	February	4,693	3,962	4,136	4,285	4,414
	March	5,001	2,647	3,518	3,761	3,777
	April	5,440	3,077	3,712	3,685	3,680
	May	4,779	3,468	3,621	3,569	3,158
	June	4,574	3,337	3,565	3,531	3,467
	July	3,965	2,180	3,965	2,286	3,965
	August	3,116	2,732	2,997	3,960	2,437
	September					
	October	2,798	2,837	3,408	3,198	2,701
	November					
	December		2,642	2,927		

No clear correlation existed between the amount of work done and the quantity of food consumed, confirming that no real regulation of food intake occurred.

By subtracting the estimated work done from the estimated food intake, discrepancies show up that should relate to changes in weight, albeit qualitatively rather than quantitatively. (Table 3 is measured in kilo-calories.)

3.

Month	Wood	Tolson	Stroud	Swan	Mear
February	549	346	99	371	674
March	677	−1,152	−1,006	−15	−634
April	2,362	941	638	205	485
May	1,158	47	158	372	−557
June	1,654	769	748	1,100	539
July	53	−485	53	−237	53
August	207	−270	−1,051	480	−483
September					
October	216	184	676	492	−74
November					
December		−1,896	−2,105		

It is remarkable that greater variations in weight did not coincide with the massive discrepancies indicated above at certain times. This argues strongly for the operation of some sort of weight control mechanisms, even though our experiments did not point to such a mechanism in all the men.

POLAR WALK RESEARCH

Our Polar journey was the longest unsupported walk ever undertaken in Antarctica and thus provided a unique opportunity to study the physiology of sustained and arduous exertion as well as to make comparisons with what is known of the details of the journeys in the 'Heroic Era' of Polar exploration. Weight limitations prevented any complex experiments from being performed *en route*, and the sinking of *Southern Quest* curtailed completion of the full bank of metabolic and fitness assessments. Nevertheless, valuable information was obtained during the walk, at the Pole, and after the return to London.

The following areas were examined: comparative analysis of diet; energy balance during the sustained manhauling; urine ketones in sustained manhauling; Basal Metabolic Rate and dietary induced thermogenesis after sustained manhauling. All results apply to the seventy days of sledging after the Polar team separated from Tolson and Stroud on 3 November.

Comparative Analysis of Diet

A normal Western diet provides between 2,000 and 3,000 kilocalories (Cals) per day from a diet of approximately the proportions shown in Table 4.

4.   *Source*   *% of Calorie intake*
      Protein   11
      Carbohydrate   46
      Fat   38
      Alcohol   5

A man doing hard manual work will use about 3,600 Cals per day, but previous studies have all placed the energy cost of manhauling far above this, with estimates ranging between 4,000 and 7,000 Cals per day.

If the intake for each member of a Polar manhauling party was significantly less than 5,000 Cals per day then the men would lose weight steadily and after one or two months would be significantly weakened. This has always been considered to be one of the factors that contributed to Scott's death, for his diet provided only 4,240 Cals up to the Beardmore Glacier, and 4,590 Cals on the plateau. On the return journey, dwindling supplies probably reduced the intake of Scott's party to below 4,000 Cals. In contrast, Amundsen's men enjoyed 4,560 Cals per day while doing less arduous work, and this intake was increased to around 5,000 Cals during his return journey.

Scott's failure also probably owed a good deal to the severe lack of vitamins, particularly of vitamin C and the vitamin B group. Generally, this has been thought to be the more significant deficiency in his diet.

The very nature of a sledge journey dictates that the food should be as light as possible, preferably weighing less than 1,000g. per man per day. We felt the only way to achieve this was to make the diet rich in fat, with its high energy content for weight (9 K.Cals/g. versus 4 K.cals/g. for protein and 3.75 K.cals/g. for carbohydrate). Table 5 shows the average daily diet on our expedition.

5.	*Total wt g.*	*Total Cals*	*Fat g.*	*Prot. g.*	*Carbo. g.*
Butter	138	1,016	113	0.5	Tr
Corn Oil	28	252	28	Tr	0
Biscuit	195	870	25	22	148
Oatmeal Blocks	95	416	16	10	62

5. *Cont.*

	Total wt g.	Total Cals	Fat g.	Prot. g.	Carbo. g.
Milk Chocolate	120	630	36	10	71
Salami	85	420	39	15	2
Instant Soups	43	144	3	3	28
Hot Chocolate Drink	100	352	6	6	73
Freeze Dried Meal*	58	306	16	12	30
Freeze Dried Vegetable*	24	83	Tr	3	19
Compressed Bacon Bar*	50	306	22	26	1
Totals	934	4,795	303	107.5	434

*The evening meal consisted of either a freeze dried meal (macaroni cheese, chicken and rice) or a compressed bacon bar, served with freeze dried potatoes and or vegetables (peas, runner beans).

These daily figures are averages for the whole journey. Not every foodstuff was eaten every day. Besides the daily 4,795 Cals, weighing 934g, each man received a supplement of approximately 15,000 Cals when they met the American field party on the Beardmore Glacier. The average intake was thus increased to 5,009 Cals. The rations carried were actually adequate to provide an average of 5,100 Cals/day, but for the first two-thirds of the journey the men did not eat all the butter allocated, and were consuming around 4,500 Cals/day. In the last third of the journey the party's good time allowed rations to be increased by raising the biscuit and butter allowance, and for the final three weeks over 5,500 Cals/day were consumed.

The proportions of the calorie intake provided by each component of the diet were: 57 per cent fat; 9 per cent protein; 34 per cent carbohydrate. This is very different from the composition of the rations used by Scott, Amundsen and Shackleton, for which the following average figures have been estimated: 36 per cent fat; 22 per cent protein; 42 per cent carbohydrate. Such a diet would have been difficult to stomach, for it is well established that a high protein load is not easily digested. A high fat content might also have caused problems of absorption, and as far as we know, the proportion of calories provided as fat in our diet was higher than any used previously. We are pleased to report that no such problems did occur.

Ours was also an unusual diet in the proportion of the

calorific intake absorbed in the form of hot drinks, for no traditional drinks, such as tea, were taken and all soups and chocolates were liberally fortified with butter. This also proved pleasant, conserved fuel and saved weight. Vitamins were provided in a high dose multivitamin tablet and through individual food items, some of which were specially fortified for expeditionary use. Although at times the men felt hungry, the diet sustained them and proved appetizing and easy to prepare.

Energy Balance during the Polar Journey

Various estimates have been made of the calorific consumption of men manhauling sledges, either measured directly by attaching apparatus to men pulling a sledge under trial conditions, or calculated from the weight change sustained on longer trips when the dietary intake has been known. On our Polar journey only the latter two methods could be used, and Table 6 summarizes the findings of the food intake method.

6.	Mear	Swan	Wood
Average daily cals	4,988	5,030*	4,988
Cal. intake in 70 days	349,130	352,130	349,130
Weight loss in g.	6,700	10,500	10,500
Calorific equivalent of weight loss **	46,900	73,500	73,500
Total Cals consumed ***	396,030	425,630	422,630
Average Cals per day	5,658	6,080	6,037

  * Swan used approx. 500g. more butter over the course of the trip.
  ** The weight loss is considered to be fat stores that can be mobilized to provide a net energy of 7 Cals/g. It was measured after full rehydration had occurred.
*** The sum of all the Cals eaten and the calories represented by the weight loss.

These figures are compatible with previous estimates, but are probably the most accurate estimates for calorie consumption when it comes to manhauling over many weeks. They are thus the most useful figures for assessing Scott's work output, for although the weight pulled per man was less, this work advantage was probably offset by using skis far less, though they did move over the same terrain at the same time of year. Previous estimates have been between 5,000 and 5,500 Cals/day and we believe that these were too low.

During the walk, the time spent in different categories of activity was approximately the same for all three men. The mean number of hours spent in each category during November, December and the first eleven days of January were as given in Table 7.

7.	Activity	November	December	January
	Walking	7.3	7.7	7.4
	Rest break	0.9	0.9	1.0
	Making camp	1.5	2.9	3.3
	Lying	5.9	4.6	4.7
	Sleeping	8.4	7.9	7.6
	Total calories	6,634	7,167	7,096

Mean estimated total calorie consumption, 6,943 Cals
Mean calorie consumption from food intake plus weight loss, 5,925 Cals

The difference between these two values could reflect inaccuracies in the literature data, particularly the value assigned to the cost of manhauling, which is given as approx. 11 Cals/min., but which this data would suggest is nearer 8.8 Cals/min. for a sustained manhauling journey.

Whichever results one accepts as accurate, the values are large and the significance of such high outputs is the startling effect on weight, with both of the heavier men on our expedition losing over 10 kg. despite an intake which was so much greater than Scott's. It seems likely, therefore, that on his expedition the weight losses must have been even more extreme. Evans might well have lost over 15 kgs. by the time he reached the Pole, with losses continuing as they turned for home. Their starvation was perhaps as debilitating as scurvy and other vitamin-related illnesses.

Urine Testing

If a person is eating less energy than he is burning, he must mobilize fat stores or body muscle to make up the difference, and this mobilization process causes chemicals called ketones to appear in the blood and the urine.

Every morning and evening, the men tested their urine for ketones, using dip sticks. The result shown in Table 8 give the percentage of tests that were positive as either a trace (Tr) or a moderate (Md) reading.

8.	Month	Mear				Wood				Swan			
			a.m.		p.m.		a.m.		p.m.		a.m.		p.m.
			%		%		%		%		%		%
	November	Tr	3.6	Tr	58	Tr	40	Tr	71	Tr	100	Tr	100
						Md	33	Md	17.6				
	December	Tr	38	Tr	54	Tr	25	Tr	50	Tr	100	Tr	100
						Md	30	Md	22				
	January	Tr	55	Tr	89	—	—	Tr	100	Tr	100	Tr	100
	Totals	Tr	27	Tr	61	Tr	32	Tr	66	Tr	100	Tr	100

The presence of ketones in the urine, particularly in the evening, was not surprising given the high work output and a diet which provided a relatively small proportion of the calories in the form of carbohydrate. It was also to be expected that Robert Swan would demonstrate this mild ketosis more than Gareth Wood who, in turn, showed it to a greater degree than Roger Mear. This probably reflects the greater discrepancy between intake and output in the larger men.

Although it proved impossible to perform all the project tests we were able to measure Roger Mear's and Robert Swan's BMR and DIT shortly after they returned to London and within two weeks of reaching the Pole. The results, compared to the mean for the year at Base are given in Table 9.

9.	Mear	Swan
Mean BMR on Base, Cals/min.	1.03	1.12
BMR after walk, Cals/min.	1.6	1.93
Mean DIT on Base, Cals/min.*	1.35	1.47
DIT after walk, Cals/min.*	1.93	2.35

*Average of increase between 45 and 90 mins after test meal over BMR.

These results show a huge increase in the men's Basal Metabolism, a phenomenon never before recorded either in sustained exercise or in prolonged cold exposure.

Why it occurred is not known, although it may have been

caused by thyroid activity. It is the thyroid gland that normally regulates the level of metabolism, and when overactive it is associated with various symptoms that the men certainly experienced, such as feeling nervous, tremulous and sweaty, and having markedly raised pulses at rest. Previous Antarctic research into thyroid levels has not demonstrated significant changes, but the situations studied have been markedly different in nature from those on our expedition, and so further work in this area should be undertaken.

APPENDIX 5   Psychological Report

by Elizabeth Holmes-Johnson, PH.D.,
LCDR, USNR

(*The opinions and assertions contained in this report are the author's own private views, and are not to be construed as official or in any way reflecting those of the Department of Navy or of the National Science Foundation, USA.*)

The United States Antarctic Research program, which has been in operation continuously for more than thirty years, is funded and managed by the Federal Government through the agency of the National Science Foundation's Division of Polar Programs. Logistical support is provided by the United States Navy Support Force Antarctica, commonly known as Operation Deep Freeze. Psychologists and psychiatrists of the United States Navy Medical Department and Naval Military Personnel Command select, screen and debrief the program's wintering personnel. I was the naval clinical psychologist sent to debrief the eighty-four people who wintered at McMurdo Station in 1985.

While in Antarctica at that time, I was also asked to assess the five members of the 'In the Footsteps of Scott' Expedition who were living at Jack Hayward Base at Cape Evans. In carrying out this assessment, I had the full co-operation of the expedition members who completed various psychological tests during their stay in Antarctica. These tests yielded a character profile of each of the five winterers and indicated also how they interacted as a group, living in isolation in an extremely confined space.

At the time of the evaluation the party was experiencing some difficulty. They had been on the ice for almost nine months and were at a point of decision-making. Who would make the journey to the Pole? The selection of three to go to the Pole could arouse severe group discord and loss of emphasis on the long-term goal. All five were individuals who were not functioning well in a group. Each made trips to Scott Base and to McMurdo in an attempt to escape from the emotional tension and friction at Cape Evans. Yet, while eliciting support from acquaintances outside their small group, they were also at pains to avoid letting on that the discord existed.

The expedition's political leader and organizer, Robert Swan, had difficulty in maintaining control over the group because it was felt that he was too involved in having the limelight, and in seeking gratification from the nearby communities of New Zealanders and Americans. While he focused on the externals, other expedition members thought him to be technically not competent to pull the group through the major forthcoming event, the time for which was rapidly drawing near. Roger Mear, the technical leader, was also behind the scenes group leader. He and Robert were probably in conflict over power and control. Though it was always accepted that these two would participate in the Polar journey, who the third member would be remained open to question. Would it be Gareth Wood or Michael Stroud? This is where the friction became apparent.

Gareth Wood was individualistic; he could complete the task and persevere to the end, but if he were chosen there would probably be a less than favourable 'group experience'. If Michael Stroud were chosen it was felt that group interaction might be more stable but the outcome less certain. Robert, Roger and Gareth would be task orientated, while Robert, Roger and Michael would be relationship orientated.

Many interesting but unresolved personality problems could have become problematic under the stress of the walk, yet the desire for a successful journey far overshadowed the desire to resolve their personal differences. So, in spite of the moral question, Robert, Roger and Gareth became the chosen team. The individual need for autonomy took precedence over the social development of the group. Each person pursued an individual quest and not group cohesiveness. There was potential for them to become so angry with each other that they would avoid speaking to each other. This would be the price to pay for failing to resolve personality difficulties.

In my terms, they might not have been 'selected' as ideal winterers because Robert, Roger and Michael had a high need for excitement and adventure, and could have experienced difficulties fitting into any group with their risk-taking behaviour. Although individualistic, Gareth on the other hand was capable of maintaining the excitement in his life. John Tolson was a good wintering candidate, being more balanced and a better group member.

The following profiles are based on the Sixteen Personality Factor Questionnaire (16PF) Manual (Copyright 1985, The Institute for Personality and Ability Testing Inc., Champion, Illinois, USA 61820).

ROGER MEAR's outstanding personality factors included being dominant, imaginative, and having undisciplined self-conflict. Next in strength were abstract thinking, tender-mindedness, shrewdness, being self-sufficient, sober, expedient and shy.

Individuals like Roger are assertive, self-assured, and independent-minded. They tend to be austere, a law to themselves, hostile or extrapunitive, authoritarian (managing others), and disregarding of authority. They tend to be unconventional, unconcerned with everyday matters, self-motivated, imaginatively creative, concerned with 'essentials', often absorbed in thought, and oblivious of particular people and physical realities. Their inner-directed interests sometimes lead to unrealistic situations accompanied by expressive outbursts. Their individuality tends to cause them to be rejected in group activities.

Roger is not bothered with will control and has little regard for social demands. He may not be overly considerate and may be impetuous.

MICHAEL STROUD had extremes in his personality greater than most of the expedition members. He sees himself as expedient, dominant, forthright, and undisciplined. Secondly and almost equally he sees himself as enthusiastic, tender-minded, imaginative and experimenting.

Individuals like Michael see themselves as assertive to agressive, authoritative, competitive and stubborn. People like him disregard rules and feel few obligations. They do not feel group pressure to conform.

Michael is not bothered with social demands and protocol. He tends to be cheerful, active, talkative, expressive and carefree. He may be impulsive in his behaviour, emotionally he is sensitive, temperamental, demanding of attention, impatient, and not always realistic. In a group his type may slow up group performance and upset group morale by undue fussiness. Being inner-directed and self-motivated while also being imaginatively creative this sometimes can lead to unrealistic situations accompanied by expressive outburst. His interests tend to be away from crude people and more towards intellectual matters. Usually his type may be skeptical, enquiring, well informed and inclined to experiment in life and tolerant of inconvenience and change. At the same time Michael also has a lot of natural warmth, genuine liking for people and is unpretentious.

ROBERT SWAN had extremes in his personality which included being quite dominant, bold (venturesome and uninhibited), tender-minded (sensitive) and forthright (open). These same characteristics which were his assets had potential to be his liabilities. He was extremely self-assured and independent minded. He felt unruffled, unshakable nerve. People like him are resilient and secure but to the point of being insensitive of when a group is not going along with them, so that they may evoke antipathies and distrust.

People like Robert are sociable, bold, ready to try new things, spontaneous and abundant in emotional response. Their 'thick-skinnedness' enables them to face wear and tear in dealing with people and grueling emotional situations without fatigue. However, they can be careless of detail, ignore danger signals, and consume much time talking. They tend to be pushy and actively interested in the opposite sex.

Robert may also be described as emotionally sensitive, daydreaming, artistically fastidious and fanciful. He would be demanding of attention, dependent, unrealistic and slow group process and upset group morale. Yet, at the same time he would expend a great deal of warmth, have genuine liking for people, be sentimental and therefore he would have a hard time hearing people's anger with him.

Robert tends to be quick to grasp ideas, a fast learner and intelligent. There is some correlation with level of culture and alertness. He would maintain his intellectual skills in the face of extreme stress.

JOHN TOLSON had no extremes of personality factors. He tended to have a balance within himself. He tended to be slightly on the shy side, practical, and self-sufficient.

Individuals who respond as John did tend to be cautious, retiring, slow in expressing themselves and prefer close friends rather than large groups. His type tend to be anxious to do the right thing, attentive to practical matters, and subject to the obvious. They are concerned with detail, keep their heads in emergencies and are responsive to the outer world situations.

He would be someone seen to be temperamentally independent, tend not to dominate and not in need of other people's agreement or support.

GARETH WOOD was extreme in only two personality factors. He was very reserved, detached, critical, cool and impersonal, while also being extremely conscientious, persevering, proper, moralistic and rule-bound.

Describing each of these factors according to similar personalities would be the following: people who score such as Gareth tend to be stiff, cool, skeptical and aloof. They like things rather than people, working alone, and avoiding compromises of viewpoints. They are likely to be precise and 'rigid' in their way of doing things and in their personal standards. In his chosen occupation these are desirable traits, in being a group member it might be a problem. They may tend, at times, to be critical, obstructive or hard. People such as Gareth tend to be exacting in character, dominated by sense of duty, persevering, responsible, planful, 'fill the unforgiving minute'. They are usually conscientious and moralistic, and prefer hard-working people to witty companions. Gareth was also very self-sufficient, serious and shy.

Bibliography

The following books have been quoted or consulted in the preparation of this text.

Roald Amundsen, *The South Pole*, John Murray, London, 1912

W. N. Bonner and D. W. H. Walton, *Key Environments – Antarctica*, Pergamon Press, Oxford, 1985

Apsley Cherry-Garrard, *The Worst Journey in the World*, Chatto & Windus, London, 1937

Ranulph Fiennes, *To the Ends of the Earth – Transglobe Expedition 1979–82*, Hodder & Stoughton, London, 1983

Sir Vivian Fuchs and Sir Edmund Hillary, *The Crossing of the Antarctic*, Cassell, London, 1958

David L. Harrowfield, *Sledging into History*, The Macmillan Company of New Zealand, Auckland, 1981

A. S. Helm and J. H. Miller, *Antarctica: The story of the New Zealand Party of the Trans-Antarctic Expedition*, R. E. Oven, Wellington, 1964

Roland Huntford, *Scott and Amundsen*, Hodder & Stoughton, London, 1979

– *Shackleton*, Hodder & Stoughton, London, 1985

Herbert G. Ponting, *The Great White South*, Duckworth, London, 1921

Reader's Digest, *Antarctica*, Reader's Digest Services Pty Ltd, NSW, 1985

R. W. Richards, *The Ross Sea Shore Party*, The Scott Polar Research Institute, Cambridge, 1962

John Rymill, *Southern Lights*, Chatto & Windus, London, 1938, reissued by The Knell Press, Malvern, 1986

Captain R. F. Scott, *The Voyage of the Discovery*, John Murray, London, 1905

– *Scott's Last Expedition*, Smith, Elder & Co., London, 1913
Sir Ernest Shackleton, *The Heart of the Antarctic*, William Heinemann, London, 1909
– *South: The Story of Shackleton's Last Expedition*, William Heinemann, London, 1919
Myrtle Simpson, *Due North*, Victor Gollancz, London, 1970
David Thomson, *Scott's Men*, Allen Lane, London, 1977
E. A. Wilson, *Diary of the Terra Nova Expedition to the Antarctic 1910–1912*, Blandford Press, London, 1972

Acknowledgments

The Expedition would like to express its deep appreciation of the friendship and generosity of those working at the New Zealand Scott Base, in the American township McMurdo and at the Amundsen-Scott Base at the South Pole. A special word of thanks is also due to Rowntree Mackintosh Confectionery for their financial support of the film of the expedition.

The prospect of writing this personal account of our expedition seemed to me at the outset almost as daunting as the Polar walk itself. Thankfully, Miriam Lande provided the peace and solitude I needed for the task, and encouragement, help and advice was always at hand. I would like to thank all the members of the expedition for their accounts of the adventure, and in particular Lynn Davis, Ken Marshall, Peter Malcolm, Mike Stroud, Robert Swan, John Tolson, Rebecca Ward and Gareth Wood, who allowed me unreserved access to their private diaries. I am greatly indebted to Lindsay Fulcher for the research and compilation of material on those hectic early days of the expedition and to Martyn Forester for his work on Robert's contribution. Also the 'Antarcticans' who were plagued by my many questions, David Wynne-Williams, Dave Rootes and Rupert Summerson, friends at British Antarctic Survey, Bob Headland at the Scott Polar Research Institute, and Min Whyman who kept me informed of reports and pronouncements made in New Zealand press.

For the use of their photographs in the book, I am grateful to John Elder (nos 12–17 of the colour illustrations), Rebecca Ward (no. 1), and Gareth Wood (no. 11). Of the black-and-white illustrations, Herbert Ponting's photographs of Scott's last Expedition were supplied by the Royal Geographical Society (nos 3, 7, 9, 10 and 12), except for no. 11 and the picture taken by Scott (no. 4) which are by courtesy of Paul Popper Ltd. The *Star* newspaper in Christchurch, New Zealand, gave permission to reproduce pictures nos 5 and 6. All other photographs are my own.

Finally, my thanks go to Tony Colwell for his tireless support as my editor at Jonathan Cape.

London
March 1987   ROGER MEAR

Supporters and Sponsors

There would have been no expedition without the support, large and small, given so enthusiastically to make the venture possible by the following individuals, societies, schools and companies:

UNITED KINDOM

HRH Princess Anne
Sir Jack Hayward

Brig. John Alexander
Jackie Antoine
Mike Banks
Sir George Bishop
Bert Bissel
Mike Blackburn
Anthony Blackwell
Chris Bonington
Nicholas Bradshaw
Ken Cameron
Guy Clapham
Ian Coombes
Lt-Col P. Cordingley
H. M. Customs
Dr Michael Davys
John Donner
Emma Drake
Mr & Mrs John Drew
Dr David Drewry
Sir Ranulph Fiennes
Sister Hilda Ford
Mark Fox-Andrews
Major Tony Gibb
Graham Boldsmith
Dr John Heap
Dr John Hemming

Wally Herbert
Major Barry Hogarth
Ric Holmes
Brian Hookman
Lord Hunt
Stuart Keir
Capt. Peter King
Chris Knowles
Ian Liddle
James McEwan
Tom Maschler
Capt. Robin Middleton
Sir John Mills
Major Brian Moore
Richard Nye
S. Peacock
Brian Pearson
Don Pratt
John Raisman
Admiral John Rawlins
Michael Roome
Lucinda Rykens
Lady Sharples
Lavinia Sidgwick
Peter Sidgwick
Duncan Smith
Fred Smith
John Stace
Keith Stanwyck
R. D. Swan
R. M. Swan

T. M. Swan
Rt Hon. Margaret
    Thatcher
Jerry Thompson
Lt-Cmdr D. Thornton
Roy Tiley
W. G. J. Trebble
Hereward Tressider
Michael Turnbull
Kevin Walton
Wilfred Watson
Stan Werner
Berry White
Nigel Winser
Shane Winser
David Wynn-Williams

Associates
HRH Prince of Wales
Gillian Acres
Frances Addison
J. Argent
K. Bannerman
Barnard Castle Inner
    Wheel
Michael & Penelope
    Barthorp
J. Bently
Joseph Berkman
N. F. Berry
Bessie Billingham

Mr & Mrs Blaney
Blue Peter (BBC TV)
J. A. Bond
Ben Bray
Dave Briffa
Mr & Mrs Robin
  Brockaway
J. Brockway
Stanley Brown
John Bruce
Lt-Col R. J. Burnaby-
  Atkins
Nancy Burton
G. S. Butler
Anne Cadbury
Anne Campbell
Mr & Mrs P. M.
  Clarkson
H. Cooper
Major J. E. Cordingly
Mary Cosgrove
J. B. Crawley
D. A. Cross
C. B. Cruikshank
Ken Davies
C. M. J. Day
J. & B. Day
G. Doggart
Mr & Mrs Donovan
Robin Duckering
R. Eastman
Mike Edwards
R. F. D. Elliot
Mildred Evans
D. Farrow
Mrs J. Fenton
J. H. Fenton
The Duke of Fife
General Robert Ford
Derek Fordham
Douglas B. Foy
Elizabeth Fulton
B. Gage
John Garnett
P. Gaston & Mike
  Coburn

Sir Geoffrey Gilbertson
F. Gill
Alistair Graham
Lucy Groelet
Michael Harbour
R. G. Harris
Emma Hayward
The Hayward Family
Charles Heneage
Arthur Hibbert
Capt M. J. Hough
N. L. Howell
George Hubert
M. C. Hutchison
Mr & Mrs A. Jameson
Mr & Mrs Johnson
Hon. James Joicey
Clive Kerfoot
N. Kershaw
John Kingerlee
Mrs Knagg
David Lentaigne
Bill Lewington
David Linton
J. Lister
Capt Lloyd-Edwards
R. MacGregor
Tony Mackintosh
Guy Madoc
M. J. Malcolm
James Marshall
J. C. Moon
John Morris
Sheila Morris
J. Muirie
I. A. Nunn
J. M. Olonan
Diana Owen
Vikram Pardy
C. Phipps
A. L. Pittinger
Norman D. Price
C. Pycraft
R. E. Ray
Mr & Mrs E.
  Richardson

Mr & Mrs Keith Roach
David Ropner
Guy Ropner
Dr Ross
R. Salter
Mr & Mrs Sasse
F. Schumann
Selbourne Bookshop
B. M. Slater
Jane Smith
Mr & Mrs Sorrell
Chris Souter
J. Steel
M. A. Straker
P. Straker
J. Sturges
Nancy Summers
R. Summerson
J. K. Swan
N. K. Theakston
R. Thomas
Ken Thomas
Michael Thronley
Roderick Usher
Susan Vigar
J. Walker
Pearl Ward
Joy Welsh
Dr Ian Whitelaw
Gwen W. Wilkinson
Dr L. Williams
M. V. C. Williams
Dr D. G. Wilson
David Yelverton
Mrs Florence Young
Helen Young

Ampleforth College
Ashdown House
Aysgarth School
Barclay Junior School
Bramcote School
Cheltenham College
City of London Club
Copthorne School

Croydon School
Eton College
Forest Comprehensive
  School
Foundation of
  Universal Unity
Francis Scott
  Charitable Trust
Godolphin Latymer
  School
Haileybury & I. S.
  School
Henfield Players
Hurworth House Prep
  School
John Lyton School
John Witty Building
  Services
King's College School
Marlborough College
The Medieval Society
Mercers Company
Northern Lights
  Theatre
The Oates Memorial
  Library
Oundle School
Peat Marwick &
  Mitchell
Queen Margaret's
  School
Redland High School
Royal Geographical
  Society
St Audries School
St Michael's School
Sandle Manor
Captain Scott Society
Sedbergh School
Ski Club of Gt Britain
South Hampstead High
  School
Sphere Drake
  Insurance
Teesdale County Fair

Terra Nova Insurance
Terra Nova School
Trinity School
Willington School

Sponsors:
ABS Pumps
ACM Pipework
Acme Electrical Co.
Air Products
Alcon Laboratories
Alexander Howden
  Insurance
Alexandra Workwear
Alfa Laval Co.
Allen and Hanbury
Allpacks
Alresford Press
Altec Edeco
Ambassador Hotel
Ambrosia Bovril
Ames Div. Miles Labs
Amphibian Sports and
  Electronics
W. R. Anderton & Co.
Andrew Mitchell Co.
Andrews Industrial
  Equipment
Andy's Guitar
  Workshop
Angears
Ansul Jones & Co.
Antartex
Antex Electronics
Apex
  Telecommunications
Apple Computers
The Arco Group
Arka Graphics
Arrow Hart Europe
Asolo Sport SRL
Associated Dairies
Baileys Hotel
Barclays Bank
Francis Barker

E. P. Barrus
Batchelor Foods
Batt Electrical
Bausch & Lomb UK
BBC
Beecham Labs
Beldam Packing &
  Rubber Co.
Belfast Ropework Co.
Belzona Molecular
BICC
Fred Bignell & Co.
Bill Switchgear
L. Bishop & Co.
Blagden Victor
BOC
Boehringer Ingelheim
L. A. Boorer & Sons
Bootham & Hillery
Boots Co.
Bostick (Textron)
Bovril
Bow Decor
Bowater Scott Corp.
Bowman (B'ham)
Bradshaw & Webb
Brammer
  Transmissions
Brett's Oils
Briggs & Marshall
Brindon Fibres &
  Plastics
The British Antarctic
  Survey
The British Edible
  Pulse Assoc.
The British Geological
  Survey
The British Marine
  Equipment Council
British Maritime
  Technology
British Mountaineering
  Council
British Rail

British Rawhide
  Belting Co.
British Ropes
British Rototherm
British Seagull Co.
British Telecom
Brooke Bond Oxo
Brooks & Walker
Brown & Tawse
Mark C. Brown
BTU Coil Co.
John M. Buchan Co.
Bureau Happold
Burgess
Burn Dep.
Burnyeats
Burton McCall
Butlers Warehousing
Butterdane
Cadbury Typhoo
Camera Care Systems
Camerons & Co.
Cannons City Gym
Cape Board & Panels
Carmel
Carrington
  Performance Fabrics
Casella London
J. J. Cash
CBS Fox Video
Celebrity Pianos
Centre for Alternative
  Technology
Children's Britannica
Lisa Childs
Chloride Batteries
Chloride Power Storage
Cirio Foods
City Electrical Factors
Clarins (UK)
Clarke Chapman
  Marine NEI
Mathew Clarke Sons
Clarkes Compressors
A. & P. Clough

Co-Ace Neptune Skip
Co-op Wholesale Soc.
Coca-Cola Export
Cochrane Shipbuilders
Coleman UK
Colmans of Norwich
Community Suppliers
Compak Systems
Compass Maritime
Cooper Tools
Cordfine Tools
Cotswold Promotions
Cottam Bros.
Cowling Burley &
  Trendall
CPC Caterplan
Crane
Crompton Parkinson
Crosslings Potter
  Cowan
Cuprinol
DAM Fishing Tackle
Damart Thermolactyl
  Thermawear
Dane & Co.
Danoff
Dearborn Chemicals
Del Monte Foods
Delta Enfield Cables
Delta Tea & Coffee
Deuta-Werke GmbH
  (Deuta UK)
George Devereau
John Dewar
Edward Doherty
  Medical
Donkins
Douglas Gill Int'l
Dow Chemical Co.
Dowding & Mills
DPS Freight Services
Draeger Safety
DRG Sellotape
DSL Deborah
  Insulation (NE)

Dufay Bitumastic
Dunlop
E. B. Communication
East Berks Boat Co.
Estgate Electrical
  Supplies
Efamol
Egg Info' Bureau
Elderpoint
Elgro
Elsan
Embassy Hotels
Enco Food Products
Encyclopaedia
  Britannica
Epson
Escombe Group
Esso Chemicals
Ethicon
Europa Sport
Eurotech Services
Everest Double
  Glazing
Fenchurch Insurance
The Fenner Group
Ferguson & Timpson
5th Royal Inniskilling
  Dragoon Guards
Finefare
Fisher Controls
Flettner Ventilator
Fluke (GB)
Footprint Tools
Graham Ford
Fortnum & Mason
Foster Refrigeration
Fothergill & Harvey
Foulkes Thomas
Charles H. Fox
Framptons
Robert Frazer & Sons
Fridge Motors
G. & J. Instruments
L Gardner & Sons
Garfunkel & Wander

Gaybo
Gazelle Group
GEC Expelair
Gilbert Gilkes &
    Gordon
GKN Steelstock
Glaxo Operations UK
W. L. Gore
Graham Builders
Graphics Factory
Greenfarm Nutritional
    Centre
Gunnebo
Guys 'n' Dolls
H. R. P.
Hackney College
Haden Moore
    Engineering
Hallrose
Hamworthy
John Harding Assoc.
Harmner & Simmons
R. T. Harris
Harvard Instruments
Mathew Harvey Co.
Hawker Siddeley
Headline Stationery
The Health Factor
Heath & Heather
Hecksher & Co.
Heinz
Helly-Hansen UK
C. Hemmings & Co.
Hendon Glass Fibre
Ken Hickman
High Jumpers
Hillsdown (Lockwood
    & Smedley)
Hilmore
Hoechst UK
Hogarth Safety Wear
Hogg Robinson
Holme & Dodsworth
Holtain
Hoover

Hub & Gillespie
    Aluminium
B. K. Huggins
Kelvin Hughes
Hysol Grafil
I. T. M. (Offshore)
ICI Pharmaceuticals
Ilford
Imperial Chemical
    Industries
Importex Development
    Int.
Industramar
Industrial Fasteners
Infinity Foods
Initial Services
Inspection Services
Institute of London
    Underwriters
Int'l Marine Coatings
Int'l Medication
    Systems (UK)
Int'l Music Pub'ns
Int'l Wool Secretariat
Invait
ITT Jabsco
J. V. C. (UK)
Jaeger
Janssen
    Pharmaceuticals
Bob Jerry & Sons
John West Foods
Keith Johnson
Johnson & Johnson
W. Jordans (Cereals)
K. P. Nuts
Kango Wolf Power
    Tools
Karrimor Int.
Katsouris Brothers
William H. Kaufman
Kaypro Corp.
Kemkleen (NE)
Klinger
Alfred Knights Pianos

Kodak
Samuel Lamont Sons
Laughton & Sons
E. Leitz (Instruments)
Le Nez Rouge
Les Vins Georges
    Duboeuf
Leyland & B'ham
    Rubber Co.
Lin Food Cash & Carry
Liquid Plastics
R. A. Lister & Co.
Henry Lloyd
London Docklands
    Develop. Corp.
London Medical Centre
Lucas Cav
Lyons Tetley
M. C. M. Marine
    Design
M. G. M. United
    Artists
McWilliam Sailmakers
Malcolm Phoebey
The Marine Society
Marlec Engineering
J. I. Marshall
May & Baker
MBS Data Efficiency
Megatron
Merck, Sharp &
    Dohme
Metcalf Components
Metcheck
Midland Bank
R. J. Miles
Miller Insulation
Millrose Electronics
Mirrlees Blackstone
MK Electric
Modern Arms Co.
Moet & Chandon
Molto Pullovers
Moriarty's Workshop
G. H. Morrison
    (Tarpaulins)

Moulinex
Mountain Equipment
Mucklow Brothers
Muddy Fox
Multifabs
Munro Cestel
Munro Deighton
Murex Welding
Music Man
Music Sales
N. E. Electric
Nabisco
National Coal Board
National Film &
    Television School
Nat West Bank
Natural Flow
Neal's Yard
Chas Newens Marine
North East Supply
Oakleaf Productions
OCL
Olympus Optical Co.
Omnisport Int'l; UK
Operation Raleigh
Ozalid UK
P. B. Joinery
Paines & Byrne
Palethorpes
Pancost Insulation
Pappadakis & Co.
Park Davis Labs
Parker Knoll
Parker Plywood
Parmley Graham
Partec Electronics
Patterson Products
F. Peart & Co.
Penguin Books
Perrier
Peterson (S. Shields)
Phoenix
    Pharmaceuticals
Picker International
Pilington P. E.

Piz Buin
Plus Products
Plysu Containers
Polyclear
Poole & Dorset
    Adventure Centre
Port of Tyne Authority
Potato Marketing
    Board
J. D. Potters
Prestige Group
R. W. Pritchard
Protectol
Pultrex
Quaker Oats
Qualitex Fabrics
Rabone Chesterman
Racal Decca (Controls,
    Navigation, and
    Service)
Radstock Midsomer
    Norton & District
Rank Audio Visual
Raven Leisure Products
RCA
Reader's Digest
Readhead's
    Shiprepairers
Readymix Drypack
Reckitt & Coleman
Regent Paper
Rheem Blagden
RHM Foods
Ridley & British
    Association of Ships'
    Suppliers
Robinson & Sons
Robinson Sheet Metal
Roche Products
Rochem
Rocol
Rodimport
Roger & Gallet
Rohan
Rolex Watch Co.

Rondanini
Ronson Division
Adele Rootstein
Rotring
Rowe & Pitman
Rowntree Mackintosh
    Confectionery
Royal Aircraft Est.
Royal Doulton
Royal Meteorological
    Society
Royal School of Signals
Ruberoid Building
    Products
Russel
Rutpen
S & G Distributors
S. A. Equipment
Sabah Timber Co.
Sabatini Taylor
St Andrews Woollen
    Mill
St Katherine's Haven
Sait Marine
Guy Salmon
Salvesen Offshore
    Services
Samcine Service
Schat Davits
School of Military
    Survey
Scott Polar Institute
Peter Scott Trust
Scottish Legal
    Assurance
Seaweather Marine
    Services
Seiko Time UK
Selkirk Chimneys
Serck Radiators
Servomex
Seton Medical
Shell UK
C. Shippam
Ships Electronic
    Services

Silva UK
Sinclair Research
Singer Co.
Slaters Electricals
Smith & Nephew
Smith & Wellstood
  Esse (1984)
Smith Kline & French
W. H. Smith (Tools)
Snowdon Mouldings
Sodastream
Solar Energy
  Developments
Solar Engineering
Soloman GB
Sony (UK)
Souter Ship's Spares
Southern Sun Hotels
Spear & Jackson
J. W. Spears & Son
Sperry
Stadium
Stafford Miller
Stanley Electronics
Steam Electric Co.
Storno
J. C. Stuart
Surrey & General
  Instruments Co.
Survival Aids
William A. Swales
Symingtons & Co.
Taylor Woodrow
TDK Tape Distributors
The Tea Council
Tees Towing
Tempex Safety
  Products
Joseph Terry & Sons
Thermos
Thomas Mercer
  Chronometers
Thomas R. Miller
Thorn EMI
Tootal Sewing Co.

Toshiba
Tower Hotel
Trade Data
Transatlantic Plastics
Travenol Labs
Travis & Arnold
Triwall
Troll Safety Equipment
Trumeter
Tyne Gangway Co.
Tyne Tees Contractors
Tyne Tugs
UBM Building Supplies
Ultimate Exercises
Unigate Dairies
Uniroyal
United Biscuits
Value Stores (E.
  Crawford)
Van Hee Transport
Van Leer UK
Vango Scotland
Vasey Fish Merchant
Vaux Breweries
Vega Instruments
Vernons Ferens Auto
  Electric Services
Vessen
Virgin Video
Waddington Games
J. T. Wade
Wade & Sons
Wailes Dove
  Bitumastics
James Walker & Co.
Walker Steel
Wander
Wapping Wire
  Warehouse
Warner Lambert UK
Wedgewood Hotel
Wednesbur Tube
Wellcome Found'n
West Export
  Pharmaceuticals

Westland Helicopters
Whyte & McKay
W. H. Wilcox & Co.
Wild Country
Wilford Polyformes
Wilkin & Sons
Wilson-Walton Int.
Woodgrange Laundry
Woodhouse Frames
Woodward Bros.
World Cargo Services
World Courier
Wuidart Engineering
Young & Cunningham
Zeals Thermometers

AUSTRALIA

Dick Smith
Australian Geographic

Sir Harold Aston
Mr Baille
Andrew Bate
Jim Beasel
Paddy Boxall
Dave & Diana Briffa
Jo Butler
Phil & Liz Castleton
Jonathan Chester
Rod & Stella Clarke
Ian Close
Pete Davies
The Dragar Family
William Franken
Diane Henry
Gillian Hunter
Glen Johns
Michael Lee
Roger & Ruth
  Meadmore
Dr Alan Meares
Richard R Miles
Peter Mitchell
E. A. Mitchener

Tim & Julie Molloy
Margaret Moore
Don Richards
Ross Vinning

Sponsors;
Acme Metal Industries
The Angliss Group
Assoc. Shipping Agents
Australian Antarctic
  Division
Australian
  Conservation F'nd'n
Australian Museum
Bill Bass Opticals
Bonds Coates Patons
Bowie Wilson & Miles
Bradmil Textiles
Brown Boverie
Bryant & May
Bulivants Lifting Gear
Bundaberg Distilling
Bushels
Centre 67
Cerebos (Australia)
Cleanaway
Clempar (Clements &
  Marshall)
Clyde Westeels
Colona Press
Commonwealth
  Industrial Gases
Computer Engineering
  Applications
Cottle Coffee
CSIRO Marine Labs
Dairy Farmers
Demeter
Dilman Navigation
Dept of Ed., NSW
Driclad Buoyance
  Leisure Industries
Dunlite Power
Ebsworth & Ebsworth
Egg Marketing Board,
  NSW

Eurunderee Stud
Exacto Knitwear
Fazaulds Henderson
Federal Broom Co.
Fibreglass Int'l
Foamed Insulation
Foodweek Magazine
Gardner Bros.
General Bindings
General Electric Co.
Gibson's
Graecross Industries
Growers Market
Habitat
Hadamore Group
Halliday & Perry Eng
Hawker Pacific
H. J. Heinz
Hernandez Coffee
Hoover Australia
Hycraft Carpets
ICI (Australia)
International Paints
Int'l Prime Exports
Jadmac Elec Services
Jadon Colour Lab
John Dewars Scotch
Letraset
McWilliams Wines
Magnus Maritec
P. Manettas
Marine Board of
  Hobart
Maritime Services
  Board
Mayfair Foods
Maypole Bakery
Monpumps (Aus.)
Neptune Engineering
Nestlés
Nexus Electronics
OCAL Agencies
Oceanic Research
  Foundation
Orlando Wines

P & O Australia
P. T. L Margarine
Page Display
Pains-Wessex
Photoguard Centre
Pork Promotion Board
Port Arthur Cider
Project Blizzard
Protect-a-Clean
Purity Supermarket
Reckitt & Coleman
RFD Safety Marine
Sachs-Dolmar (Aus.)
Samuelson Film Service
Seaways Disposa
H. B. Selbey
Shell (Australia)
Sigma
Sims Metal
Dick Smith Adventure
Socomin
Spicers Paper Ind
Streets Ice Cream
Sydney Opera House
  Trust
T. R. & B. M. Wood
Taslabs
Tasmaid Foods
Tasmanian Museum &
  Art Gallery
Telecom
Thermos
Toshiba (Aus.)
Triad Film
Trident Video
TVT 6
Unemployed People's
  Union
United Milk (Tas.)
Verbation Australia
Vizden
Wander/Jarch
The Wash House
John West
Westpak Bank

Wild Leitz (Aus.)
W. E. Woods
Woodwards Fine Cars
Yvonne Liechti
Zodiac Inflatable Boats

AUSTRIA

Siegfried Glanznig
Ernest Gritzner
Walter Nagl
Peter Sova
Anton Stepana

Koflach GmbH
Stift Schotten

CANADA

Adventure Network
Bart Lewis
Kaufman Footwear
Martyn Williams
Maureen Garrity
Patrick Morrow
One Step Beyond

NEW ZEALAND

Sir Edmund Hillary

Harry Ayres
R. F. Ballantyne
John D. Barber
M. R. Barnett
Sir David Beattie
Elizabeth Bellfield
British High
   Commission
Bill Burton
David Carter
John Claydon
Warren Collins
Gerald Davies
Bill Dolan
Ian Duff

Graham Dunston
Arthur Ellis
Mel Foster
Tony Gemmell
Tony Giddal
Laurie Greenfield
David Harrowield
Rod Hurst
John Kelso
F. M. B. Kight
W. G. Lloyd
Lyttleton Historical
   Society
Lt-Col R. S. Mackenzie
Paul Mansa
Baden Norris
A. W. Robinson
Russel Scoular
Michael Short
Tony Simmons
Peter J. Skellerup
George Spakman
Mr & Mrs Stace
Denise Stewart
Sir Robertson & Lady
   Adrienne Stewart
Mayor Sir John & Lady
   Thorn
Min Whyman & Family

Associates:
J. Allen
A. J. Barton
A. M. Begg
J. Bristead
J. Dillon
M. A. Ferrier
J. Forman
A. R. Grace
M. K. Griffiths
P. Guilford
Jeff Hart
Hugh Irving
Mr & Mrs D. M. Kerr
A. F. Laity

G. E. S. Lowe
Alistair McGregor
N. D. McRae
M. Nathan
R. J. Osborne
A. Ryall
David Whale
E. P. Wilding
Jim Wills

Sponsors:
Abacus the Micro Shop
Ernest Adam
Air New Zealand
Alliance Freeze Dried
   Foods
Alp Sport
Avis
Arthur Barnetts
Alliance Textiles
Bently Poultry Farm
Bowers Eggs
Brent Stanley
Brett's DCA
Cadbury Fry Hudsons
Canterbury Clothing
Cerebos (NZ)
Chateau Regency Hotel
Christchurch Council
City Motors
Clarendon Hotel
Corbans Wines
Duncan Cotterill
W. H. & H. M.
   Cranfield
Daryl Sumonds
Dawn Meat
Diesel Services
D & W Ford Motors
Diversey NZ
Donaghys Industries
Dunedin City Council
ETA Foods
Fairydown
W. R. Fletcher

Flight Group
Foodstuffs NZ
Geoff Beaver
  Motorbike Hire
Globe Fisheries
Growers Direct Market
Gus Wholesalers
Hertz
James Cook Hotel
Jarden & Co
Lion Breweries
R. A. Lister (NZ)
Lucas Services
Lyttleton Pilots
Monochrome Services
Mono Packaging
Moray Industries
Metropolitan Milk
Nestlé NZ
NZ Breweries
NZ Dairy Board
NZ Express
Newmans Rentals
Noel Leeming TV
PDL Holdings
Pacific Metals
P & O Synco (NZ)
Port Chalmers Council
Port Chalmers Pilots
Otago Harbour Board
Radford & Co.
J. Rattray
Ravensdown Fertilizer
  Co-op
Residents of Port
  Chalmers & Port
  Lyttleton
R. F. D. (NZ)
RNZ Signals
  Directorate
Safeway Scaffolding
Shell Oil NZ
Skellerup Industries
Skope Industries
Sleeps Foods

Sports Marine
Tainui Associates
Team Hutchinson
  (Ford Motors)
Trigon Industries
U. E. B. Industries
Villa Maria Wines
Waitaki Refrigeration
Whitcoulls
Willson Distillers
Wing on Wholesale
Mr Wood-Mancy
L. L. Wright

SOUTH AFRICA

Robert Reinecke
Theopil Steinmann

Josephine Brouard
Charlotte Brown
Diana Campbell
Pam Cornwall
Capt. Damerall
Alice Goldin
Bernard Hill
Dr Pat Josephson
D. G. Jupp
Keith & Ann Lamb
Robert Lamb
J. P. Leask
Tom Larkin
Adele Lucas
Leon Markovitz
Jonathan Ritchie
B. Wallace-Bradley
Roger Williams

Associates:
Di Davis
Mr & Mrs M. Rabett
Tony Sanderson
Hamish Wares
Laurie Whale
Squatter Williams

Sponsors:
Alfa Laval SA
Max Arcus & Son
Atkinson Audio Visual
Avis
Baltic Timbers Co.
Camp & Climb
Cape Times
Century Pharmacy
CFC Coastal Chemicals
Chandling Int'l
Citrus Exchange
Database Computers
Eveready SA
Exclusive Books
Federated Timbers
Frank & Hirsh
Freight Marine Co.
Glenryk Pilchards
Globe Engineering
Haggie Rand
Hamrad
Heuer
Hohenort Hotel
Intermark
Irvin & Johnson
Karos Arthur's Seat
  Hotel
D. Killa & Sons
Kodak
Koo Products
Kovisco
Landdrost Hotel
Lionel & Brian's
  Garage
Liquid Fruit
Lodge Service
Marine Navigation
  Systems
Marine Service
Mountain Club of SA
National Trading Co.
OCL Containers
The Owl Club
P & G Timbers

Peter Styne Books
Pick 'n' Pay
Plascon-Parthenon
  Paint Co.
Richard Summers
  Photography
Romatex Ropes &
  Twines
Royal Cape Yacht
  Club
SA Breweries
SA Marine Corp.
SA Navy Bank
SAF Marine
Safmarine & Safleisure
Sanlam Golden Acre
SAS Unity

The Schoenstatt
  Catholic Movement
Sealink
Shell SA
The Ship Society
Sperry Electronics
Teescape SA (Pty)
Three Spears Africa
United SA Brush
Wild & Leitz SA

USA

Alison Landes
Bill Graves
A16
Alpine Research Inc.

Cascade Designs
Chouinard Equipment
Explorers Club of NY
Gibbs Products
Hughes Aircraft Co.
Marlane Environmental
  Systems
Mountain Safety
  Research
Mountain Smith
National Geographical
  Magazine
Oregon Freeze Dried
  Foods
Philadelphia Resins
Survival International
Brian Winthrop

Index

Index